EIGHTH EDITION

Strategic Analysis and Action

MARY M. CROSSAN
Richard Ivey School of Business,
University of Western Ontario

MICHAEL J. ROUSE
Richard Ivey School of Business,
University of Western Ontario

JOSEPH N. FRY
Richard Ivey School of Business,
University of Western Ontario

J. PETER KILLING
Institute for Management Development,
Lausanne, Switzerland

PEARSON

Toronto

Vice-President, Editorial Director: Gary Bennett
Editor-in-Chief: Nicole Lukach
Acquisitions Editor: Nick Durie
Marketing Manager: Jenna Wulff
Supervising Developmental Editor: Madhu Ranadive
Project Manager: Jessica Hellen
Manufacturing Manager: Susan Johnson
Production Editor: Lila Campbell
Proofreader: Susan Bindernagel
Compositor: MPS Limited, a Macmillan Company
Permissions Researcher: Joanne Tang
Art Director: Julia Hall
Cover and Interior Designer: Anthony Leung
Cover Image: Neliyana Kostadinova, Shutterstock images

---

10 9 8 [EBM]

Library and Archives Canada Cataloguing in Publication

Strategic analysis & action / Mary M.
Crossan . . . [et al.]. — 8th ed.

First–4th eds. written by Joseph N. Fry, J. Peter
Killing. 5th–8th eds. written by Mary M. Crossan et al.
Includes bibliographical references and index.
ISBN 978-0-13-215810-7

1. Business planning—Textbooks. 2. Strategic planning—Textbooks. I. Crossan, Mary M.
II. Title: Strategic analysis and action.

HD31.F79 2011   658.4'012   C2011-907005-7

ISBN 978-0-13-215810-7

Contents

Preface

This book was written to complement case analysis in university and company strategic management courses. It takes the point of view of the general manager and presents a consistent, operational approach to analyzing and acting on strategic problems. Our intent is to introduce you to the breadth of material in strategic management, yet enable you to apply it in a decision-making process. In doing so, we venture beyond current strategic management texts to help reconcile the diversity, breadth and complexity of the field.

As we point out in Chapter 1, general managers run businesses and other types of organizations, and, while their responsibility may be for a small business, a not-for-profit, public sector, or large corporation, they face the common challenge of guiding their organizations to success in competitive environments. The aim of this book is to develop the basic general management skills required to understand a business organization, sense the opportunities and problems that it faces, deal effectively with strategic decisions, and to set in place the people, structures, and operations to implement those decisions.

In preparing the text materials, we have concentrated on analytic concepts that contribute to a practical understanding of specific strategic issues and to the translation of this understanding into personal action. Further, we have linked these discrete concepts into a comprehensive framework—the Diamond-E framework—to ensure that the whole of the situation facing the business is appreciated and that priorities are set for both analysis and action.

We have made two assumptions about our readers. First, we have assumed that they are engaged in trying to solve strategic problems—as students of business doing case analyses or field projects, or as managers on the job. Application and practice are the prime vehicles for understanding the power and limitations of the concepts in this text and, more importantly, for developing general management skills. Second, we have assumed that our readers possess a basic understanding of the background disciplines and functional areas of business, such as the financial analysis and marketing skills provided in early courses in university business programs.

NEW TO THIS EDITION

The first edition of this book was published in 1986. In revising it for this eighth edition, we have updated both the examples and recent theory that support the practical and user-friendly aspects of the seventh edition. We have made some formatting changes to make the book more user-friendly for readers.

Many of the changes in theory and practice in recent years have been towards fragmentation of concepts and pitting one approach against another. We have found this to be counter-productive. For example, emphasizing a dynamic approach to strategy does not negate the importance of understanding strategic positioning at a point in time. Thus, in this edition, we have tried to make connections between concepts that have become increasingly fragmented or polarized.

Throughout the many editions our consistent aim has been to increase the relevance of the materials for solving general management problems in the field or in the form of written cases.

ACKNOWLEDGEMENTS

We have been fortunate to work for many years in institutions that value good teaching and professional relevance. These cultural attributes have been developed and reinforced by many people. In all editions we have benefited from the new ideas and continuing support of our colleagues in the university and in the private sector. We would particularly like to acknowledge our immediate colleagues at the Richard Ivey School of Business and at IMD who, over the years, have included professors Jay Anand, Tima Bansal, Paul Beamish, Oana Branzei, Laurence Capron, the late Harold Crookell, Jim Dowd, Tony Frost, Michael Geringer, Louis Hébert, Gerald Higgins, Amy Hillman, Ariff Kachra, Mike Levenhagen, Peter Lorange, Pat MacDonald, Cara Maurer, Alan Morrison, Eric Morse, Charlene Nicholls-Nixon, Tom Poynter, Glenn Rowe, Paul Strebel, Don Thain, Stewart Thornhill, Rod White, Mark Zbaracki and Charlene Zietsma.

We are also extremely grateful to the following reviewers for their comments and suggestions: Gary J. Bissonette, Queen's University; Ray Chateau, Humber College; Elizabeth Croft, University of Northern British Columbia; P. Fitzgerald, Saint Mary's University; Terry Power, Royal Roads University; Jianyun Tang, Memorial University of Newfoundland.

We are indebted to our publisher, Pearson Canada, and in particular Madhu Ranadive and Nick Durie for their help in producing and promoting this book. At Ivey we are obliged to Manu Mahbubani for his research support. Finally, we extend a big thank you to Michele Foster, Courtney Hambides, and Penni Pring for their diligent and industrious effort in bringing everything together.

Mary M. Crossan,

Joseph N. Fry,

Michael J. Rouse

London, Ontario

J. Peter Killing

Lausanne, Switzerland

SUPPLEMENTS

Test Item File (978-0-13-294393-2)

The Test Item File is new to this edition. This test bank in Microsoft Word format includes over 300 question. There are approximately 30 questions per chapter, including multiple choice, true/false, and short answer. The Test Item File is available for download from a password protected section of Pearson Canada's online catalogue. Navigate to your book's catalogue page to view a list of those supplements that are available. See your local sales representative for details and access.

CourseSmart for Instructors (ISBN 978-0-13-215812-1)

CourseSmart goes beyond traditional expectations—providing instant, online access to the textbooks and course materials you need at a lower cost for students. And even as students save money, you can save time and hassle with a digital eTextbook that allows you to search for the most relevant content at the very moment you need it. Whether it's evaluating textbooks or creating lecture notes to help students with difficult concepts, CourseSmart can make life a little easier. See how when you visit www.coursesmart.com/instructors.

CourseSmart for Students (ISBN 978-0-13-215812-1)

CourseSmart goes beyond traditional expectations—providing instant, online access to the textbooks and course materials you need at an average savings of 60%. With instant access from any computer and the ability to search your text, you'll find the content you need quickly, no matter where you are. And with online tools like highlighting and note-taking, you can save time and study efficiently. See all the benefits at www.coursesmart.com/students.

Technology Specialists

Pearson's Technology Specialists work with faculty and campus course designers to ensure that Pearson technology products, assessment tools, and online course materials are tailored to meet your specific needs. This highly qualified team is dedicated to helping schools take full advantage of a wide range of educational resources, by assisting in the integration of a variety of instructional materials and media formats. Your local Pearson Canada sales representative can provide you with more details on this service program.

Introduction

This introduction explains the approach and organization of the book and suggests how you can use it to best advantage.

APPROACH

The book was prepared as a practical guide for strategic analysis and action. We have designed it for readers who are working on applied strategic problems, either through case studies or on-the-job assignments. It provides an organized set of concepts and procedures to help readers identify strategic issues, make choices, and implement decisions.

The point of view we take on strategic issues is that of a general manager. We assume that you are willing to share this perspective—to see yourself as responsible for the overall direction and success of an organization or business unit. As a general manager, you must think in comprehensive terms of the total problem you are dealing with, taking into account the full breadth of its meaning and consequences for the business. Partial analyses from a specialist or a functional perspective may be helpful, but they do not meet the general manager's need for the best overall approach to a situation. In addition to the broad issues of direction, you must worry about the specific steps of execution—about closing the gaps between strategic choice and practical, personal action. Again, the recommendations of a consultant or staff specialist may be useful, but their advice will usually address only the directional aspects of the general manager's concerns. In short, we ask you to step into a particularly challenging position in which you must think of problems in terms of a total business, set priorities, and plan for tangible, practical action.

Three threads weave their way through the fabric of the text: value, advantage, and globalization. General managers are fundamentally charged with the responsibility for guiding their organizations to generate and capture value with an eye to how that value is distributed among various stakeholders, including shareholders. Our perspective is that organizations are a mechanism invented by society to generate value that individuals cannot generate on their own. The value that organizations generate takes many forms (e.g., profit, jobs, self-actualization, goods, and services), and different organizations generate different types of value. All organizations, however, must generate value—that is the reason they exist.

Organizational growth or even survivability depends not merely on the generation of value; businesses must also have comparative or competitive advantage. Why should customers buy your valuable product or service rather than another firm's? As a general manager, you must ensure that your value generating organization has competitive advantages.

Thirdly, today's environments are global. Very few industries are not impacted in some meaningful way by global forces. We deal with some specific issues related to global diversification strategies, but a basic assumption that we hold, and that we encourage you to consider as a general manager, is that globalization is no longer a separate, optional consideration. Globalization is a fundamental element for strategic analysis and action.

Understanding that the role of the general manager has changed in recent years, we have chosen to underscore this change with the new term "Cross-Enterprise Leadership." We summarized these changes, and the distinctions between the general manager and the Cross-Enterprise Leader in an Ivey Business Journal article. There, we concluded that the forces of globalization, rapid change, and time-based competition had redefined the role of the general manager and that organizations, as single entities controlling their own fate, had been supplanted by networks and alliances of enterprises.

> *Whereas general management focused on integrating the various functions within an organization, the business imperative today requires an approach—Cross-Enterprise Leadership—that can create, capture and distribute value across a network of companies, not just within a company. Second, these networks, which we call enterprises, are complex and dynamic, and must be able to respond as a whole to the emergent challenges that are continually presented. Third, no one leader can "manage" the enterprise, and therefore leadership needs to be distributed. Finally, these changes require an approach to leadership over-and-above that possessed by traditional business leaders. At its core, Cross-Enterprise Leadership recognizes that managers operate in a complex world in which the boundaries of organizations are fluid and dynamic, cutting across functional designations, departments, business units, companies, geography and cultures.*[1]

That value is created cross-enterprise is demonstrated by Coca-Cola and Nestle who are competitors in bottled water and several beverage categories around the world. But in North America, Coca-Cola is the primary distributor for Nestle's Nestea product. Toshiba reduces its shipping costs by having UPS undertake repairs of Toshiba products and Singapore based Flextronics undertakes design and manufacturing services for companies in the automotive, industrial, medical and technology sectors. Health care networks have become a necessary means to deliver on health care needs. While we take the organization as the primary focus, our perspective acknowledges that the boundaries of the organization are often blurry and models of strategy need the flexibility to take this into account.

For the purpose of this book, we will retain the term "general manager", however our view of the role of the general manager has changed, and these changes are reflected in the materials presented. The choice and presentation of material in the book have been guided by experience and practical utility. Our aim has been to provide useful tools organized into one consistent and comprehensive framework. Our intent is to present the diversity and complexity of the field, but distill it so that it can be applied in a decision-making process. Additional readings are suggested, where appropriate, at the end of chapters for those who wish to explore specific subjects in greater depth.

Throughout the book, we have frequently used examples to make the connection between the concepts, which have to be somewhat general for flexibility and breadth of application, and specific strategic issues. As you read, you might find it useful to think of examples from your own experience and test the applicability of the concepts against them.

ORGANIZATION

The book is organized according to a general pattern: problem identification to decision to execution. This is a natural, logical sequence and is effective for the cumulative presentation of concepts. But we do not mean to imply that actual strategic problems can be dealt with in such a neat, serial fashion. On the contrary, most strategic problems require an iterative approach, in which the analysis moves back and forth between choice and action. This point will become evident as you read through the book. Its immediate application, however, is that you should not expect to find business situations, or case problems describing them, that neatly conform to the flow of the text.

Throughout the book we use the terms business, organization, and firm interchangeably. Whether a not-for-profit or for-profit organization, a small entrepreneurial firm or a large multi-national, a public or private sector enterprise, the concepts apply to all types of organizations. If there is a particular distinction to be made for a specific type of organization, such as a not-for-profit, we will flag it. However, these instances will be rare as the fundamentals of strategy apply to all types of organizations in all geographic contexts.

There are 11 chapters in the book. Chapters 1 and 2 position the concept of strategy as a crucial general management tool and then provide an operational understanding and definition of it. Chapter 3 introduces the Diamond-E framework and the fundamental logic of strategic analysis. Chapters 4 through 8 elaborate on the processes of analysis by working through the individual components of the Diamond-E framework with a view to building a comprehensive position on strategic needs and priorities. Chapter 9 discusses the dynamic nature of strategy, providing a transition to Chapters 10 and 11, which concentrate on developing personal action plans to move from the analytic results to the implementation of strategic changes.

SUGGESTIONS FOR USE

At the outset we suggest that you read Chapters 1 through 3 thoroughly. This will provide a perspective for your thinking and a basic framework for your analysis. Skim the rest of the book so that you know where to turn as specific circumstances dictate.

As you deal with problems, use the book selectively. Try to work back and forth between the problem that you are addressing and the relevant parts of the book. Use the concepts to check your analysis and, as necessary, to expand it. Common sense is very important here. Do not try to force the concepts and procedures on a problem; instead use them to enrich the analysis.

Study the book after you have spent some time working on strategic problems. At that point you will more readily appreciate the general analytical approach and see the applicability of particular concepts. From then on, the building of skills in strategic analysis and action is a matter of practice and more practice. Remember, you are dealing with the most complex problems in business. Good luck!

Notes

1. Crossan, M., Olivera, F. "Cross-Enterprise Leadership: A New Approach for the 21st Century," *Ivey Business Journal*, May June, 2006.

Chapter 1
A General Management Perspective

A general manager is someone who has responsibility for all functional facets of the business. General managers run businesses and organizations of all kinds, such as for-profit businesses, public sector and not-for-profit organizations.[1] A fundamental challenge facing general managers today stems from the fact that the external environment in which their organization operates—which includes current customers, potential customers, competitors, technological innovation, government, suppliers, global forces and so on—is changing so rapidly that the firm, with its finite resources and limited organizational capabilities, is hard-pressed to keep up. Keep up it must, however, because in a rapidly changing environment, sticking with yesterday's strategy, no matter how successful it has been, is often a recipe for tomorrow's disaster.

Although the general manager holds a particular position in the organization, any individual in a functional position can have a general management perspective, and we argue that having one will assist employees throughout the organization. A general management perspective means having the capacity to understand and to appreciate issues facing individuals who are placed in the specific role of a general manager. Often, strategic decisions require difficult trade-offs. To the degree that employees understand why decisions have been made and what needs to be done, personal performance and organizational performance will be enhanced. A general management perspective also helps you to identify relevant data, information, and knowledge that are important to strategic analysis and action. Strategic decisions need to draw on the collective intelligence of the workforce. The general manager does not act in isolation. Throughout the text we refer to the General Manager, which is intended to capture all persons seeking to develop a general management perspective.

THE JOB OF THE GENERAL MANAGER

The job of the general manager is to create value for the enterprise. As a general manager you need to recognize emerging opportunities and challenges, prepare a response, and ensure the success of whatever plan of action you decide upon.

By way of example, consider the rapidly changing competitive situation in the consumer smartphone industry over the last few years. This is an industry that has grown rapidly and undergone rapid innovation. Research in Motion (RIM), a company that had a dominant position in the enterprise smartphone market, entered the consumer smart-phone market to increase its revenues and market share. As an early entrant in the industry it initially had good success capturing higher market share each year. But this came at the cost of reduced margins which the Co-CEO Jim Balisille described as a deliberate strategy of a "land grab."

"So we could have a sweeter margin for a couple of quarters and we might not torque the growth quite as much and then we will rue that for the next 20 years, that we gave up the key land for a little bit of interim gratification."[2]

While RIM's blackberry smartphone devices offered a superior email experience, the release of Apple's iPhone in 2007 started chipping away at RIM's market share and by the second quarter of 2011 Apple had achieved the top position in the smartphone space while RIM was in fourth place, with a market share that had declined over the previous year. What was even more worrisome was the fact that RIM was behind the curve in its response to Apple's release of the iPad and when RIM did release a competitive product, the market response was critical due to high defect rates and insufficient functionality. What had gone wrong? How could a company that had a leading position in the enterprise smartphone market come up so short in the consumer segment? Many analysts pinned the failure down to RIM's capabilities and resources that, while finely honed to understand and lead the enterprise market, did not seem to understand the needs of the consumer market and RIM was therefore slow to react to changes in, let alone lead, the market.

Having established a long-term direction, and created the strategy, the general manager's work is not done. In fact, the most difficult part is just beginning. While RIM's CEOs established long-term direction and created the strategy early on, not enough was done to develop the capability to allow the organization to provide leadership in both the enterprise and consumer market. Capabilities that were deemed as superior in RIM's highly protected enterprise market where inadequate in the far more competitive consumer market. Further, many capabilities required for success in consumer products were lacking.

This example illustrates three of the fundamental components of the general manager's job: setting direction, creating strategy, and implementing change. One further crucial aspect of the job, shown in Figure 1.1, is assessing performance—both current and longer term. Without a good feel for how well the organization is performing at any point in time, a general manager could get the other three components of the job very wrong. Emphasizing lofty but distant goals when the company may not survive the coming year could lead to disaster; acting as if there is a crisis when a slower pace of change would be more appropriate can be just as damaging.

A competent general manager will perform all four of these tasks. The tasks will not be addressed sequentially or in isolation from each other, but as a continuously changing mix of activities. The double-headed arrows in Figure 1.1 are intended to convey this interconnectedness.

The primary focus of this book is on the processes and tools you will need for creating strategy and managing strategic change. Before you embark on the strategy-making

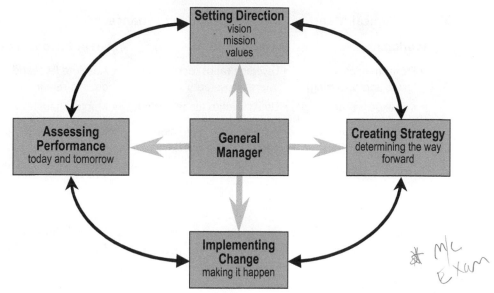

Figure 1.1 The Job of the General Manager

process you need to make sure that you know your starting position, which means that you need a solid assessment of current performance. You also need a high-level view of what you are trying to achieve, which will be captured in your vision, mission, and values. In the remainder of this chapter we address these topics.

ASSESSING PERFORMANCE

We begin with a discussion of performance assessment because the general manager who is not skilled at this task will have great difficulty with the other aspects of the job. Many corporate tragedies are rooted in the fact that senior managers had a false idea of how well their organization was performing. Take, for example, McDonald's, which in 2003 announced its first-ever quarterly loss since becoming a public company in 1965. As a franchisor, McDonald's collects royalties that amount to four percent of sales. However, it is also a real estate company, owning the land and buildings of many of the franchised locations, with rent amounting to about 10 percent of sales. Focused on its profitable real estate, which prompted expansive growth, McDonald's lost sight of deteriorating measures of performance such as same-store sales, which had been stagnant for a decade, and service, where it had ranked at the bottom of the fast-food industry since 1994. To turn things around, management had to reverse its strategy by dramatically reducing the number of store openings worldwide and, instead, focusing its attention on getting more customers into existing stores. The results were impressive. In 2010, McDonald's had achieved growth in same-store sales for eight consecutive years. From 2003 to 2010, revenues increased by 40 percent and net income more than trebled.

Table 1.1 Typical Measures of Operating Performance

Profitability	Financial Position	Market Performance
• Profit margins (gross and operating)	• Leverage ratios (debt/equity, interest coverage)	• Absolute level and growth rate in sales
• Key expense ratios	• Liquidity ratios (units, revenue)	• Market share
• Return on equity, assets	• Activity ratios (e.g., asset and inventory turnover)	• New products as % of sales
• Economic value added		

There are many approaches to take in sizing up performance, and each industry and company will have its own metrics based on the key performance drivers. Financial services provider Charles Schwab, for example, keeps its focus on maintaining strong client relationships through its "client promoter score" that measures the likelihood that a current client will recommend Schwab to their family or friends. Other organizations seek a balance among multiple performance indicators. For a useful approach to creating multiple performance measures, see Kaplan and Norton's "Balanced Scorecard."[3]

Our assessment of organizational performance is based on two sets of measures: *operating performance* and *organizational health*. Operating performance includes the "hard" or more quantitative measures of financial and market performance. Some typical measures of operating performance are included in Table 1.1. In any given situation some of these measures may be more important than others. Whatever your circumstances, beware of relying on only a single measure of operating performance, or on solely internal measures.

Measures of organizational health are generally "softer" and more qualitative than those of operating performance, and include such things as management and worker enthusiasm, the ability to work across boundaries, and the ability of the organization to learn. These and other factors are described in Table 1.2. Again, you might put more emphasis on some of these factors than others as you are assessing the health of your organization, but here too we recommend that you focus on more than a single measure, and assess how these factors are changing over time.

The danger that many senior management teams face is that they think they know where the business stands in terms of organizational health, when often they do not. This could be because negative communication to the top of the organization is implicitly or explicitly discouraged, it could be the result of middle managers choosing to filter information before it reaches the top, or simply that senior managers do not listen well. One response in many firms has been to use anonymous employee surveys on a large scale to try to get a realistic assessment of these measures.

It is also important to recognize that the drivers of performance for any company or industry are often inter-related in important ways with key leading and lagging indicators. For example, a fast food chain developed a causal model proposing the drivers of strategic

Tool #3 Org Health

Table 1.2 Typical Measures of Organizational Health

Enthusiasm	Boundaries	Problem Solving	Learning	Sustainability
How enthusiastic are managers and employees about their work?	Do individuals identify with narrow sub-groups, or with the organization as a whole?	Are problem areas identified and dealt with, or hidden and ignored?	Does the organization learn from its experiences? From others' experiences?	Can the pace at which people are working be sustained?

Source: Adapted from R. Pascale, M. Millimann, and L. Gioja, "Changing the Way We Change," *Harvard Business Review*, (November–December 1997).

success. They found that choices in selection and staffing impacted employee satisfaction, which in turn affected the value employees were able to add to the business. Employee value-add affected customer satisfaction, which affected customer buying behavior, profitability, and overall shareholder value.[4]

Using the Performance Matrix

We use the performance matrix to classify operating performance and organizational health as roughly positive or negative and ask three questions: (1) where was your business three years ago, (2) where is it today, and (3) which way is it currently moving? Our main emphasis is on the current position of the business, but a discussion of this naturally leads to consideration of where the business has been and which way it is moving. In Figure 1.2 we have illustrated the hypothetical case of a business that has moved from Quadrant 2 (Q2) through Q4 and is currently in Q3, hoping to move upward to Q1.

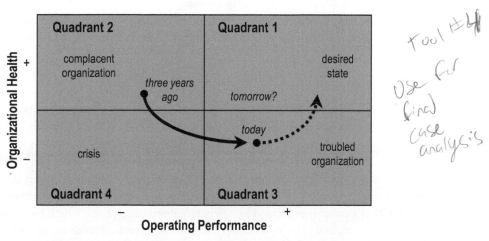

Tool #4
Use for final case analysis

Figure 1.2 The Performance Matrix (with illustrative example)

Clearly, the desired state is Quadrant 1, in which operating performance and organizational health are both positive. If your analysis suggests that your business is in this quadrant, and you expect it to stay there, your strategy review will probably be a question of fine tuning, and perhaps taking a farther than usual look into the future. But do not take the strategy assessment process lightly. You need to ensure that you have placed yourself in this quadrant as a result of thorough analysis, not complacency or wishful thinking.

The picture in Quadrant 2, on the other hand, may be of an inward-looking and complacent organization where people enjoy their work, but collectively are performing inadequately in terms of market and financial standards. There may be recognition by a few that there is a need to change, but getting a meaningful strategic review under way may be difficult, as currently happy employees will not want to face the prospect of making uncomfortable changes to improve operating performance.

In Quadrant 3 the business is achieving its operating objectives at the expense of organizational health. This may arise because management has applied pressure for short-term profits, often via downsizing, without upgrading the skills of their people. Management also may have given little thought to the processes by which work should be done. It is a classic case of doing the same work with fewer people, and everyone is burned out.

Quadrant 4 represents a clear-cut problem situation in which immediate and comprehensive action is necessary. It may well be a crisis; if so, strategic analysis had better be fast. Shortcuts may have to be taken, but our hope is that if your firm is in crisis a quick look through this book will at least help you decide where to start, and which parts of the strategy creation process will quickly yield the most value to you and your business team.

In later chapters we will discuss other perspectives on performance. In Chapter 5, for example, we will ask you to predict the likely performance of your business if it continues with its existing strategy; this is your "base case" scenario. In the last two chapters of the book, which deal with the management of change, we will discuss the crisis curve concept, which involves tracing the past, current, and projected future performance of a business to determine the urgency for change.

We now turn to another task of the general manager that needs to be considered before we turn to strategic analysis: that of establishing the overall direction for the business.

SETTING DIRECTION: VISION, MISSION, VALUES

Organizations need a strong sense of direction—a vision—to bring coherence to the many strategic and operating decisions that managers at all levels are constantly called upon to make. There are three basic reasons for starting strategic analysis with work on visioning. The first is to resolve confusion over the purpose of the business: why it exists. For example, some of the most visible instances are in family-owned companies, when disagreements arise among the family shareholders over such issues as dividend income or family employment. Other examples are found in newly privatized enterprises, which have long been an arm of the state, and now have to decide on fundamental objectives, and whom they are to serve. All organizations, though, need a clear sense of what and who they are.

The second reason for developing or changing a company's vision is to revitalize it. Here the pursuit of a new vision alerts people to the need for change. When Steve Jobs resumed control of Apple Computer, he brought with him his vision to change the world through technology. What began as a focusing of resources on key products has revitalized the company, setting the stage for a new strategy in 2004 to make Macs a hub in a networked world of digital devices. *Fortune* magazine described Jobs as having

> . . . exercised his increasing power with the facility of a jujitsu master. Consider: He elbowed aside the likes of Sony to change the dynamics of consumer electronics with the iPod. He persuaded the music industry, the television networks, and Hollywood to let him show them how to distribute their wares in the Digital Age with the iTunes Music Store. He employed the arch austerity of his hugely successful Apple Stores to give the big-box boys a lesson in high-margin, high-touch retailing. And this year, at the height of his creative and promotional powers, Jobs orchestrated Apple's over-the-top entry into the cellular telephone business with the iPhone, a lozenge of glass and aluminum encasing a do-everything digital device.[5]

According to the International Data Corporation, in the second quarter of 2011 Apple's iPhone had captured the top market share of the global smart phone market. In a few short years, Apple went from not having a product in the smartphone market to being the leader.[6] Finally, you might decide to prepare a mission statement when your business is operating reasonably well, but you think that creating one might be useful to reinforce your existing informal "sense of vision". You might also see it perhaps as a public relations exercise, to better present the business to shareholders, customers, or regulators.

The challenge in developing a vision is simultaneously to raise people's sights, give them direction, and stay realistic. While it usually helps to formalize agreements about vision, mission, and values in an explicit mission statement, the existence of a formal statement may actually mean very little; the critical factor is whether the vision has permeated the organization. Achieving a powerful sense of mission depends very heavily on the day-to-day decisions and actions of an organization's leaders. People look to actions, not words, for guidance. If a purpose like "to be the best and most successful company in the airline business" is to have real motivating power and directional meaning, then the actions of senior management in everything from investment decisions for aircraft to the budgets for cleaning cabins had better be consistent with that vision.

There are many frameworks and references on the subject of vision, mission, and values. A list of references is provided at the end of this chapter. Collins and Porras studied highly successful companies and found that what they had in common was an enduring set of core values and purpose, unique to each company, that remain fixed even though their business strategies evolved over time.[7]

The Collins and Porras framework is a good example since it is based on solid research, yet provides a practical approach for applying the concepts. Collins and Porras state that "at the broadest level, vision consists of two major components—a Guiding Philosophy that, in the context of expected future environments, leads to a Tangible Image."[8]

In the Collins and Porras framework, the Guiding Philosophy includes the core purpose and core values of the organization. The core purpose and core values need to be translated into a Tangible Image in the form of a mission and a vivid description of that mission. Whereas in the case of strategy, environmental analysis plays a pivotal role, in the case of vision, it plays more of a moderating role in translating purpose into mission. Aspiration plays a stronger role with vision such that there is a fine line between the possible and impossible. Although Collins and Porras advocate that strategic analysis should be done after the vision and mission-setting process, this is rarely the case. The practical matter is that vision and strategy operate in tandem as we discuss later in this chapter.

Guiding Philosophy

The guiding philosophy has two elements, the core purpose and core values. The core values are the starting point for the guiding philosophy.

Values Values represent the basic beliefs that govern individual and group behaviour in an organization. This may be brief and at a high level of abstraction, or much more detailed and specific. To support its mission to, "establish Starbucks as the premier purveyor of the finest coffee in the world while maintaining our uncompromising principles as we grow," Starbucks has six guiding principles:[9]

- Provide a great work environment and treat each other with respect and dignity
- Embrace diversity as an essential component in the way we do business
- Apply the highest standards of excellence to the purchasing, roasting and fresh delivery of our coffee
- Develop enthusiastically satisfied customers all of the time
- Contribute positively to our communities and our environment
- Recognize that profitability is essential to our future success

At first glance, you may find this a rather straightforward list. There is certainly very little here with which to disagree. Surely every company wants to treat people with respect and dignity. On the other hand, Starbucks really lives these values, as can be seen by the employee stock plan, benefits, a first-class working environment, a heavy investment in training, an obsessive focus on the customer, and other measures.

It is not surprising that Starbucks imbues these values since they are strongly held by CEO Howard Schultz. Schultz was deeply affected by the experiences of his father, stating that "My father was a broken-down blue collar worker . . . He was not valued and not respected, and it made him very bitter and angry. I wanted Starbucks to be a company that didn't leave anyone behind."[10] Having witnessed the financial stress on his family when his father was out of work with a broken ankle and no medical benefits, Schultz is committed to treat everyone with respect and dignity. As a result, thousands of part-time Starbucks workers have full medical benefits. The proof of the values is that Schultz is not willing to compromise. Although his profit margins are lower than other fast-food or restaurant businesses, Schultz says that it is the price you have to pay for doing business his way.

Since Starbucks has achieved these things, then it is indeed different from many other companies. Creating a values list that looks good is not so difficult; living up to your values is a tougher task. After Schultz left as CEO, performance at Starbucks between 2005 and 2008 fell and its stock declined by over 50%. On his return as CEO in 2008, Schultz attributed the decline to Starbucks moving away from its values.

> *Success is not sustainable if it is defined by how big you become or by growth for growth's sake. Success is very shallow if it doesn't have emotional meaning. I think there was a herd mentality—a reason for being that somehow became linked to PE, the stock price, and a group of people who felt they were invincible.*[11]

He goes on to say:

> *You have to have a 100% belief in your core reason for being. There was tremendous pressure . . . to dramatically change the strategy and the business model of the company. The marketplace was saying, "Starbucks needs to undo all these company-owned stores and franchise the system." That would have given us a war chest of cash and significantly increased return on capital. It's a good argument economically. It's a good argument for shareholder value. But it would have fractured the culture of the company. You have to be authentic, you have to be true, and you have to believe in your heart that this is going to work. Someone said to me, "You are roasting 400 million pounds of coffee a year. If you reduce the quality 5%, no one would know. That's a few hundred million dollars!" We would never do that.*[12]

We do not have to look far to see examples of companies like Enron and Tyco that had a set of values they could not live up to.

We add a final caveat on the issue of values. One might expect that an enduring set of values could only be beneficial to a company, but this is not necessarily the case. For many years, under the leadership of Akio Morita, Sony Corporation of Japan operated with the strongly held core value that Sony is a pioneer, and does not follow others. This was very motivating, especially to the researchers and engineers in Sony's laboratories, and the company introduced a long list of innovative products, such as the Walkman, that were clear firsts on the market. The pioneering spirit was an important element of Sony's success.

However, concerned that it might lose its preeminent position in home entertainment as the computer business and the home entertainment business converge, Sony chose to develop a personal computer. Working with Intel and Microsoft, Sony's entry in the personal computer business was clearly not a pioneering move. Sony engineers had to learn to work with others. Nobukuyi Idei, the successor to Morita, started to talk about modified values. His key words were *originality*, *passion*, *openness*, and *change*. Originality is closely tied to the previous pioneering concept, but openness, in particular, was a new idea, and what Idei was promoting was an openness to ideas from other companies, to soften Sony's often isolationist stance. And under Sir Howard Stringer, Idei's successor, Sony continued to partner with other companies, such as its partnership with HID Global and Google in 2010, while at the same it also worked on improving its operational efficiency to allow it to regain its leadership in innovation.

Core Purpose Core purpose defines the reason for being and may never be fully realized, in contrast to goals and objectives, which are formulated specifically to be achievable. Collins and Porras provide some examples of core purpose. For 3M it is to "solve unsolved problems innovatively." For Merck it is "to preserve and improve human life", and for Wal-Mart it is "to give ordinary folk the chance to buy the same things as rich people." Collins and Porras argue that maximizing shareholder wealth is the "standard off-the-shelf purpose for those organizations that have not yet identified their true core purpose. It is a substitute—and a weak one at that."[13]

Tangible Image

In the Collins and Porras framework, core values and core purpose need to be paired with an envisioned future, including a vivid description that is reachable in a 10- to 30-year time frame.

Mission Statement "A mission is a clear and compelling goal that serves to unify an organization's efforts. An effective mission must stretch and challenge the organization, yet be achievable. It translates the abstractness of philosophy into a tangible, energizing, highly focused goal that draws the organization forward. It is crisp, clear, engaging—it reaches out and grabs people in the gut."[14] The example Collins and Porras provide of an effective mission statement is that made by President Kennedy in 1961—"Achieving the goal, before this decade is out, of landing a man on the moon and returning him safely to earth."[15]

Vivid Description Collins and Porras point to Henry Ford's vision to democratize the automobile, supported by the following vivid description.

> I will build a motor car for the great multitude . . . It will be so low in price that no man making a good salary will be unable to own one and enjoy with his family the blessing of hours of pleasure in God's great open spaces . . . When I'm through, everybody will be able to afford one, and everyone will have one. The horse will have disappeared from our highways, the automobile will be taken for granted . . . [and we will] give a large number of men employment at good wages.

Reasonable Expectations of a Vision Process

The Collins and Porras framework helps to organize the components of vision, which include a guiding philosophy of core values and purpose, and a tangible image with a mission and vivid description. Some reasonable expectations follow from applying such a framework and, in fact, provide a test for the outcome of pursuing the process. They are that the vision, mission, and value outcomes (1) settle some fundamental questions about the purpose of the business; (2) prompt and reinforce the day-to-day actions that are consistent with their meaning; and (3) provide direction in the formulation of the more specific strategy of the firm. In this respect, consider the following example.

Schindler Elevator of Switzerland has a simply-stated vision, "*leadership through service.*" At first glance, this seems rather innocuous, and unlikely to be very motivating. However, a closer look suggests otherwise. As Schindler is number two in its industry, behind Otis, achieving leadership in sales volume is a very challenging task. "Leadership" as Schindler defines it, also includes leadership in quality, safety, innovation, employee motivation, and responsiveness to customers. Furthermore, to ensure that the company's operating units around the world pay more than lip service to the vision, objectives are set and performance is measured in each of these areas. In terms of customer satisfaction, for example, every Schindler operation is to be ranked higher than the competition in its served markets, and at a minimum must achieve greater than 45 percent of respondents ranking the company a "5" (i.e., excellent) on a five-point scale. Less than three percent of responses are allowed at the "1" or "2" level. Similar objectives exist for employee motivation and market share position. If you work anywhere in the Schindler world, this vision is difficult to ignore.

In addition to spelling out the company's destination, which is "leadership" in its industry, Schindler's mission statement indicates how that destination is to be reached: through "service." Once again, this does not sound particularly exciting. However "service" is a motivating and differentiating concept for the Schindler organization for several reasons. First, Otis and Mitsubishi, both major competitors, have visions which emphasize leadership through technology, so Schindler's mission statement is differentiating it from its most important rivals. Second, Schindler has traditionally been a manufacturing and technology-driven company, and emphasizing that the company will compete on service is a new concept which will drive change in many areas of the organization. Finally, as Peter Zbinden, the president of Schindler, commented:

> When we say "service," we mean service to both internal and external customers. So this is a statement about how we will work together, as well as how we treat our customers. The difference between a good company and a great company today is the way it delivers its overall service. Our vision captures both where we are going and how we are going to compete.

In Schindler's case, the company sets very specific, measurable, three-year objectives tied directly to its mission statement which, in turn, is a distillation of its long-term vision. Objectives are renewed and extended annually, and provide what the company calls "measurable feedback on progress made towards achievement of the company's vision."

Process Concerns

Visions and visionary ideas may arise from a variety of sources, ranging from the singular imagination of a strong leader to an elaborate process of employee involvement. If you tap the knowledge and aspirations of the key people of an organization, the argument goes, you can achieve creativity and commitment at the same time. Indeed, if the process is carefully managed this can be true, but there are some risks and limits in this approach that should be recognized.

One management group went through a very elaborate visioning process and were quite disillusioned by the outcome. They had just spent a lot of time and effort trying to define their company as they thought it should look five years in the future. The process even involved a technology by which they could vote secretly on specific suggestions as they came up in the discussions! Ultimately a "vision" was produced which represented the mechanical consensus of the group. Then the difficulties surfaced. Some managers thought the outcome was ridiculous because it failed to properly recognize the constraints under which the company was operating. Others found it simply irrelevant—it seemed to have little to do with the very real problems that they were facing right now. Everyone was disappointed. This was a process gone wrong. The construction of a vision, any vision, had become the object of the exercise, at the expense of a real debate about the identity, direction, opportunities, and problems in front of the company and what should be done.

A Final Vision Check

There are three basic questions to put to an emerging vision. First, does it portray a desirable *and* feasible destination? Second, does it do so without jeopardizing management's flexibility to maneuver as circumstances change? Third, does it stretch the organization? The question of desirability is much easier to answer than that of feasibility. For desirability, just ask people: employees, friends, customers, suppliers, investors. For feasibility and flexibility, however, you need to do some careful analysis.

Feasibility The question of whether you can reasonably expect to get to your visionary destination cannot be answered in the abstract. A vision will not stand on its own. You need to relate it to the realities of your situation. To do this, you need to express the vision first in the more definitive terms of a supporting strategy, and second, to test that strategy. Does it make sense?

Flexibility Much of the power of a vision lies in the fact that it is a public commitment for the whole organization. A vision must also be flexible, however, because circumstances may change in unanticipated ways. Management may hesitate to change a public commitment that is no longer appropriate. Even if management does change its position, the momentum behind the now obsolete vision may persist in various parts of the organization for reasons ranging from ignorance, to disagreement, to willful pursuit of self-serving activities.

Stretch Sometimes organizations focus on a vision that is too easily reached under the false rationalization that they are ensuring feasibility. A vision should go further than what is doable with today's resources and capabilities. Rather, it should motivate people, it should inspire and enthuse the firm with a sense of purpose and the need for exploration and discovery. Leading companies often began with visions that were, at the time, out of proportion to their then current resources and capabilities. Visions that require organizations to stretch are ambitious conceptions of what the organization will be in the future.

There is clearly a fine line here. A powerful vision that grasps an organization also makes it difficult to change quickly, and this risk must be considered before an organization is fired up to pursue it. A vision provides stretch and flexibility but must be close enough to what is realistic. As with feasibility, the risk of an inflexible visionary commitment can only be thoroughly identified by going through the steps of putting the vision into strategic terms and checking for sustainability.

FROM VISION, MISSION, AND VALUES TO STRATEGY

Linking the vision, which is intended to inspire and motivate people, with the strategy, which provides guidance and direction, is a critical task of general management. Firms often get trapped in defining a vision and fail to translate the vision into a strategy. The result is often strategic drift. We show the relationship between vision, strategy and tactics in Table 1.3.

Vision, mission, and values are very useful, but also very general leadership tools. Properly developed, they will inspire an organization and give it a basic sense of direction and broad guidelines for getting there.

Table 1.3 Vision, Strategy, and Tactics

Vision	Strategy	Tactics
Diverse audiences	Decision makers	Operational executors
Broad direction	General priorities	Specific actions
Long-term	Medium-term	Short-term
Inspirational	Declaring	Doing
Enduring	Stable	Changing
Energy	Direction	Map

STRATEGIC ANALYSIS, PLANNING, AND BUSINESS PLANS

While this book focuses on strategic analysis, the link to strategic planning and business plans can be readily made. Simply put, if you understand strategic analysis and action, you are well positioned for both strategic planning and preparing business plans. Strategic planning is the approach to undertaking strategic analysis on a recurring basis and it deals with who develops the strategy, how it happens and when it takes place. We discuss strategic planning in Chapter 9 after presenting the various elements of strategic analysis. While strategic analysis is a process, the development of business plans is an output or outcome of that analysis. Many organizations undertake strategic analysis with a view to making a particular strategic decision or perhaps to developing a strategic plan. Occasionally, business plans are required to communicate to others, such as investors, the value of a particular strategic proposal.

Business plans come in many forms. The underlying analysis required to write a strong business plan is the focus of this text. How that analysis is communicated in the form of a business plan must be customized to the particular situation. Yet there are some standard elements that are typically required in any business plan, which we set out in detail in Chapter 9. But the realities of general management—which call, among other things, for judgments about the precise viability of ideas in a competitive market, the resolution of often conflicting interests, and the achievement of change in the face of inertia and resistance—demand a more flexible tool than planning and a more precise tool than vision to deal with ends and means. This is what we attempt to capture in the idea of strategy, the topic of the next chapter.

SUMMARY

This chapter has concentrated on two aspects of the general manager's job that need attention before you become immersed in the strategy-making process: assessing performance and setting the direction for the business. We suggest that your performance assessment focus on both operating performance and organizational health. Both need to be understood before you turn to strategy. In terms of direction setting, we have concentrated on vision, mission, and values. These things do not need to be formalized into a written document, but they do need to be agreed upon, and shared within the organization. Without them, you will be creating strategy in a vacuum.

Notes

1. The concepts utilized in the book have wide applicability to organizations generally—not just to for-profit business organizations. We use the terms "business", "firm" and

"organization" interchangeably but draw most of our examples from, and use language that is perhaps more common to, for-profit businesses.

2. McInnes, Kyle "Rim makes "land grab" with consumer market despite small margins." BlackBerry Cool, March 30, 2009. Web. 28 Sept. 2011. <www.blackberrycool.com/2009/03/30/rim-makes-land-grab-with-consumer-market-despite-small-margins/>.

3. Kaplan, Robert S., and David P. Norton. "The Balanced Scorecard—Measures That Drive Performance." *Harvard Business Review* 70 (January–February 1992): 71–80. Print.

4. Ittner, Christopher D., and David F. Larcker. "Coming Up Short on Nonfinancial Performance Measurement." *Harvard Business Review* 81 (November 2003): 88–97. Print.

5. Schlender, B., et al. "Power 25." *Fortune* 156.12 (Dec 10, 2007): 116. Print.

6. "Apple Rises to the Top as Worldwide Smartphone Market Grows 65.4% in the Second Quarter of 2011, IDC Finds." *IDC Press Release*. IDC (Aug 4, 2011). Web. 28 Sept. 2011. <www.idc.com/getdoc.jsp?containerId=prUS22974611>.

7. Collins, James C., and Jerry I. Porras. "Organizational Vision and Visionary Organizations." *California Management Review* 34 (Fall 1991): 30–52. Print.

8. Collins, James C. and Jerry I. Porras. "Organizational Vision and Visionary Organizations." *California Management Review* 34 (Fall 1991): 33. Print.

9. "Our Starbucks Mission Statement." Starbucks Corporation (2011). Web. 28 Sept. 2011. <www.starbucks.com/aboutus/environment.asp>.

10. Daniels, Cora. "Mr. Coffee." *Fortune* 147 (April 14, 2003): 139–141. Print.

11. Ignatius, Adi. "We Had to Own the Mistakes." *Harvard Business Review* 88.7/8 (2010): 108–115. *Business Source Complete, EBSCO*. Web. 16 Aug. 2011.

12. Ignatius, Adi. "We Had to Own the Mistakes." *Harvard Business Review* 88.7/8 (2010): 108–115. *Business Source Complete, EBSCO*. Web. 16 Aug. 2011.

13. Collins, James C., and Jerry I. Porras. "Building Your Company's Vision." *Harvard Business Review* 74 (September–October 1996): 65-78. Print.

14. Collins, James C., and Jerry I. Porras. "Organizational Vision and Visionary Organizations." *California Management Review* 34 (Fall 1991): 42. Print.

15. Collins, James C., and Jerry I. Porras. "Organizational Vision and Visionary Organizations." *California Management Review* 34 (Fall 1991): 42. Print.

Additional Readings

1. Alexander, John W. "Sharing the Vision." *Business Horizons* 32 (May–June 1989): 56-59. Print.

2. Bartlett, Christopher, and Sumantra Ghoshal. "Changing the Role of Top Management: Beyond Strategy to Purpose." *Harvard Business Review* 72 (November–December 1994): 79–89. Print.

3. Campbell, Andrew, Marion Devine, and David Young. *A Sense of Mission*. London: Hutchinson Books Limited, 1990. Print.

4. Collins, James C., and Jerry I. Porras. *Built to Last: Successful Habits of Visionary Companies*. New York: Harper Business, 1994. Print.

5. Collins, James C., and Jerry I. Porras. "The Ultimate Vision." *Across The Board* 32 (January 1995): 19–23. Print.

6. De Geus, Arie. "The Living Company." *Harvard Business Review* 75 (March–April 1997): 51–59. Print.

7. Fry, N., and P. Killing. "Vision Check." *Business Quarterly* 54 (Autumn 1989): 64-70. Print.

8. Langeler, Gerald H. "The Vision Trap." *Harvard Business Review* 70 (March–April 1992): 46–54. Print.

9. Leavitt, Harold J. *Corporate Pathfinders*. New York: Penguin Books, 1986. Print.

10. Schmincke, Donald R. "Strategic Thinking: A Perspective For Success." *Management Review* 79 (August 1990): 16–19. Print.

11. Simons, Robert. *Levers of Control*. Boston: Harvard Business School Press, 1995. Print.

12. Smith, Bryan. "Vision: A Time To Take Stock." *Business Quarterly* 54 (Autumn 1989): 80–84. Print.

13. Stewart, Thomas A. "A Refreshing Change: Vision Statements That Make Sense." *Fortune* 134 (September 30, 1996): 195–196. Print.

14. "The Vision Thing," *The Economist* 332 (September 3, 1994): 67. Print.

15. Thornberry, Neal. "A View about 'Vision'." *European Management Journal* 15 (February 1997): 28–34. Print.

16. Wright, Norman B., and Peter M. Tobia. "Strategic Vision at Consumers Packaging." *Business Quarterly* 54 (Autumn 1989): 70–74. Print.

Chapter 2
Strategy

Strategy is a concrete expression of how an organization intends to compete and win in its marketplace. As such, strategy is the definitive tool for building, communicating, and maintaining the direction of a business. The intention of strategy is to take the basic ideas of a business, such as those reflected in the vision, mission, and values, and to express them in operational terms—in terms that are directly useful for analysis and action.

Many organizations have no stated strategy. In fact, Collis and Rukstad suggest that "It's a dirty little secret: Most executives cannot articulate the objective, scope, and advantage of their business in a simple statement".[1] However, every organization has an implied strategy, which can be inferred from the decisions and actions taken. Even in cases where an organization has a stated strategy, the strategy needs to be closely examined. Often, the stated strategy is really more like a vision given the high level of abstraction. Conversely, a stated strategy may actually be a set of tactics given the detailed set of actions. There are many views about what constitutes a strategy. We will begin by focusing on one model and conclude the chapter with other perspectives on strategy.

In this chapter we present a practical model for developing the concept of strategy. We suggest that a useful way for you to visualize business strategy is to think of it in terms of four related components: goals, product market focus, value proposition, and core activities. After a short elaboration of this model and a discussion of its utility we will explore these building block components in some depth, one by one and then together, first in the relatively simple context of a single business, and later in multibusiness applications.

THE ESSENTIALS OF THE STRATEGY MODEL

Our conception of strategy is presented in Figure 2.1. Taken alone, each component in this model refers to a distinct aspect of a strategy. Your first step in trying to understand the strategy of a business, or to describe its strategic intentions, is to focus on these separate components and to address such questions as the following:

1. *Goals*: What does the business propose to achieve? What are its aims, for example, with respect to growth, profitability and risk?

2. *Product Market Focus*: What are the products and/or services that the business plans to sell, and to what specific markets?

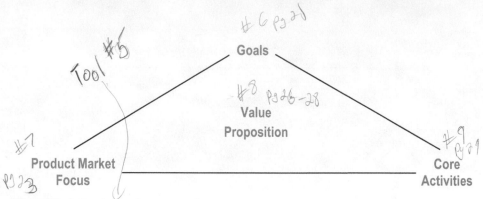

Figure 2.1 Business Strategy Components

3. *Value Proposition:* How does the business intend to attract customers? What benefits constitute its "offer" or "value proposition" in the marketplace?

4. *Core Activities:* What are the primary value-adding activities that the business intends to perform and how does it intend to perform them?

Remember as you pursue this process that every firm *has* a strategy; but you will often have to look beyond formal statements to the decision behaviour of management over time to figure out what that strategy is. As an understanding of each of the individual components starts to emerge, your second step is to bring these findings together, as reflected in the schematic presentation, and to study the overall picture for clarity and consistency. If you find a reasonably coherent picture, you have the necessary base point from which to probe the past success (or failure) of the business, or to analyze its future prospects. However, if you are saddled with ambiguity you will have to start your work from scratch and deal with questions about why such a situation exists, what its consequences have been, and what needs to be done to resolve it.

THE ROLE OF STRATEGY

Strategy plays a central role in the efforts of general managers to establish, sustain, and monitor the direction of their businesses. In fact, the absence of strategy can cause considerable frustration. Take for example, some typical complaints identified by Collis and Rukstad: "I tried for months to get an initiative off the ground, and then it is shut down because 'it doesn't fit the strategy.' Why didn't anyone tell me that at the beginning?" Or, "Why are we bidding on this customer's business again? We lost it last year, and I thought we agreed then not to waste our time chasing the contract!".[2] Our favourite question, often heard from the support functions of businesses is: "How are we supposed to prioritize our services when we don't even know what the business strategy is?" Consider the following examples of the ways in which strategy can help.

A Hub for Analysis In a retrospective sense, the concept of strategy provides a base point for organizing and discussing your understanding of what a business is all about.

Most businesses are more complex and subtle than they seem on first view. The concept of strategy will help you to sort out what a business is doing and what it is doing differently than its competitors, and to communicate and discuss your views on these points. This understanding supplies a needed basis for a further analysis of why a business has been a success (or failure) and what legacy of position and momentum is implicit in this success (or failure).

In a prospective sense, the concept of strategy provides you with a starting point for analyzing and debating choices that affect the future direction of the business. There is a "base case" choice in most situations, for example, which consists essentially of pressing forward with the current strategy. Does this "base case" make sense relative to future markets and competition? What performance can you expect and at what level of risk? As you move forward, new strategic initiatives are likely to be more complex and subtle. Virtually any decision that is hard to reverse needs to be considered in relation to the intended direction of the business. Many of these emerge spontaneously as people sense an opportunity or move to deal with a specific problem. A great advantage of the strategy framework is that it helps you to highlight the ramifications of such spontaneous initiatives and to keep your subsequent analysis and decision focused on essential matters.

A Link to Action Strategy provides a vehicle for you to translate general ideas about direction and performance, for example, into more explicit, actionable terms. *Goals* set up the targets against which progress and performance can be assessed. *Product market focus* provides critical direction to people throughout the business so that they can focus their effort on targeted markets and products and, just as importantly, avoid wasting their time on tangential opportunities. Much the same can be said for the *value proposition*; this strategy component provides a beacon for employees everywhere, illuminating specifically what the business is trying to do for its customers and, by inference, the requirements of their particular role. The choice of *core activities* highlights the key jobs that will have to be done and the capabilities that need most to be developed and reinforced. Decisions to alter any or all of the components set up the requirements for achieving change.

Strategy also provides a touchstone for continuous improvement. It puts your interpretation of vision, mission, and values into a testable framework that can be used to reinforce continuity where appropriate and to drive change where necessary. In this way strategy can and will be changed, usually incrementally, to adapt to changing circumstances. As such, it provides general managers with an everyday tool to help keep their organizations on track and to put their effort where it really counts.

STRATEGY IN A SINGLE BUSINESS

For the time being we will focus our discussion of the four strategy components by assuming that we are dealing with a single business. This business may be an independent entity or a strategic business unit (SBU) in a larger corporation. An SBU sells a distinct set of products or services to an identifiable group of customers and it is accountable for distinct revenues, costs, and investments, directly or by reasonable allocation. Some organizations are distinct businesses with one overall business strategy. Others have several business strategies and these strategies fall under the broader umbrella of corporate strategy. Whereas business strategy focuses on how an organization will create value within a particular line of business, corporate strategy deals with the portfolio of business strategies and how they relate to each other. We discuss corporate strategy at the end of this chapter.

In describing business strategy there is no required starting point. However, two of the four elements tend to be easier entry points into the strategy. If a vision or mission exists, it is quite possible that the goals will develop as a natural extension. Alternatively, the value proposition is often easier to articulate when you focus on how value is created in the eyes of the customer. Regardless of where you start, it is often necessary to iterate through the various components to ensure they are aligned. Occasionally one of the four elements may act as an anchor point, but more typically, all are in some degree of flux and insight is required to determine how changes in one might affect the other.

GOALS

Strategic goals are an expression, in measurable terms, of what a business intends to achieve—absolutely and relative to competition. In contrast to a vision, which may include very long-term goals, strategic goals are more immediate. It is helpful to distinguish between two broad categories of goals, which we call *hard goals* and *soft goals*. Some examples of specific goals within these two categories are presented in Table 2.1. In this classification, the hard goals focus on the aims and performance of the business as a classic economic entity whether it be for profit or not for profit, revealing measurable targets and time frames. A business, for example, may intend to grow revenues at a rate of 10 percent, be first or second in sales in the market it serves, and earn a 15 percent return on shareholder equity by year five. A hospital might focus on patient safety measures, while a food bank might target the growth in food donations year over year.

The soft goals of a business set out targets for the social conduct of the business. They focus on the intentions of the business with respect to its managers, employees, and in the community at large. Soft goals may be overlooked in strategic analyses that focus too narrowly on a faceless economic conception of a business; and unfortunately so, for soft goals can be compelling elements for shaping the direction of a business. It would be difficult for you to develop strategy in a family firm, for example, if you did not understand the critical roles played by soft goals with respect to such matters as family status and employment.

Soft goals are also more difficult to state in measurable terms, which may be another reason why they are often overlooked. But measurability is essential in order to use goals to manage and influence the conduct of the business. There is very little point in espousing

Table 2.1 Examples of Business Goals

Hard Goals	Soft Goals
Profitability	**Management**
• Return on sales, net assets employed, and equity • Economic value added (EVA) • Total return to shareholders key expense ratios	• Autonomy • Status
Market Position	**Employees**
• Rank by sales, assets, etc. in industry • Leader or follower in new products, marketing practices • Share of market	• Economic security • Opportunities to advance • Working conditions
Growth	**Community**
• Increase in sales, assets, earnings • Growth in earnings per share	• Control of externalities • Contributions to welfare, cultural life
Risk	**Society**
• Financial risk • Operating risk	• General benefits through innovation, efficiency, responsible political environment
Healthcare Organization Goals **Hard**	**Soft**
• Mortality rates • Re-infection rates	• Patient satisfaction • Perceptions of community health and well being

a high standard of workplace safety, for example, unless you put measures and targets and reporting systems into place.

Goal Structures

Businesses typically pursue a variety of goals simultaneously, so it is useful to think in terms of a business goal structure. In general, a goal structure should represent, in scope and balance, the important aims of the business. This would be true, for example, if they reflected the "balanced scorecard" notion proposed by Kaplan and Norton[3], which requires a consistent, broadly based set of goals that reflect a firm's ambitions. When this applies, as we pointed out in Chapter 1, there is a natural and easy tie to performance measurement. More often than not, however, the construction of a coherent goal structure is a tough job that calls for some very serious decisions.

Describing Goal Structures

As goals proliferate, so too do the opportunities for conflict and confusion. To avoid this, the several goals of a business must be placed in some order of priority or what we call a goal structure. Consider the challenge faced by our students as they address an assignment to describe the goal structure of the business in which they have worked. It is reasonably easy for the students to assemble a list of goals from experience, from talking to colleagues, and from reviewing business documents. These goal lists often range across a broad spectrum of desirable ends, from high growth, to increasing profitability, to employee morale. But simple lists are not enough because one can usually anticipate that the coincident pursuit of the various goals will result in conflicts, for example, between spending to build market share and current profitability. The telling question at this point is what goal drives the resolution of the conflict: will it be share position or current profits? Determining goal priorities is a tough but critical job; tough because in many businesses goal priorities are not well spelled out and must often be derived from informal understandings and behaviour; critical because, without a sense of priorities, a simple list of goals can be meaningless, even misleading. Imagine the consternation of some students when they discover a gap between the professed and real goals of the business unit! If the goal structure of a business is obscure, or inconsistent, people will be truly confused and the business cannot be said to have a coherent strategy.

The essential nature of a goal structure can be caught, for example, in the use of the shorthand terms *growth, harvest,* and *divest* to describe different generic goal structures. A growth strategy implies a priority on market, plant and personnel investments to grow the business, if necessary at the expense of current profitability. A harvest strategy implies a stingy approach to investment and spending as priority is given to milking cash and profits from a business. Divest means to give priority to those actions that prepare and initiate the sale of the business. While such terms as these need to be developed with specifics in individual situations, they do capture the overall notion of a coherent set of priorities in the goals of a business.

As you go about developing the goal structure of a business, you may have to resolve some difficult conflicts between the external forces on the business and its internal interests and capabilities. External forces are represented, for example, by competitive challenges or shareholder demands. Internal influences arise from such factors as the expectations and limitations of the firm's employees. You are now well into the process of strategy formulation. Further, as circumstances change, so too, must the goal structure.

Consider a classic example of the need to adapt goal structures to a changing environment. From its start-up in 1974 to the stock market meltdown in 2001, the brokerage firm Charles Schwab Corp. put a high priority on unusual (for the industry) personnel priorities such as hiring unconventional people, eliminating commission-based pay, and treating staff as family.[4] Layoffs were anathema and team play was fundamental. These goals were consistent with the company's equally unconventional pursuit of discount brokerage that helped to fuel Schwab's amazing growth to $5.8 billion in revenues and some

16,000 employees by 2000. Then the bottom fell out of the market, and as it did it became clear that there were new competitive issues in the industry that had been disguised by rapid growth. Schwab needed not only to downsize, but to change the way it did business. Management hesitated, understandably, but acted as the cumulative impact of the environmental changes took their toll. By the end of 2003 Schwab had laid off over 6,500 employees and the company was working by way of internal transition and acquisition to become a broad-based financial services firm. With this, of course, the company's personnel policies began to mirror the industry, raising a fundamental question: how does Schwab intend to differentiate itself in the future? It did so by changing its focus from capital market products to addressing the needs of the individual investor and set a new goal; to help everyone be financially fit. Schwab changed its focus to concentrate on client relationships and making decisions "Through Clients' Eyes."[5]

Goals and Competitive Advantage

Businesses may elect to use their goal structures as one way of distinguishing themselves from competitors and achieving competitive advantage. They may choose, for example, to take greater risks, or to be more aggressive, or to be more patient than others in their industry. Boeing's willingness to "bet the company" on new aircraft models kept it ahead of competition for decades. (Interestingly, as Boeing's appetite for this level of risk diminished, so did their industry dominance). Microsoft's highly aggressive (and controversial) approach to market leadership has frustrated and deflected competitors for many years. Toyota's patient, grinding approach to building a global leadership position in automobiles resulted in Toyota achieving the top sales position spot in the global automobile market by 2008.

PRODUCT MARKET FOCUS

The product market focus component of strategy spells out the nature of the products and/or services that a business intends to offer and the characteristics of the markets that it intends to compete in. Think of your favourite radio station. What is its emphasis in programming (rock, rap, country, easy listening, etc.) and from this, who is the implied audience (demographics, shopping habits, etc.)? Your answer will be a pretty good indication of the station's choice of product market focus. Many of the strategic decisions that firms face are product or market choices. The scope of the product/market, that is whether the product is existing or new and whether the market is existing or new, frames this type of strategic choice. This can be depicted in the classic two by two matrix with market choice on one axis and product choice on the other.

Firms can choose to focus on existing products and markets through a penetration strategy. A penetration strategy suggests that there is market share to be gained by focusing on the current products and markets, or perhaps there is growth in the market that would provide for growth even if market share were to remain the same. Alternatively, they can choose to develop new products for existing markets with a new product development strategy. This is often the case when companies try to leverage their market base as McDonald's did, for example, when it began to offer a breakfast menu. Offering existing products to new markets using a market development strategy is typically the case when we consider geographic expansion of the strategy. Finally, firms may choose to diversify both products and markets.

The usual application of the product market focus concept is in looking downstream at choices of product line scope, customer groups, geographic areas, and so on. This is where most businesses face competition and where, as a consequence, the strategically most important distinctions need to be made. Do not let the notion of competition deter you if you are in the not-for-profit sector. Simply put, there are scarce resources in the organization and the environment, and the notion of competition is intended to capture the view that everyone must make choices about how they allocate scarce resources such as time and money. For example, we observed hospital administrators and physicians grapple with the notion of their market share for various services and come to the realization that in the area of transplantation they should be focusing their attention on the more complicated multi-organ transplants rather than single organ. They realized that having been at the forefront in the early stages of transplantation, they continued to do surgeries that had become fairly routine, when their distinctiveness and expertise was in more complex areas.

Although we often look downstream to customers in considering product market focus, in resource industries, downstream markets are usually commodity markets and the critical competition occurs on the upstream side, where businesses must compete for access and continuity of supply for oil, timber, minerals, and like reserves. Unlike many of its broadly based competitors, the oil and gas company Encana Corporation, for example, has built a strong position by focusing on deep natural gas plays in the Rocky Mountains, where its accumulated experience gives it an advantage. In 2009 Encana further refined its focus by spinning out its oil business to make Encana a pure-play natural gas company. The important point here for your analytic process is to concentrate your product market definition on the markets—either upstream or downstream—in which the business is facing the keenest competition.

Describing Product Market Focus

If you are dealing with a business that encompasses multiple products and markets, you will find it helpful to visualize the product market focus using a cross-reference format, or matrix, that arranges product entries against market segments. By entering appropriate classification data into the cells of this matrix (revenues, assets employed, profits, etc.), it is possible to build a quite precise picture of the current or intended product market emphasis of the business. The example that follows illustrates the major steps in preparing such a matrix.

Building a Product Market Matrix: An Example Olympia Mills produced a line of tufted carpets in its Spokane facilities. The carpets were sold throughout the northwest market area. One conception of the company's product market matrix is illustrated in Table 2.2. In this matrix the product and market categories were chosen to represent aggregates that Olympia could do something about in a strategic sense—such as dropping a line, or changing segment emphasis.

The product line distinctions in Table 2.2 were chosen on the basis of manufacturing requirements and marketing considerations. Solid-coloured carpets could be tufted from yarn that was spun in the company's spinning mill and dyed in the carpet mill. This product type was particularly favoured by the residential contract market. Multicolour carpet was produced from pre-dyed yarns and was particularly important for the commercial market. Foam-backed carpet required special equipment and was suited to the lower-priced segments of the retail market.

The market segment distinctions in the matrix were chosen to reflect differences in product requirements, buying processes, and competition. The retail segment represented sales through retailers to home owners, largely for replacement. A wide style, colour, and quality range was required together with fast, reliable delivery. The residential contract market comprised sales through builders to new-home buyers and required sharp pricing to match competition on large orders. The commercial market consisted of sales for new or replacement carpeting to commercial real estate developers and their tenants. It frequently involved custom design and specifications.

The data chosen for the cells are indicative rather than complete. The share-of-market figures are based on the geographic market served. Additional information on product line contribution, assets employed, total market potential, etc., might be useful for further analysis.

The classifications clearly involve a number of judgments. Why were the products not broken down into further quality and style classifications? Why was the retail market

Table 2.2 Olympia Mills Product Market Matrix ($000,000)

	Retail	Residential	Commercial	Total
Total Revenue	5.2	13.8	3.3	22.3
Share Regional Market	6%	23%	5%	11%
Solid-Colour Carpet Revenue	3.8	11.0	1.0	15.8
Share Solid-Colour Market	9%	31%	6%	16%
Multicolour Carpet Revenue	1.2	2.8	2.3	6.3
Share Multicolour Market	3%	12%	5%	6%
Foam-Backed Market Revenue	0.2	—	—	0.2
Share Foam-Backed Market	—	—	—	—

classification not further developed, for example, to identify sales direct from the mill to retailers as compared to those made through distributors? You might ask a host of other reasonable questions, for which the answer is essentially that the classifications are a matter of judgment based on an understanding of the purpose at hand. What we have described at this point is a business that is heavily reliant on the solid-coloured/residential contract market. The classifications can be further refined as emerging strategic questions and choices dictate. There are no issues of right or wrong in building a product market matrix, only those of utility.

Product Market Focus and Competitive Advantage

A business may select a particular product market focus as a way of achieving competitive differentiation and advantage. A quite typical choice, for example, is to concentrate on product market niches where competitors are relatively weak or simply uninterested.

McCain, for example, used this approach to build its worldwide french-fried potato business. Over a period of three decades the company moved from its Canadian base to England, Australia, continental Europe, and so on, while taking advantage of weaker competitors and avoiding the strong and entrenched competitors in the U.S. marketplace. Then, in the mid 1990s, the company, which was now well armed in scale and technology, was ready to make a serious commitment to the U.S. domestic market.

VALUE PROPOSITION

A business's value proposition is a statement of the fundamental benefit or benefits that it has chosen to "offer" in the marketplace. Michael Porter presents two generic value propositions, or what he calls "generic strategies"—low cost and differentiation. A low cost strategy endeavours to provide products and services at a lower cost than competitors, and therefore enables firms to compete on price. The Dow Chemical Company is an example of a firm following a "low cost" strategy. A differentiation strategy is broadly defined to include anything such as service, quality, or features that sets a product or service apart from competitors. Pfizer, the pharmaceuticals company, follows a "differentiation" strategy. Porter warns against being stuck in the middle between a low cost and differentiation value proposition. He argues that the core activities required to support a low cost strategy are significantly different than those supporting a differentiation strategy. For example, he states that "cost leadership requires aggressive construction of efficient-scale facilities, vigorous pursuit of cost reductions from experience, tight cost and overhead control, avoidance of marginal customer accounts, and cost minimization in areas like R&D, service, sales force, advertising, and so on."[6] In addition, it is likely that different segments will respond differently to each value proposition. For example, Porter suggests that "differentiation may sometimes preclude gaining a high market share. It often requires a perception of exclusivity, which is incompatible with high market share. More commonly, however, achieving differentiation will imply a trade-off with cost position if the activities required in creating it are inherently costly, such as extensive research, product design, high quality materials, or intensive customer support."[7]

There are critics of Porter's view that firms cannot pursue low cost and differentiation. For example, Kim and Mauborgne state that an alignment between low cost and differentiation "enables a company to open new market space by breaking the existing value-cost trade-off".[8] This is the basis for their Blue Ocean Strategy, which we discuss in Chapter 4. Kim and Mauborgne attempt to pit what they term a "structuralist approach" to strategy, in which industry structure is taken largely for granted and strategy must be aligned around low cost or differentiation, against a "reconstructionist approach," in which strategy can shape industry structure and firms may pursue low cost and differentiation simultaneously. Kim and Mauborgne present the example of Dubai as a country employing a strategy that provides a package for investors that is low cost and differentiated. We see these two approaches as an artificial distinction since industry structure is not a given, nor is there anything that prevents a firm from achieving low cost and differentiation if the other components of the strategy can support it. The warning is that it is difficult, but not impossible to achieve the alignment.

Describing Value Propositions

The key to a useful expression of the value proposition of a business is to work with variables that are important to customers and to simplify them to basic themes. Customers are interested in what a product or service does for them. They do not particularly care, for example, that a business wants to be the industry's low cost producer. This is only important to the customer if the low costs get translated into low relative prices or other benefits. The aim therefore should be to express value propositions in terms of fundamental customer benefits such as price, features, service, and execution.

It is also important to stick to simple, fundamental themes, which may be quite a task since there are a variety of ways in which a basic value proposition may be presented in a market, as illustrated in Table 2.3. A value proposition based on price, for example, might be delivered by any of a combination of dozens of direct price or indirect economic benefits. From a strategic standpoint, however, the important reality is that the business's value proposition is based on price. The precise tactics for conveying these benefits are important, of course, but only after the fundamental approach has been established.

Ultimately, the scope and detail required in expressing a value proposition rests on the utility of the result. The critical question is whether the value proposition, as described, is sufficiently developed to provide a meaningful sense of direction and to support subsequent tests for effectiveness, feasibility, and sustainability. For example, you might find a proposal to compete on "customer intimacy"—a concept developed by Treacy and Wiersema in their book *The Discipline of Market Leaders*[9]—too vague to work with. Here you need to press further to define the particulars of the proposed relationships between business and customer that lie behind the expression. On the other hand, pushing for detail, particularly in the early steps of evaluating or building a strategy, might bog

Tool #8

Table 2.3 Subsidiary Value Proposition Variables

Price	Features	Execution
Direct	**Tangible**	**Availability**
• List price	• Quality	• Timing
• Discount structure	• Performance	• Convenience
• Rebates	• Proprietary properties	• Delivery
• Credit rates	• Pre- and post-sale service	**Reliability**
Indirect	• Options, choice	• As promised, when promised, etc.
• Financial assistance	• Guarantees	**Intensity**
• Capital vs. operating cost balance	**Intangible (Image)**	• Sales hustle
• Life cycle cost	• Design	• Service hustle
• Cost absorption (delivery, training, etc.)	• Fashions	• Friendliness
	• Prestige	
	• "Personality" and "event" associations	

you down in incidentals and restrict your flexibility. It usually makes sense to start with a very basic theme and incorporate greater detail as necessary as the analysis proceeds.

Finally, by redefining the "customer" we can apply the idea of value proposition to supply (upstream) markets. Thus, a junior oil company might define the private or governmental holders of mineral rights in a particular area as its customers and address the question of the value proposition it intends to put forward to secure those rights. Another example is a residential real estate business that targets top-rate agents as its supply-side customers and addresses the value proposition by which it intends to secure and hold those resources.

It is sometimes helpful to broaden the notion of customer to one of key stakeholder. For example, business schools typically need to consider the value proposition for students, recruiters, and alumni. Whenever there is a portfolio of "customers" it is important to ensure that the fundamental elements of the value proposition are aligned. It is not uncommon for organizations to exist within a network of stakeholders that may be fruitfully considered as customers for which there must be alignment in the underlying value proposition. Furthermore, it is not uncommon that "customer" may actually refer to an internal customer to the organization. Often there are sub-groups within the organization that need to define a strategy relative to the overall business strategy. The same concepts apply, yet the value proposition relates to how the group will provide value to its internal customers. Functions such as logistics, human resource management, legal services, etc., could be outsourced. In designing strategy to service an internal customer, it is helpful to consider the value proposition you provide to the organization relative to the value proposition should it be outsourced.

The Value Proposition and Competitive Advantage

The choice of a value proposition is perhaps the most obvious way in which a business attempts to differentiate itself from competition. To the extent that a proposed value proposition is important to customers, different from competitors, and hard for competitors to match, it will constitute a competitive advantage. Consider the following examples.

- The warehouse retailer Costco competes by offering customers low unit prices on "quantity" purchases of food and general merchandise items. The price advantage is important to small commercial customers and to householders with the cash and storage capacity to put items into "inventory." The prices are hard for competitors to match so long as they incur the costs associated with the smaller package and lot sizes that many customers want.

- Whole Foods, which is the fastest growing grocery chain in the United States, differentiates itself through its emphasis on unique product features such as pesticide-free produce, hormone-free meat, and preservative–free processed foods. These are important features to some customers and when they are offered in depth and variety in large stores they become difficult for competitors to match in their conventionally merchandised facilities.

Although many companies fall into the trap of just listing all the benefits to customers, the key is to understand those benefits that provide differentiation and are particularly resonant with the customer.[10] In many industries it is relatively easy for competitors to quickly copy new product or service innovations. What major parcel service does not promise fast, reliable delivery? What real estate company does not promise the best in personal attention and advice? To create a competitive advantage in such circumstances, a business may put a more subtle value proposition to work—the fact that it will actually deliver on its promise, that it will be superior in execution. What differentiates such companies is not their claim to fast service or personal attention, for example, but the credibility of their claims, and behind this the building of businesses that can actually execute the promises better than their competitors.

CORE ACTIVITIES   Tool #9

In the "value chain" of activities that constitutes an industry, a business needs to make choices about which particular activities it intends to perform and how it intends to perform them. Further, among the activities that it decides to perform, there will be some that are critical to the effective operation of the business; these are called *core* activities. A firm's determination of its core activities is a critical aspect of its strategy since these choices will have a fundamental impact on its market and operations control, cost structure, capabilities, and flexibility. Take the example of

Kmart. Over a decade ago, before it started its slide into bankruptcy, Kmart decided first to outsource its transportation activities and later, to outsource its information technology. The explanation given at the time was that these moves would allow its people to concentrate on "merchandising." This seemed reasonable on the surface, but less so in reference to the competitive imperatives of the industry. Here, Wal-Mart, which saw itself as a logistics and merchandising business, was investing heavily in distribution and information technology. Soon Kmart could not match Wal-Mart's costs, partly because it simply did not have control over some of the fundamental cost elements of the business. Losses mounted as Kmart attempted to remain competitive, but no amount of "merchandising" would save the day. Kmart's failure rose from many causes; not the least of these were the early decisions on core activities, which essentially sent management to battle with one arm tied behind its back.

The description of core activities relates to the notion of cross-enterprise leadership. Since the boundaries of the organization have become more blurred with partnerships and joint ventures that can often deliver products and services in a seamless fashion, the description of core activities need not be bounded by those that are delivered solely by your organization. Clearly, as in the case of Kmart, when a firm has outsourced an activity and has little control over it, the activity can no longer be considered core. However, a critical activity over which the organization has some degree of control or influence may be considered a core activity.

Describing Core Activities

The challenge in describing the core activities component of a business strategy is in determining the degree of scope and detail that suits the issues being considered. The scope of issues may vary from the very broad perspective of a business dealing with fundamental matters of vertical integration to the very specific process perspective of a firm considering the best way in which to weave together internal and outside activities in building a sales and service system. The focus and detail utilized in identifying and analyzing core activities should vary accordingly. In the examples below, we have illustrated this principle for what we might call broad, intermediate, and process levels of generality.

In pursuing issues of vertical integration, for example, you will have to decide on what basic building blocks in the industry value chain you intend to perform and those you will access through a market. From this broad perspective, your core activities would be best described in terms of the building blocks that represent fundamental aspects of the industry such as raw material supply, manufacturing, distribution and so on. For example, Starbucks has a close relationship with its many suppliers to ensure a steady supply of high quality coffee beans. It controls the value chain from that point on with its own in-house proprietary roasting capability and a logistics operation that ensures timely delivery of product to its stores. Starbucks has not opted for a franchise model because it seeks to maintain control over its retail outlets. It has its own real estate group to ensure growth is achieved in the best locations. The broad, building block approach described above is usually sufficient for industry studies and basic corporate decisions on vertical integration.

If you are trying to determine how best to proceed in pursuing a particular product market opportunity, however, the focus and detail of the core activity description will probably have to move to a functional base and deal with such categories as product and process research and development, component supply, assembly, marketing, distribution, sales and service, and so on. The aim at this intermediate level of analysis is to identify where the business has material and realistic opportunities to perform or not to perform a function and the consequences of the choices that it might make on these matters. In setting up its regional jet aircraft business, for example, Bombardier chose to focus on design, testing and systems coordination, final assembly, and marketing, and to bring in partners for manufacturing, such as Taiwan's Aerospace Industrial for mid- and rear-section fabrication and Japan's Mitsubishi Heavy Industries for wing production. These core activity choices by Bombardier represented a strategic trade-off of potential value added and control, particularly in wing manufacturing technology, for greater financial and manufacturing capacity and possible market access.

In the broad and intermediate levels of generality, the emphasis is on describing the basic activities that a business has chosen to perform and less so on how it intends to link and perform them. At the process level, the focus turns to mapping activity *systems* in sufficient detail to support operations planning and coordination, systems development, and quite detailed comparisons with competitors. Here, of course, it is possible to elaborate the description into dozens and even hundreds of different, but still reasonably significant, activities. Take for example the Shouldice Hospital, located just outside Toronto, that focuses on hernia surgeries. A process level comparison with other hospitals on how it performs its pre-surgery, surgery, and the multiple day post-surgery processes will help you understand how Shouldice has successfully competed with hospitals that have significantly more resources at their disposal. As you proceed to more detailed descriptions, moreover, you will be faced with the question of how far to take the analysis. At some point your elaboration of the activities goes beyond major commitments that are hard to reverse and the analysis becomes more operational than strategic. This is where you stop. That is not to say that the operational issues are not important, just different, and subject to prior decisions on strategic position. For the most part, for strategic analysis and action the intermediate levels of scope and detail will usually be sufficient and should certainly be the starting point. Further detail can then be pursued as specific situations warrant. Porter maps the activity system of IKEA to illustrate how it supports major strategic elements such as self-selection by customers (including inventory management and store layout), limited customer service (including in-store displays, knock-down packaging, and ease of transport), low manufacturing costs (including design and long-term supplier relationships) and modular furniture design (including in-house design and knock-down packaging). All of these elements support that value proposition of low price and unique products.[11]

Core Activities and Competitive Advantage

In most industries there are many potential differences in the core activity sets that a business might choose to perform. This provides an equivalently wide range of possibilities for competitive positioning and competitive advantage. To illustrate, consider the choices with respect to vertical integration that are open to a business as it seeks advantages in market or supply control, cost, focus, and flexibility.

Vertical integration forward, for market control, or backward, for supply control, may provide a business with an advantage over its rivals. In the broadcasting industry, for example, Bell Canada Enterprises (BCE), a provider of infrastructure for broadcasting media content and programming, among other services, recently acquired CTV, a producer of media content and programming. The acquisition allows BCE to modify CTV's programming in order to deliver it not only to televisions but also to personal computers and mobile devices. The enhanced offering to deliver the same content on multiple platforms, plus its ability to restrict some of CTV's more popular programming to BCE's own distribution channels only, may potentially give BCE an advantage over its competitors.

The pursuit of advantageous costs may be the critical driver behind the choice and structuring of core activities. As we have mentioned, a key element of Wal-Mart's strategy over the years, for example, has been to pursue low cost by internalizing all of the key activities in its supply and distribution value chain. This system ranges from suppliers, who are "virtually" integrated with Wal-Mart by operating policies and electronic data interchange, through the logistics functions of warehousing and transportation, to store operations and the checkout counter. As a pioneer of this approach, Wal-Mart built up a significant cost leadership over its less integrated and rigorously managed competitors and has maintained this advantage for decades.

The pursuit of differentiation may also be a critical factor behind the choice and structuring of core activities. In the athletic footwear market, for example, the big brands like Nike, Reebok, and Adidas have built formidable capabilities in design, sourcing, and marketing, but they rely on overseas contract manufacturers for supply. Marketing is critical: each company spends tens of millions to keep its designs up to date, to secure the endorsement of high-profile athletes and to support mass-media advertising. A smaller competitor, New Balance, differentiates itself from the giants by stressing function over fashion, manufacturing over marketing. It emphasizes the fit and performance of its shoes; there is less glitz. Its focus on manufacturing extends to the production of many of its shoes in five U.S.-based factories. In the marketplace it employs an "endorsed by no one" policy, spends very little media money, and gives priority to building retail relationships. This differentiation works for the company; it is growing rapidly (outpacing the industry) and it fully intends to sustain its unique approach.

PUTTING THE STRATEGY COMPONENTS TOGETHER

In the process of creating and testing new strategic ideas, it is often useful to focus your thinking on only one or two of the four strategy components at a time. A proposal for a business to compete on price, for example, requires considerable development and

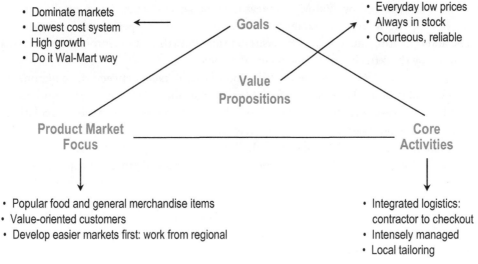

Figure 2.2 The Wal-Mart Business Strategy

analysis in its own right before it is subjected to wider scrutiny. At some point, however, you will have to pull all of the strategic components together to see if they present an internally consistent and comprehensive picture of the direction of the business. This total view of strategy is a critical step in building an accurate understanding of a business and in evaluating its future development.

Consider, for example, the simplified, version of Wal-Mart's strategy as pictured in Figure 2.2. An overview like this is intended to help you to simultaneously grasp several dimensions of a very remarkable business. You can better appreciate the power of the company in the marketplace as you observe the consistency of the strategy components, from the goals of achieving low cost by pursuing its unique "Wal-Mart" way, to the product focus on basic, popular merchandise, to the value proposition of everyday low prices, and on to delivery through a highly integrated set of core activities. For example, Wal-Mart has stringent criteria for suppliers before it admits them into its network, negotiates aggressively with them to keep prices low, and insists suppliers innovate continuously to lower prices. At the same time it invests heavily in technology and its supply management system to keep inventories low, and links suppliers electronically to ensure that they have current information on product sales and inventories. All these activities contribute to reducing product costs. Costs are further kept down through lower labour costs, a non-unionized work force, and a highly flexible work scheduling system. By keeping costs down, customers are offered lower prices, which in turn generate higher volumes. The higher volumes give suppliers motivation to reduce prices further and also contribute to achieving a dominant position in a given market. Customer throughput and volume are also increased through Wal-Mart's value propositions such as being always in stock and providing courteous reliable service. Wal-Mart's employees are motivated to provide such a service and keep costs down through the company-wide emphasis on the "Wal-Mart Way".

All this is re-enforced by Wal-Mart's measurement system. This system tracks, among other things, the increase in same-store sales to measure the performance of existing stores, and operating income growth versus net sales growth and inventory growth versus net sales growth to track improvements in efficiency,

It is easy to underestimate the contribution of the linkages between the components to a successful strategy. For example, Wal-Mart's expansion into Germany was unsuccessful partly due to resistance to Wal-Mart's workplace practices and government regulations that restricted store hour openings, ultimately leading to Wal-Mart withdrawal from the German market. In India, Wal-Mart had challenges integrating local supply management and distribution. By 2010, Wal-Mart's entry into India was still proceeding at a slow pace due to these issues and the regulatory restrictions on foreign direct investments in the retail sector.

You have the basis in such a conception of Wal-Mart's strategy to pursue your understanding of the path that the company has followed in the past and to ask if this direction makes sense for the future.

There are two lines of inquiry to follow as you assemble the components of strategy into one picture. The first is whether the components complement and reinforce each other. In the case of Wal-Mart they do. But what would you make of a bank that wants to be "all things to all people" and compete on customer intimacy or of a manufacturer that wants to be the lowest cost producer in its industry, but fails to include supply chain management as a core activity? Gaps and inconsistencies among the elements of a business strategy are problem markers. How big a problem they represent depends on broader circumstances, such as industry competitiveness. Monopolies and regulated businesses, for example, may get away for some time with serious internal logical flaws in their strategies.

The second line of inquiry is a central theme of this book. Given a strategy description, one that reflects the reality of your business, in nature, in clarity or ambiguity, in logical consistency or conflict, how does the strategy stand up as you test it against the other elements of the Diamond-E framework? We turn to this pursuit in subsequent chapters of the book.

It is possible to take the components and summarize them into a statement of strategy, but this can be tricky and takes substantial work on each of the four elements to develop an overall statement that is coherent. Collis and Rukstad provide the example of Edward Jones, the fourth-largest brokerage firm in the United States that has quadrupled its market share over the last two decades and continues to be listed in *Fortune*'s top companies to work for. They suggest that just about every one of the 37,000 employees could express the strategy to "grow to 17,000 financial advisers by 2012 by offering trusted and convenient face-to-face financial advice to conservative individual investors who delegate their financial decisions, through a national network of one-financial-adviser offices."[12] This statement is an overview of the goals, product market focus, value proposition, and core activities. No doubt there is more, such as financial targets and core activities; however, such a statement could serve is a driving force in the organization.

OTHER STRATEGY PERSPECTIVES

Although we have presented one strategy model, there are many models of strategy that can be employed. One of the factors differentiating types of models is the concept of strategy on which the model is based. Mintzberg presents five different types of strategy, which he called the 5Ps for obvious reasons (plan, position, ploy, perspective, pattern).[13] Sometimes strategy is viewed as a "plan" or a blueprint that will guide the business. Closely associated with the view of strategy as a plan, is the view of strategy as a "position" that identifies how the company intends to apply its resources and capabilities to position itself within the competitive environment. The four components of strategy we have identified clearly provide a sense of the strategic position, but could also be construed as a plan. These two perspectives are the most common view of strategy.

However, many firms actually treat strategy as a "ploy" or set of tactics on which to compete. We like to refer to these tactics as strategic initiatives that should be based on an understanding of the four components of strategy. Unfortunately, many organizations embark on strategic initiatives with no coherent sense of the underlying strategy. For example, it is not uncommon to hear declarations of strategic investments in employees, new technology, or perhaps an acquisition without any sense of how such investments relate to the overall business strategy.

The way some firms describe their strategy may be closer to a "perspective" about the way they do things. This perspective sometimes approximates a vision or set of values about how the firm competes. Finally, Mintzberg suggests that strategy may be a "pattern" of actions with no stated plan or position. As a result, the strategy is inferred from the actions taken. We acknowledge this may be the case, but suggest that it is possible to identify the components of strategy from the pattern of actions.

It is important to acknowledge these different perspectives on strategy so that you can better understand the conversations and initiatives undertaken around strategy. The term strategy is often used quite loosely and, therefore, being aware of its different uses will help you to direct your organization's efforts to developing a coherent strategy. Even with concepts of strategy that are close approximations to what we have presented here, different terms are used, so it is important not to get stuck on the terms but instead focus on the intent. For example, Collis and Rukstad suggest three components of strategy: objective, scope, and advantage.[14] Objective is a close approximation to Goals. Scope is a close approximation to Product Market Focus. Advantage is a close approximation to value proposition; however, it encompasses elements of core activities as well. It essentially describes elements of the strategy that provide differentiation vis-à-vis other organizations. The subtle but important difference is that differentiation and advantage arise from all four components. Notice that in the foregoing sections when we described each of the strategy components we also described how they support competitive advantage. We believe a strategy statement is well served by first describing the components. Aspects of each are necessary but not sufficient to provide an advantage and it is by examining the four strategy components and their inter-relationship that you can begin to understand how the strategy provides competitive advantage.

The foregoing represents some broad differences in the use of the term strategy. Mintzberg, Ahlstrand, and Lampel, in their book "*Strategy Safari*," present ten different schools of strategy[15] (a helpful "mind mapping" of the Strategy Safari book can be found at http://www.shearonforschools.com/Strategy_Safari.htm). It is not our intent to describe all ten schools, but rather to introduce the notion that perspectives on strategy can be quite different. For example, three of the schools, the design, planning, and positioning schools, take a very rational orientation to strategy as creating a fit between the internal and external environment. The schools fit well with the definition of strategy as either a plan or a position and are based on a rational perspective of strategy: goal-oriented, instrumental rationality, reflecting the origins of the concept in theories of industrial organization and neoclassical microeconomics. Six schools (cognitive, entrepreneurial, learning, political, cultural, environmental) take more of a behavioural and process view to explain how strategy arises and is enacted. Our perspective of strategy is in line with what Mintzberg et al., termed the configuration school. They suggest that it "differs from all the others in one fundamental respect: it offers the possibility of reconciliation, one way to integrate the messages of the other schools."[16]

The Diamond-E model takes into account how a firm positions itself and designs a strategy that enables it to leverage its resources and capabilities to create value. However, we also draw on other perspectives of strategy to augment the traditional rational view of strategy. The management preference component of the Diamond-E acknowledges the individual elements that arise from the cognitive, political, entrepreneurial and cultural perspectives. As well, we delve more deeply into the cognitive and learning schools in Chapter 9 as we transition from formulation to execution.

It is important to note that the field of strategy and strategic analysis in many organizations is strongly influenced by three of the schools (design school, planning school, positioning school). Mintzberg describes the three dominant schools as follows:

> . . . the 'design school' considers strategy making as an informal process of conception, typically in a leader's conscious mind. The design school model, sometimes called SWOT, also underlies the second, which I call the 'planning school' and which accepts the premises of the former, save two—that the process be informal and the chief executive be the key actor . . . The third, which I call the 'positioning school,' focuses on the content of strategies more than on the processes by which they are prescribed to be made.[17]

These strategy schools and definitions have tended to coalesce around two overriding views about strategy content, and two on strategy process. On the content side, the emphasis placed on either the external (industry) or internal (company) has been a differentiating factor on "what" strategy includes. On the process side, the emphasis placed on either strategy as a well-defined analytical process or strategy as an emergent and perhaps chaotic process has differentiated "how" strategy arises.

We provide a broad and comprehensive view of strategy. On the content side, we incorporate both the external and internal approaches, and on the process side we acknowledge the analytical building blocks of strategy, but recognize the dynamic nature of strategy, which includes emergent and chaotic components. We develop these ideas further in Chapters 9, 10, and 11.

It is also helpful to define what strategy is not. As Porter points out, operational effectiveness is not strategy. He argues that the "quest for productivity, quality, and speed has spawned a remarkable number of management tools and techniques: total quality management, benchmarking, time-based competition, outsourcing, partnering, reengineering, change management. Although the resulting operational improvements have often been dramatic, many companies have been frustrated by their inability to translate those gains into sustainable profitability. And bit by bit, almost imperceptibly, management tools have taken the place of strategy. As managers push to improve on all fronts, they move farther away from viable competitive positions."[18] In many instances operational improvements can be quickly copied by competitors and provide little in the way of a sustainable competitive advantage. While necessary, operational excellence is insufficient, since a sound competitive strategy rests on unique activities. Rather, it is the unique configuration of goals, product market focus, value proposition, and core activities that provides a sustainable competitive advantage.

Porter describes strategy that focuses on a uniqueness in the product market focus as "variety-based positioning" and the alignment between the value proposition and product market focus as being "needs-based positioning," whereas aligning the core activities to deliver the value proposition in a unique way is "access-based positioning." He acknowledges that these approaches are not mutually exclusive. Given the many configurations of the four strategy components, we are inclined to suggest that there are many different options for creating different configurations. We agree with Porter that strategy dictates trade-offs. Too often organizations try to copy another organization's strategy but end up with an ill-defined strategy with components that no longer align. For example, Continental Airlines maintained its position as a full-service airline with all its associated core activities such as working with travel agents, a mixed fleet of planes, baggage checking, and seat assignments while it tried to copy Southwest's point-to-point "no frills" operation.[19]

CORPORATE STRATEGY

To this point we have focused on the identification and the description of the strategy of an individual business unit. This same process remains essential as we look at the corporate strategy of multibusiness enterprises, because the strategy of the constituent businesses in a multibusiness firm is a fundamental building block for describing and understanding its corporate strategy. We proceed here with some explanatory background on the distinction between corporate and business strategy and then we turn to the tangible tasks of identifying and evaluating corporate strategy.

Traditional views of strategy have assumed fairly distinct boundaries between the firm and its industry, as well as between industries. As a result there has been a clear

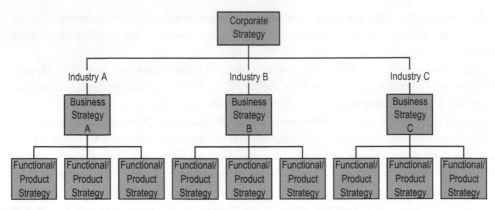

Figure 2.3 Corporate, Business, and Functional Strategy

distinction between corporate strategy, business strategy and functional or product strategy. Corporate strategy has traditionally looked at decisions about the management of businesses across industries. Business-level strategy deals with creating competitive advantage within an industry, while functional or product strategies are the means of executing the business strategy as shown in Figure 2.3.

The typical multibusiness corporation consists of a management hierarchy, which passes from a corporate entity to the business groups and thence to individual business units that the corporation encompasses. In this hierarchy, the corporate office establishes a corporate strategy and from this a set of strategic guidelines for the groups. The groups, in turn, develop group strategies and set up guidelines for their individual units. In general, as you move down this hierarchy from the corporate level to the unit level, the emphasis passes from broad positions to increasingly specific initiatives. Andrews, looking at the hierarchy from the bottom up, sets out the distinctions very clearly:

> As we ascend from a specific strategy to a corporate strategy, we pass from specific economic objectives to broader organization goals. More weight is given to such characteristics as unity, coherence, consistency, purpose, and concern for the future. The time horizon grows more distant and market-share percentages give way to a more comprehensive vision of the company's future development as an institution.[20]

The corporate level of the multibusiness organization is an intermediary—it stands between the individual businesses and the capital markets. As such, it has to address three critical questions: What businesses/industries should we be operating in?; 2) How should we manage these businesses?; and 3) Is the cost of corporate headquarters less than the value created by having different businesses in one corporation? Overall, what is it that the corporate office does that results in the businesses under its umbrella being worth more standing together than they would be standing independently, or held by another more effective corporate group? From a shareholder perspective, what is the economic justification of the multibusiness structure? Corporate strategy, in this perspective, is an explanation of the way in which the corporate entity intends to compete and to provide superior shareholder value relative to these alternatives.

Describing Corporate Strategy

You can develop a practical description of corporate strategy by focusing, as suggested by Collis and Montgomery,[21] on three observable aspects of a multibusiness operation: its businesses portfolio, corporate resources, and corporate management processes.

The first step in the descriptive process is to identify the businesses that the corporation encompasses, which is not difficult, and the essential similarities and differences among these businesses, which is more of a challenge. This is where an understanding of each business's strategy comes in. By comparing, in particular, the product market focuses and value propositions of the businesses, you can develop a good understanding of the ways and the degree to which the businesses are, or are not, related. Newell Rubbermaid encompasses a wide range of businesses from window blinds to office stationery to plastic household items. While they look diverse in nature, the commonalities of the businesses are substantial; they are all prosaic, low technology, long lifecycle products and their target market is the mass merchandiser operators such as Wal-Mart. They share a common value proposition of exceptional service as defined by the merchandiser. Brascan Corporation, in contrast, encompasses such businesses as forest products, commercial real estate, and financial services. There are no common elements across their business strategies; this is what is called a conglomerate enterprise.

The second step in describing corporate strategy is to identify the resources (financial, technical, personnel, etc.) that are treated as "corporate property" to be shared by, and transferred between, the businesses. In Newell Rubbermaid, for example, the information technology requirements of all the businesses are handled at the corporate level and the corporate office is actively engaged in developing and transferring management personnel. A common mode of managing the customer interface, a key corporate advantage, is reinforced through employee development and transfers across businesses. At Brascan the corporate office manages financial resources for the firm, but the office is very small and the businesses must stand, for the most part, on their own feet. One can see pretty clearly from the above examples that the more related the businesses, the greater the potential role for the corporate office.

The third step of description is to identify the ways and the degree to which corporate management is engaged in the business-level decisions about strategy, operations, and performance. In Newell Rubbermaid, corporate management operates hand in glove with the businesses through frequent strategic and operating reviews and detailed performance assessment. At Brascan, corporate management operates more at arm's length, vetting and facilitating major strategic decisions such as acquisitions and monitoring longer cycle performance.

The pursuit of these three aspects of corporate activity provides a reasonably comprehensive picture of the role of the corporate level in the business. We can readily see the differences in corporate strategy at Newell Rubbermaid and Brascan. These understandings set up the more critical pursuit of whether the corporate level makes a contribution to the businesses that is greater than its costs.

By understanding these elements of corporate strategy, it is possible to identify the type of corporate strategy being employed. Corporate strategy can range from a situation where there may be a dominant business unit (between 70 and 95 percent of revenue comes from a single business) to unrelated diversification, often called conglomerates, where less than 70 percent of revenue comes from a dominant business and there are no common links between the businesses such as found in Brascan. In between there is "related constrained" in which less than 70 percent of revenue comes from a dominant business but the underlying businesses are quite linked in terms of product, technology, and distribution as found with Newell Rubbermaid. "Related linked" describes corporate strategy where less than 70 percent of revenue comes from a dominant business and there are limited links between the businesses as characterized by Johnson & Johnson.[22]

Keep in mind that different types of corporate strategy require different types of corporate structure, corporate controls, and corporate/divisional rewards. For example, in terms of the multidivisional structure (often called M-form), the businesses could be set up as distinct strategic business units (SBUs), they could share some joint processes in a cooperative form, or they could actually take a competitive form as was the case with Beaver Lumber and Aikenheads (the forerunner of Home Depot in Canada) when Molson's owned both. Corporate controls could be strategic and financial, or simply financial in cases where unrelated diversification precludes any standardized or in-depth comparison with respect to strategy. Finally, rewards could be based on a combination of corporate and business unit performance or simply the business unit.[23]

Corporate Strategy and Competitive Advantage

The purpose of corporate level management (and thus, ultimately its justification) is to add competitive advantage to its constituent business units. If it does, then the businesses will be worth more under the corporate umbrella than operating separately; if it does not, then the opposite applies. Given our understanding of corporate strategy as described above, we can investigate this issue.

In a related business corporation, such as Newell Rubbermaid, there are numerous ways in which corporate management can add value by providing the businesses, for example, with the opportunity to achieve cost synergies (through the sharing of corporate resources), revenue synergies (through scale in pursuing market relationships), resilience (through access to a management pool), and discipline (through rigorous business reviews). These potential advantages can be highlighted by pulling a specific business out of the corporate context and asking what additional challenges it would have to meet if it were standing alone. In Newell Rubbermaid, for example, the window blind business would face major costs if, on its own, it had to set up and support a vendor system to satisfy Wal-Mart, to say nothing of having to negotiate all alone in the marketplace. The logic is there; the remaining question is whether corporate management is doing a good job of execution, something that has to be pursued through a case-by-case study of the performance of the corporation and its businesses.

In a conglomerate, such as Brascan, it is much harder to make a logical case for the corporate structure—so much so, in fact, that conglomerates routinely trade at a discount to the sum of estimated value of their individual holdings. While the conglomerate format is often defended as providing diversification, in efficient markets the individual investor can achieve the equivalent without paying for corporate management. The question then is just what can corporate management do to add value? Given the differences in the businesses, the possibilities are limited. Given the range of businesses it would take truly remarkable managers to add substantively to strategy and operations. In fact, however sincere their intentions, it is quite possible that corporate managers who become involved in businesses they cannot really know will have a negative impact on those businesses. So the justification for the conglomerate format usually falls back on: 1) raising funds and allocating funds at rates and with effectiveness superior to the capital markets, which, of course, is suspect; and 2) implementing management incentives and controls at the business level, which will give results superior to those available by way of a simple single business structure, which, too, is debatable. General Electric (GE), has often been viewed as an outlier and exemplar in how the corporate office can create value. As described by Rowe, White, Lehmberg, and Phillips, "GE has not only survived as a conglomerate, it has prospered and become one of the largest, most successful, diversified firms in the world."[24] GE has demonstrated excellence in implementing management processes across the range of businesses that have not only allowed its businesses to prosper, but it has had an enduring effect on its leaders as it proves to be an excellent breeding ground for future business leaders. Remarkably, Rowe and his colleagues found that "firms led by CEOs who were trained at GE will outperform firms led by CEOs who were not."[25]

Corporate Strategy and Corporate General Management

The central challenge to corporate general management is to create a coherent corporate strategy that adds value to its individual business units. Campbell, Goold, and Alexander have noted how difficult it is for the corporate office to do this.[26,27] Any multibusiness endeavour for which corporate management cannot articulate a coherent and persuasive strategy should be marked as suspect—the corporate association is probably not adding value and may, in fact, be destroying value as corporate politics and misdirection get in the way of the progress of the individual business entities.

The proof of the pudding as to whether a corporate strategy makes sense, and whether corporate management is doing a worthwhile job, is in performance. But performance in the case of multibusiness enterprises can be a tricky measure to pin down, because of the inherent complexity of the situation and the fact that the most relevant criterion—the potential performance of the businesses on a separate basis or with another parent—is inevitably a hypothetical estimate. This gives corporate general managers considerable license, particularly in the short term, to fool themselves and their shareholders. An important counter in these circumstances of performance ambiguity is for corporate managers to be particularly careful that they define and work to a strategy, adjusting it as circumstances suggest, and for shareholders to insist on the same. When Christopher Galvin stepped down in late 2003 after six years as Motorola's CEO, for example, analysts and shareholders pressed the company to spin off one or more of its six business sectors, something Galvin had refused to do. Over the previous years, Motorola's performance had faltered and the outside view, at least, was that it needed to focus, and that divestment of its semiconductor sector, in particular, would be to the benefit of both the corporation and the individual business. In 2004 Motorola divested its semiconductor business and over the next few years its financial performance improved significantly with net income jumping fourfold between 2003 and 2006. Losses once again mounted during and after the 2008 recession. Finally, in 2010 Motorola announced that it would split its remaining business into two separate companies: one for their mobile devices and home business, Motorola Solutions, and the other for mobile and wireline digital communications, Motorola Mobility Holdings. Many shareholders and analysts felt that the two separate companies would be more nimble and responsive to market needs. On the day of the announcement Motorola shares jumped 7.5%. The spin-off was completed in January 2011 and on the first day of trading the stock price of both the companies closed higher. While both companies have seen initial improvement in financial performance, it will be interesting to see if they can sustain their growth as independent companies and deliver superior returns to shareholders. However, in the case where corporate management remains obstinate in the face of poor performance, the ultimate remedy is a takeover bid. Just the threat of a takeover bid can stimulate dramatic action as it did in the case of Novell Inc., which received a hostile takeover offer that ultimately resulted in the sale of a portion of its patent portfolio and its more friendly takeover by Attachmate Corporation.

SUMMARY

This chapter has concentrated on the task of identifying the strategy of a business in terms that are easy to communicate and open to logical tests. We have defined strategy in terms of four related components: goals, product market focus, value proposition, and core activities. Each of these components represents a distinct facet of strategy and each needs to be individually described and understood. We have suggested some general approaches to this task, all of which emphasize the ultimate utility of the interpretation for the strategic decisions at hand. Finally, we have emphasized the need to draw the components together to see how they relate and co-determine the direction of the business. We are now ready to proceed with the next steps of strategic analysis.

Notes

1. Collis, David J., and Michael G. Rukstad. "Can You Say What Your Strategy Is?" *Harvard Business Review* 86.4 (2008): 82–90. *Business Source Complete, EBSCO*. Web. 15 Aug. 2011.

2. Collis, David J., and Michael G. Rukstad. "Can You Say What Your Strategy Is?" *Harvard Business Review* 86.4 (2008): 84. *Business Source Complete, EBSCO*. Web. 15 Aug. 2011.

3. Kaplan, Robert S., and David P. Norton. "The Balanced Scorecard—Measures That Drive Performance." *Harvard Business Review* 70 (January–February 1992): 71–79. Print.

4. Morris, Betsy. "When Bad Things Happen To Good Companies." *Fortune* (December 8, 2003): 80–88. Print.

5. "The Charles Schwab Corporation 2010 Annual Report." Charles Schwab Corporation (2011): 1. Web. 28 Sept. 2011. <www.aboutschwab.com/images/uploads/10ar_10k.pdf>.

6. Porter, Michael, *Competitive Strategy: Techniques for Analyzing Industries and Competitors*. New York: The Free Press, 1980, p. 35.

7. Porter, Michael. *Competitive Strategy: Techniques for Analyzing Industries and Competitors*. New York: The Free Press, 1980, p.35.

8. Kim, W. Chan, and Renée Mauborgne. "How Strategy Shapes Structure." *Harvard Business Review* 87.9 (2009): 72–80. *Business Source Complete, EBSCO*. Web. 15 Aug. 2011.

9. Treacy, Michael, and Fred Wiersema. *The Discipline of Market Leaders.* Reading: Addison-Wesley Publishing Company, 1995. Print.

   The authors use the terms "operational excellence," "product leadership," and "customer intimacy" to describe the key "value disciplines" that a business might pursue. These terms are consistent, respectively, with price, features, and execution.

10. Anderson, James C., James A. Narus, and Wouter van Rossum. "Customer Value Propositions in Business Markets." *Harvard Business Review* 84.3 (2006): 90–99. *Business Source Complete, EBSCO*. Web. 15 Aug. 2011.

11. Porter, Michael E. "What Is Strategy?" *Harvard Business Review* 74.6 (1996): 61–78. *Business Source Complete, EBSCO*. Web. 16 Aug. 2011.

12. Collis, David J., and Michael G. Rukstad. "Can You Say What Your Strategy Is?" *Harvard Business Review* 86.4 (2008): 82–90. *Business Source Complete, EBSCO*. Web. 15 Aug. 2011.

13. Mintzberg, Henry. "The Strategy Concept I: Five Ps for Strategy." *California Management Review* 30 (Fall 1987): 11. Print.

14. Collis, David J., and Michael G. Rukstad. "Can You Say What Your Strategy Is?" *Harvard Business Review* 86.4 (2008): 82–90. *Business Source Complete, EBSCO*. Web. 15 Aug. 2011.

15. Mintzberg, Henry, Bruce Ahlstrand, and Joseph Lampel, *Strategy Safari: A guided tour through the wilds of strategic management*. New York: Free Press, 1998. Print.

16. Mintzberg, Henry, Bruce Ahlstrand, and Joseph Lampel, *Strategy Safari: A guided tour through the wilds of strategic management*. New York: Free Press, 1998. 302. Print.

17. Mintzberg, Henry. *The Rise and Fall of Strategic Planning*. New York: Free Press, 1994. 2. Print.

18. Porter, Michael E. "What Is Strategy?" *Harvard Business Review* 74.6 (1996): 61–78. *Business Source Complete, EBSCO*. Web. 16 Aug. 2011,

19. Porter, Michael E. "What Is Strategy?" *Harvard Business Review* 74.6 (1996): 61–78. *Business Source Complete, EBSCO*. Web. 16 Aug. 2011.

20. Andrews, Kenneth R. *The Concept of Corporate Strategy*. Rev. ed. Homewood, Illinois: Richard D. Irwin, Inc., 1980. chapter 2. Print.

21. Collis, David J., and Cynthia Montgomery. "Creating Corporate Advantage." *Harvard Business Review* 76 (May–June 1998): 70–83. Print.

22. Hitt, Michael, et al. *Strategic Management: Competitiveness and Globalization – Concepts*. 3rd Canadian ed. Toronto: Nelson Education, 2009. chapter 7. Print.

23. Hitt, Michael, et al. *Strategic Management: Competitiveness and Globalization – Concepts*. 3rd Canadian ed. Toronto: Nelson Education, 2009. chapter 12. Print.

24. Rowe, W. Glenn, et al. "General Electric: An Outlier in CEO Talent Development." *Ivey Business Journal* 73.1 (2009): 2. *Business Source Complete, EBSCO*. Web. 17 Aug. 2011.

25. Rowe, W. Glenn, et al. "General Electric: An Outlier in CEO Talent Development." *Ivey Business Journal* 73.1 (2009): 2. *Business Source Complete, EBSCO*. Web. 17 Aug. 2011.

26. Goold, Michael, and Andrew Campbell. "Desperately Seeking Synergy." *Harvard Business Review* 76 (September–October 1998): 130–143. Print.

27. Campbell, Andrew, Michael Goold, and Marcus Alexander. "Corporate Strategy: The Quest for Parenting Advantage." *Harvard Business Review* 73 (March 1995): 120–132. Print.

Additional Readings

1. Donaldson, Gordon, and Jay W. Lorsch. *Decision Making at the Top: The Shaping of Strategic Direction*. New York: Basic Books Inc., 1983. Print.

2. Grant, Robert M. *Contemporary Strategy Analysis*. Cambridge: Blackwell Publishers, 1995. chapters 1 and 2. Print.

3. Hamel, Gary. "Strategy as Revolution." *Harvard Business Review* 74 (July–August 1996): 69–81. Print.

4. Hamel, Gary, and C.K. Prahalad. "Competing for the Future." *Harvard Business Review* 72 (July–August 1994): 122–129. Print.

5. Hamel, Gary. and C.K. Prahalad. "Strategy as Stretch and Leverage." *Harvard Business Review* 71 (March–April 1993): 75–85. Print.

6. Hamel, Gary, and C.K. Prahalad. "Strategic Intent." *Harvard Business Review* 67 (May–June 1989): 63–77. Print.

7. Mintzberg, Henry. "The Fall and Rise of Strategic Planning." *Harvard Business Review* 72 (January–February 1994): 107–115. Print.

8. Mintzberg, Henry. "Crafting Strategy." *Harvard Business Review* 65 (July–August 1987): 66–76. Print.

9. Ohmae, Kenichi. "Getting Back to Strategy." *Harvard Business Review* 66 (November–December 1988): 149–157. Print.

10. Porter, Michael E. "What Is Strategy?" *Harvard Business Review* 74 (November–December 1996): 61–78. Print.

11. Porter, Michael E. "From Competitive Advantage to Corporate Strategy." *Harvard Business Review* 65 (May–June 1987): 43–60. Print.

12. Wrapp, Edward H. "Good Managers Don't Make Policy Decisions." *Harvard Business Review*, 62 (July–August 1984): 8–16. Print.

Chapter 3
The Diamond-E Framework

This chapter describes the basic steps involved in creating, revising, and evaluating strategies. We present a comprehensive model, which we call the *Diamond-E framework*, to help you identify and relate the broad forces that must be considered in building and testing strategies, and we suggest a sequence of steps for you to follow to put the model to work. In later chapters we will elaborate on the variables in the Diamond-E framework and on our suggestions for incorporating them into the creative and analytic process.

INTRODUCING THE DIAMOND-E FRAMEWORK

The Diamond-E model, as presented in Figure 3.1, is, in effect, a high-level road map for strategic analysis. It identifies the key variables that need to be considered in the analysis and it structures the critical relationships among them. Strategy is the critical linking variable in the model. Strategy tells you what opportunities the business is pursuing in the environment and, by inference, what resources, organizational capabilities, and management preferences are required for effective execution. The double-headed arrows in the diagram indicate that any of the variables can either drive strategy (in the sense, for example, that an environment change forces a strategy change, or that a new strategic initiative is launched to exploit a unique resource) or constrain strategy (as, for example, when resources are insufficient to support a contemplated strategic change).

Each variable in the Diamond-E relates directly or indirectly to each of the others. Within the business, for example, management preferences will directly influence strategic choices and organizational factors, and these in turn will influence resource development. The precise nature of the relationships will vary in different situations, but it is vitally important to appreciate the dynamic consequences of the linkages; changes in any one variable will likely affect all the other variables.

THE CRITERION OF CONSISTENCY

The principal logic underlying the Diamond-E framework is that of consistency, or alignment. The idea is that high consistency among the component variables in the Diamond-E will lead to successful performance, while conflict or inconsistencies will

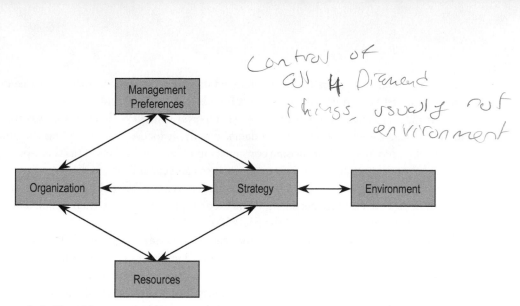

Handwritten annotation: Control of all 4 Diamend things, usually not environment

Figure 3.1 The Diamond-E Framework

lead to poor performance. It follows that a viable strategy needs to be in alignment with the opportunities and challenges of the environment on the one hand, and with the internal capabilities, drives, and constraints of the business on the other hand. To persist with a course of action in the face of serious inconsistencies is to court disaster. As one of our students remarked, "if you took apart a pound of diamond and a pound of graphite, you would be left with identical piles of carbon atoms. There are simply more and better bonds between the carbon atoms in diamonds. Likewise, the Diamond-E can be either a shining example of cogence, or a brittle substance relegated to the interior of pencils. It all comes down to the strength of the linkages." This does not mean that strategy is static. Quite the contrary. In a dynamic environment with shifting customer preferences and competition the strategy needs to be nimble, as does the organization. Similarly, there could be dramatic changes in resources that may dictate strategic change.

The Diamond-E model and the criterion of consistency may seem disarmingly simple. The rub is that a strategy must satisfy both the external and internal circumstances *simultaneously*. For example, a strategic initiative that addresses a major challenge or opportunity will be doomed to failure if it makes unrealistic demands on resources and organization.

Consider the situation facing A.G. Lafley when he took over as CEO of Procter & Gamble (P&G) in 2000. His predecessor, Durk Jager, had resigned suddenly after a 17-month tenure in which he had pressed the company into a near frenzy of new product and brand launches. In the abstract, the strategy seemed appealing; in recent years P&G had lost its growth momentum in the face of tougher brand and private label competition. But Jager's aggressive, all-fronts, forced march assault proved to be too much, even for P&G's vaunted development and marketing capabilities. Failures mounted, costs escalated, and morale tumbled. Enter Lafley with a simple, powerful, "back to the basics" recovery plan. P&G refocused on its core brands, sold off marginal products, pulled out of product launches, and cut overheads. Lafley brought P&G back to what it could effectively execute. Under his leadership, P&G changed its growth strategy to focus on three main areas. The first was on its core and largest brands that could provide access to the largest and strongest retailers and win in the most important markets. The second was to shift focus to beauty and personal care products. Finally, it focused on extending the affordability of its products to low-income consumers in emerging markets. This three-pronged, focused strategy leveraged P&G internal resources and capabilities to the changing external environment and paid off. Over the next ten years P&G delivered a 12% annual growth in its core earnings per share, its market capitalization more than doubled, and its stock price handily outperformed the S&P 500.

The P&G example illustrates a further catch in the seemingly simple balances of the Diamond-E, in that the linkages must be developed and sustained over time, even as circumstances change. A strategy that is in alignment for some time will eventually fall into inconsistency, just as inevitably as environments change, if it, and all the other internal variables in the business, are not kept up to date. Over the years, P&G's strategy and execution had lost their differentiating edge. Something significant needed to be done to revitalize the company by bringing the linkages of the Diamond-E back into a productive balance.

In reality, total consistency and perfect alignment are elusive. The variables in play are too complex and too dynamic to expect this. The principle of alignment remains the driving concern in strategic analysis, however, and it becomes a matter of management judgment to decide which inconsistencies the firm can live with, which can be resolved or mitigated within the existing strategic approach, and which are so significant and difficult to address that major strategic changes are required.

Consistency, Opportunity, and Risk

Since the principle of consistency is an ideal, virtually every strategy will be associated with some current and future inconsistencies. A critical aspect of strategic analysis, therefore, is to identify these inconsistencies and to assess the degree of risk associated with them. The risks can then be weighed against the opportunity that the initiative offers. A broad classification of the risks arising from inconsistencies is given in Figure 3.2.

		TIME HORIZON	
		SHORT-TERM	LONG-TERM
RISKS	ENVIRONMENTAL	Errors in reading the environment cause strategic failure	Environmental changes make the strategy obsolete
	CAPABILITY	Strategic demands exceed the capacity to execute	Internal capabilities develop inconsistently with strategy

Figure 3.2 Strategic Risks

Environmental risks arise from potential inconsistencies between strategy and environment. In the short run, the risk is usually one of miscalculating timing, or potential, or competitive reaction: you think that a strategic initiative will work but there is a chance that you may be misreading the situation. Canon's early, heavy investment in digital photography, for example, was a risky move in light of the uncertainties around the speed of market development for this innovation, but it proved to be a sound one. In the long run, the risk is usually one of missing or underestimating environment changes: you think you are okay, but your perceptions are biased by past success and present ambiguity. Kodak, for example, procrastinated for years before deciding to go after digital photography in a big way and is now having to play catch up in an industry in which it was once the unquestioned leader. By 2010, while Kodak had regained a strong position in a number of its markets, it was far from being the unquestioned leader.

To address the viability of your strategy, or core business, as Zook[1] calls it, he suggests that it is important to take a close look at customers to determine the state of their profitability, market share, retention rate, loyalty, and share of wallet. With respect to competition, you can look at relative cost position, degree of differentiation, and emerging business models of competitors. In summary, the environmental risks will manifest themselves in industry profits, so it is important to keep an eye on the growth in the industry, associated costs and revenues, and the way in which value is created, captured and distributed.

Capability risks arise from inconsistencies between strategy and the capabilities and drives within the firm. In the short run, a new strategy may simply demand too much. We saw that in the earlier P&G example. In the long run, capabilities may not develop adequately to support a consistent but continuously more demanding strategy. In many firms this takes the form of a slow, insidious process. The demands of the strategy notch up as the environment evolves, but internal capabilities actually erode as complacency sets in and takes its toll on innovation and costs. Zook suggests looking at the core capabilities and also the organization and its associated culture to determine any stress points arising from undesired attrition, energy, motivation, or bottlenecks to growth.[2] The business slowly slides from positive operating performance and organizational health to a negative situation. Ultimately, and hopefully sooner than later, a wake-up call rings, often to be followed by a new CEO. In 2010, for example, Omar Ishrak was brought in from GE Healthcare, a world leader in its market, to take on the role of CEO at Medtronics whose share performance had languished over the previous decade.

Bear in mind that risk is unavoidable—do not trap yourself in a fruitless quest for a risk-free strategy. Be conscious of risks, certainly, but be sure to weigh them against needs and opportunities. Opportunities may lie in untapped insights into customers, an unexploited capability, or a strategy that is not tightly aligned. Apple and its venture into music is a classic example. Zook points out that Apple exploited its capability in user-friendly design and imaginative marketing to build a business that accounts for 50 percent of its revenues and 40 percent of its profits[3]. Strategies that intelligently stretch what is possible in the market and what is possible to implement are those most likely to provide high returns and competitive advantage.[4]

Strategy, Strategic Proposals, and Strategic Analysis

In Chapter 2 we described business strategy in terms of four related components—goals, product market focus, value proposition, and core activities. It is important for you to remember, as you describe and evaluate strategy in these terms, that you are usually dealing with the result of an evolutionary process—the cumulative outcome of a series of small steps taken one at a time over an extended period of time. It would actually be quite unusual for a strategy, as you identify it, to be the end point of some grand plan. Rather, it is more likely to be the product of a series of important but limited strategic decisions—each made on the basis of what made sense at the time. Wal-Mart's strategy, as we described it in Chapter 2, for example, was not the end result of a master plan that Sam Walton had in his mind when he started into the business, but rather of a series of smart moves that he made over the years to exploit insights and opportunities as they occurred.

What this means for strategic analysis is that as you move from diagnosis to the consideration of new ideas you will be working for the most part with one or more strategic proposals. Strategic proposals are discrete ideas or action plans that will have significant implications for one or more of the components of strategy and thus for the strategy of the business as a whole. A new product initiative, such as Rogers Communications' consideration of entry into the voice over internet phone (VoIP) business, or an acquisition, such as Encana's bid for Tom Brown, are examples of strategic proposals. A decision on the desirability of such proposals must therefore consider their (1) implications for the ongoing strategy of the business; (2) consistency with the other variables in the Diamond-E framework; and ultimately (3) their promise of profitability. This is a big job, but at least we are not trying to reinvent the whole strategy. Fortunately, we do not have to start at the beginning to create a totally new strategy very often, although in cases of major environmental changes and company crises this is pretty much the case.

Some strategic proposals, such as those above that involve new product launches or acquisitions, are easily identified. Others are less obvious and may even be disguised, either deliberately or inadvertently. A division manager may, for example, push for the selection of a larger plant site, leaving submerged the questions of whether the corporation should expand, or even be in the business. Similarly, management may appraise a new compensation scheme on the basis of its equity, technical, and tax merits, but not fully explore its potential impact on the goals of the organization. The implication, again, is that you must take a broad approach to strategic analysis, remaining sensitive to the strategic implications of what may seem to be everyday decisions.

USING THE DIAMOND-E FRAMEWORK

In the description of the process of strategic analysis that follows, we refer to the use of the *Diamond-E analysis*. This is shorthand for a systematic review of each of the key linkages in the Diamond-E framework—strategy with environment, resources, management preferences, and organization. The objectives of the analysis, depending on circumstances, are to help (1) assess the appropriateness of the firm's current strategy; (2) generate new ideas and strategic proposals; and (3) evaluate specific strategic proposals.

The Strategy-Environment Linkage

In a typical analysis using the Diamond-E, the first task is to deal with the strategy-environment linkage. This requires a careful assessment of the forces at work in the environment and the translation of these observations into their implications for the business in terms of specific strategic opportunities and challenges. With these opportunities and challenges in hand you can proceed to check the existing strategy of the business for consistency, to evaluate a proposal that has been put forward for analysis, or to work at generating new strategic proposals. A final step in working through the strategy-environment linkage is to put together a performance forecast for the proposal(s) under study based on the assumption (to be tested later in the analysis) that it could be successfully implemented. The analysis of the strategy-environment linkage will be expanded in Chapters 4 and 5.

The Strategy-Resources Linkage

The first step in checking the strategy-resources linkage is to identify the resource requirements for the current strategy or new strategic proposal. This is followed by a comparison of the required resources with those available, or readily available, to the business and with this the identification of resource gaps. A judgment follows on the probabilities of being able to close the resource gaps, the consequences of failing to do so, and ultimately the wisdom of proceeding with the strategy under study. In the meantime a great deal has been learned about the resources of the business and this can be woven into the process through the creation of new proposals.

This last point, the idea of coming up with new strategic proposals while in the middle of a process aimed at examining established ones, is a critical aspect of the Diamond-E analysis. It emphasizes that we are not proposing a linear, closed system of logic, but an open system of analysis that should recycle to incorporate learning and insights as it proceeds. In this sense, the Diamond-E involves much more trial and error and iterative logic than may first be assumed. The analysis of the strategy-resources linkage is expanded in Chapter 6.

The Strategy-Management Preferences Linkage

Most models for strategic planning and analysis focus on the alignment of strategy, environment, resources, and organization. These models are fine as far as they go, but we believe that they are seriously flawed by not including the strategic preferences of the key managers in the business. Managers, after all, are the authors and implementers of strategy. Their preferences constitute strategic drives and constraints just as surely as do resources and organizational capabilities. The beliefs of Ingvar Kamprad, for example, that well-designed, well-built furniture should be available to the common family at affordable prices, were of central importance in the development of IKEA's business strategy. Our position, in general, is that you cannot expect to do an effective job of understanding, creating, and analyzing strategies if you ignore preferences.

The analysis of the strategy-management preferences linkage starts with the identification of preferences that would be consistent with the successful execution of the strategy. These are then compared with the preferences of the business managers who are critical to the execution process. If these required and observed preferences are consistent, the analysis can move on. But there are two kinds of problems that might arise. First, you may find that the preferences of the various managers are quite similar, but at odds with the strategic proposal. The proposal may call for a significantly more aggressive attitude towards innovation and risk, for example, than is currently prevalent in the management ranks. Such a situation will call for a judgment on whether the preferences can reasonably be modified by organizational action, or whether this is just asking for too much. If the latter is the case, you may have to abandon the proposal. This would be a painful move, because any proposal that has come this far has passed the consistency checks with environment and resources.

Second, you may find that differences in individual strategic preferences are causing conflict among the managers as well as with the strategy. This is actually quite common, since managers in different roles such as marketing, manufacturing, research and development, and so on will quite naturally reflect different orientations to strategic content, timing, and risk. Recall that one of the prime functions of strategy is to get these different managers working towards the same goals and vision. As you begin to understand the nature of these conflicts you can determine the best steps to bring their preferences into alignment, and the time and risk factors involved in doing so. The analysis of the strategy-management preferences linkage is expanded in Chapter 7.

The Strategy-Organization Linkage

The assessment of the strategy-organization linkage is usually the last step in the Diamond-E analysis. If a proposed strategy has made it this far through the analysis you are usually reasonably happy with it, and want to determine whether the organization will implement it effectively. Thus, if you find problems in the strategy-organization linkage, your first response will be to try to change the organization to develop new capabilities. Only if this does not appear feasible should you consider changing the strategy.

You should start the strategy-organization analysis by identifying the organizational capabilities required to implement the strategy, as deduced directly by the strategy and indirectly from the gaps identified in the resource and preference analysis. The next step is to check for consistency between the required capabilities and those evident in the organization. If these are consistent you can move on to forecast performance, make choices, and work on execution. If there are gaps, however, you will need to determine the nature and feasibility of the changes to develop the missing capabilities. As we will explain in Chapter 8, there are four critical variables that have a major impact on your organization's capabilities. These are leadership, structure, management processes, and culture. What changes will be required in these variables, and how difficult will it be to make the changes?

Having completed an assessment of the consistency of the strategy-organization linkage, and at least one tour around the Diamond-E, it is time to return to the conditional performance forecast coming out of the earlier strategy-environment analysis. Does the forecast stand up in the light of implementation issues? If so, the strategy and its promise can be carried forward to further comparisons and decision. If not, either the performance forecast will have to be revised to reflect the implementation issues, or the strategy itself will have to be modified and the analysis recycled.

STRATEGIC TENSION

Another way to think about the Diamond-E framework is by examining some of the fundamental tensions that exist between the elements. The notion of "tension" is critical to this concept of strategy. It suggests there is no perfect strategic choice and firms will always experience some stretch or tension. Figure 3.3 shows that firms must manage the tension between what they "need" to do given the competitive environment, what they "can" do given their organization, resources and capabilities, and what they "want" to do given management preferences. All that we have done here is simplify the internal side of the Diamond-E by combining organization with resources.

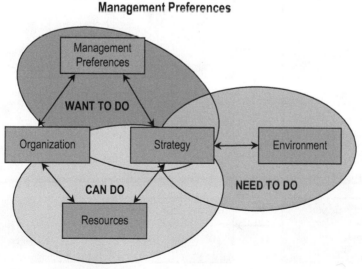

Figure 3.3 Diamond E Framework: Tensions

In trying to satisfy a market "need," a strategy, may stretch what a firm "can" deliver. Alternatively, a firm may satisfy key stakeholder interests at the expense of not delivering exactly what the market needs, as found in many entrepreneurial firms who are guided by what an entrepreneur "wants" to do.

THE PROCESS OF STRATEGIC ANALYSIS

The Diamond-E framework is the focal point of a more comprehensive process of strategic analysis as described in Figure 3.4. This is a full strategic review that works from an assessment of the current performance and strategy of the business, through creation and assessment of strategic options, to decision and execution. Such full and formal analyses are appropriate (1) on a periodic basis, such as once a year, as determined by senior management; (2) in light of current or anticipated poor performance; (3) when the business confronts a suddenly perceived opportunity or threat; or (4) to fully assess a spontaneous proposal originating within the organization.

Formal strategic reviews are very important, but there is an equivalently significant contribution to be gained from employing this same process informally on an ongoing basis. If this analytic process also becomes an informal and continuous part of the way managers think about the future of their business, there will be big dividends in the timeliness of recognizing new possibilities and in the flexibility to address them. There is no need here for numbers and surveys and presentations; rather, you try on an ongoing basis to put everyday events and experience together in a format that pushes you to think about long-term implications. Then, as circumstances unfold, you are ready for timely action or

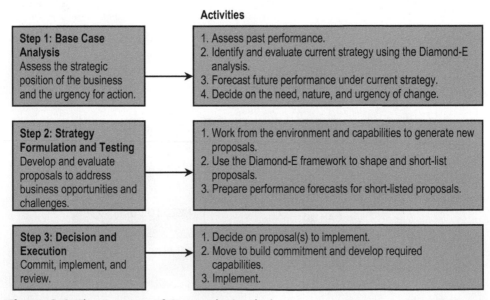

Figure 3.4 The Process of Strategic Analysis

perhaps to initiate a more formal review. In this sense the process of strategic analysis, or strategic thinking, becomes an integral part of the everyday agenda of management.

Whatever the initiating conditions, and at whatever point you enter the strategic review process, there are three steps or stages of work that need to be completed. In logical sequence, which you should understand may not reflect your entry point, these are (1) base case analysis; (2) strategy formulation and testing; and (3) decision and execution. As illustrated in Figure 3.4, the Diamond-E is central to Steps 1 and 2 of this process. The following sections describe each of these steps.

Step 1: Base Case Analysis

The objective of this step of analysis is to establish what will happen if you simply continue to employ the current strategy, or modest variations of it, and from this determine the urgency for strategic action.

Assess Performance A careful analysis of the performance of your business is a fundamental first step in base case analysis. Unless you are on the brink of a dramatic change in the environment, performance trends that are on target suggest that you have the strategy about right. Performance difficulties, on the other hand, mean that your business strategy does not suit competitive conditions, or that your capabilities are inadequate, or both. Diagnosis will always require detective work, and a sensitive analysis of performance factors will provide essential clues to the location and the extent of strategic problems.

First, test the performance of your business against internal goals and external pressures using the measures of operating performance and organizational health that we suggested in Chapter 1. Pay particular attention to your most important strategic goals. If the generation of new products is a critical goal, how are you doing? If you need to gain market share at the expense of a certain competitor in a particular segment, ensure that you have the data you need to monitor progress. Bear in mind that these measures of performance relative to your own goals are important, but not conclusive. You will still have to evaluate, as part of your subsequent Diamond-E analysis, whether the goals, as set, are appropriate and realistic.

Second, you need to measure the firm's performance against external reference standards and benchmarks. How well is the business doing relative to the current expectations of shareholders, bankers, customers, labour markets, suppliers, government agencies, and so on? These judgments will identify the areas in which the firm is well positioned as well as those in which it is vulnerable.

The results of the performance assessment will help to set the agenda for the rest of your analysis. If the business is having difficulties, your approach should be one of diagnosing the problems and developing remedies. On the other hand, if the business is performing well, your approach should be to check vulnerabilities and build strategies to take advantage of new opportunities. The steps of subsequent analysis will be the same as those illustrated in Figure 3.4, but the focus will be on different issues.

Identify the Strategy To move forward from the performance assessment you need a clear understanding of your current business strategy. This is the platform for looking outward at the environment on one hand, and inward to the company on the other hand, and for deciding what forces and circumstances should be given priority attention. Sometimes your strategy will be well formed and consistent, sometimes not. But recall that your business will always have a strategy, albeit in some circumstances implicit, incomplete, or confused. Your job here is to identify the priorities that are driving the business, whatever they are.

Evaluate the Strategy Using your organization's current strategy as a point of departure, assess the consistency of the relationships in the Diamond-E framework. What you are aiming for in this application of the Diamond-E is a forecast of the future performance of the business, assuming that it continues to employ the current strategy. This forecast, in effect, summarizes the impact of the consistent and inconsistent relationships that you have identified in your analysis.

Decide on the Nature and Urgency of Required Changes The base case Diamond-E analysis and performance forecast will provide you with the grounds for judgments about the prospects of continuing with your present strategy. If the forecast looks good, how long can you expect it to continue? How can you make it even better? In some situations you will decide that minor changes in strategy, or in the elements of the Diamond-E supporting strategy, are all that is required, and that their urgency is low. In other cases the forecast will look dire and you will have to move very quickly to implement some radical changes in strategy and operations. Sometimes the outlook will be satisfactory but could be improved with relatively modest strategic action.

Step 2: Strategy Formulation and Testing

As you move to create new strategic proposals, you can rely heavily on your earlier work to dictate the issues that take priority, the time frame that you have to work in, and the rough scale of action that makes sense.

Generate Strategic Proposals Unless you have begun the process of strategic analysis with some concrete strategic proposals in mind, you are likely to find that your primary source of new ideas is the analysis that you have just completed. As you evaluated your current performance and strategy and worked through the Diamond-E, you were undoubtedly struck by some new insights. Now is the time to review these, to develop a list of new opportunities and problems, and to assemble proposals that address the most attractive possibilities or the most urgent challenges. Fresh ideas may also arise spontaneously, of course, and these should be added to the inventory. In general, the more thorough the preparatory work, the better the set of options you will have to consider, and the easier it will be to create new strategic proposals.

Evaluate Strategic Proposals The most promising strategic proposals should be assessed by means of the Diamond-E analysis. The workload will not be quite as high this time because you can rely on much of the analysis that you have already done in evaluating the current strategy. To make sure that the door stays open for other proposals and for new ideas, your first applications of the Diamond-E should be fast and provisional. There is no need at this point for you to make detailed, formal performance forecasts. Work with consistency and inconsistency and be pretty quick to disqualify proposals encumbered by inconsistencies. The aim at the outset is to sort the proposals quickly and to assemble a short list of the promising possibilities. Then you will need to apply the full rigour of the Diamond-E, culminating with performance forecasts.

The performance forecasts for the most attractive strategic proposals will need to be carefully reviewed. You will have to make crucial judgments about whether the performance estimates will actually be met. Are the forecasts credible? Do they reflect an acceptable balance of risk and opportunity? All things considered, which of the proposals looks the best? Finally, do you have an answer yet or do you have to recycle in search of a strategy that is more promising and convincing than those uncovered to this point?

Step 3: Decision and Execution

At this stage, you may be in the happy position of having a number of new strategic proposals to choose from, all of which you find attractive. More often, managers find that they are torn between adopting one of several imperfect proposals. Whatever the situation, the time has come to make a choice. Doing the analysis that we have suggested is important, but it should not be converted into an excuse for endless delay, with calls for more and more information, or more and more analysis.

When your choice is made, it is time to plan for execution. If your choice represents a significant change to your firm, you will want to look at Chapters 10 and 11, which deal with the implementation of strategic change. Furthermore, your analysis of implementation should inform the formulation of strategy. As you consider what it will take to implement the strategy, you will likely need to revisit your underlying assumptions about the strategy to ensure they are still valid.

SUMMARY

This chapter has presented a general framework for strategic analysis. The Diamond-E framework identifies the basic building blocks and relationships to consider in dealing with strategy problems. The Diamond-E analysis provides a systematic way to evaluate strategies in light of the critical linkages defined in the model. It serves as a crucial phase of a broader process of strategic analysis, which encompasses a sequence of steps leading from base case analysis to strategic choice. It is important to note that there are many approaches to strategic analysis, but all approaches stem from the basic building blocks that are inherent in the Diamond E framework. Take, for example, Zook's seven steps to a new core business in which he suggests the following:

1. Define the core of your business. Reach consensus on the true state of the core.

2. Assess the core's full potential and the durability of its key differentiation.

3. Develop a point of view about the future, and define the status quo.

4. Identify the full range of options for redefining the core from the inside and from the outside.

5. Identify your hidden assets, and ask whether they create new options or enable others.

6. Use key criteria (leadership, profit pool, repeatability, chances of implementation) in deciding which assets to employ in redefining your core.

7. Set up a program office to help initiate, track, and manage course corrections.[5]

Although Zook is vague in his discussion of what the "core" means, the four elements of strategy provide good definition around its elements: goals, product market focus, value proposition and core activities. Differentiation typically refers to how well differentiated the value proposition is, but it could also refer to differentiation in the other strategy elements. Identifying hidden assets involves looking both inside to capabilities and resources and outside to customer needs that may be unmet by competitors. As we move through subsequent chapters, the importance of implementation will become paramount since many strategies sound good on paper but fail because of poor execution and implementation.

The emphasis in the chapter has been on basic tools and logic. Subsequent chapters will go into the substance and detail required to apply the framework and process to specific strategic problems.

Notes

1. Zook, Chris. "Finding Your Next CORE Business." *Harvard Business Review* 85.4 (2007): 66–75. *Business Source Complete, EBSCO*. Web. 15 Aug. 2011..

2. Zook, Chris. "Finding Your Next CORE Business." *Harvard Business Review* 85.4 (2007): 66–75. *Business Source Complete, EBSCO*. Web. 15 Aug. 2011.

3. Zook, Chris. "Finding Your Next CORE Business." *Harvard Business Review* 85.4 (2007): 66–75. *Business Source Complete, EBSCO*. Web. 15 Aug. 2011.

4. For a further discussion of the idea of stretch, see Hamel, Gary, and C. K. Prahalad. "Strategy as Stretch and Leverage," *Harvard Business Review* 71 (March–April 1993): 75–84. Print.

5. Zook, Chris. "Finding Your Next CORE Business." *Harvard Business Review* 85.4 (2007): 66–75. *Business Source Complete, EBSCO*. Web. 15 Aug. 2011.

Chapter 4
Tools for Environment Analysis

In market economies businesses must compete for survival and prosperity. They succeed if their strategies address customer needs and create competitive advantages. They fail if their strategies are inconsistent with market forces. The catch, of course, is that you have to evaluate strategy in terms of the future, not the past, and these cut-and-dried realities are much easier to see in retrospect than they are in prospect.

Environment analysis, or industry analysis as it is often called, has two significant implications for the overall strategic analysis. The first is that not all industries are equally attractive. Although studies have varied in their estimates, it is generally accepted that, on average, 10 to 20 percent of a firm's profitability can be attributed to the industry within which it operates. Therefore, the decision to make initial or further investment in an industry depends on the industry attractiveness. However, it is important to note that the relationship between strategy and the environment, or what is often termed the industry structure, is a two-way street. Structure shapes strategy but strategy shapes structure as well. The notion that strategy shapes structure is the basis for approaches such as the Blue Ocean Strategy that we will discuss later in this chapter.[1]

Second, regardless of the industry attractiveness, we need to assess the industry economics, drivers of profitability, and the key success factors (KSFs) to understand what it takes to win in the industry. There are many models of industry analysis that provide different perspectives and approaches. We begin this chapter by reviewing some of the more salient models. We then compare and contrast the models and address how they can be used in conducting industry analysis. The following models are examined:

- Porter's Five Forces Model
- Industry Value Chain
- Cooperation and Competition: Game Theory
- PEST
- Scenario Planning
- New Economy Models
- Blue Ocean Strategy
- Global Industry Models
- Stakeholder Analysis.

Later, in Chapter 5, we attempt to reconcile the complexity of the environment analysis tools presented in this chapter with a general and practical approach to conducting environment analysis.

PORTER'S FIVE FORCES MODEL

One of the earliest models used to examine industry economics and industry attractiveness is Michael Porter's Five Forces Model (Figure 4.1).[2] Rooted in economic theory, Porter suggests that there are five competitive forces at play in any industry that will determine that industry's profitability: competitive rivalry, threat of new entrants, supplier power, buyer power, and threat of substitute products. The weaker these forces, which describe the key structural features of the industry, the greater the opportunity for superior performance by firms within the industry; the stronger these forces, the more difficult it will be. Understanding industry structure is therefore the starting point for strategic analysis and strategy formulation. As well, examining the five forces helps organizations understand how value that is created by companies, is actually captured by the industry players.

Threat of Entry The rationale behind new entrants as a major competitive force relates to basic economic models suggesting that the greater the number of competitors, the closer the industry is to perfect competition. In contrast, where there is only one competitor a monopoly exists. The fewer the competitors, the greater the likelihood of higher profits. In addition, new entrants who are diversifying from outside an industry may be able to leverage capabilities or offset costs, such that they alter the economics of how firms compete in an industry, as Apple did when it entered the music industry.[3] Porter suggests there are six major barriers to entry: economies of scale, product differentiation, capital requirements, cost disadvantages independent of size, access to distribution channels, and

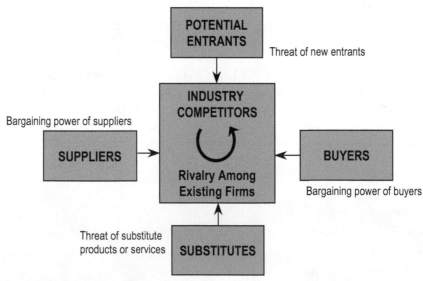

Figure 4.1 Porter's Five Forces Model

↳ Industry Tool

government policy. The key with each is to consider the impact on costs, price, and thus profitability.

Economies of Scale There are supply-side economies of scale whereby, as the absolute volume of production increases, unit costs per product tend to decrease, resulting in economies of scale. As such, existing firms that have already made significant investments in manufacturing (or marketing, distribution, purchasing, sales force utilization, etc.) will likely hold an absolute cost advantage over potential new entrants. Furthermore, multi-business firms may also be able to create scale economies by sharing operational or functional costs with other business units in the company or by exploiting existing vertically integrated production and distribution systems. There are also demand-side economies of scale called network effects when the likelihood of customers purchasing a product or service increases with volume. For example, eBay has demand-side economics in its favour in the on-line auction industry.[4] Economies of scale, therefore, pose a barrier to entry by either forcing new entrants to come into the industry at a larger scale with great risk, or at a smaller scale with cost disadvantages.

Product Differentiation Established firms may also enjoy the benefits of brand recognition and customer loyalty that have been built on past marketing, advertising, and sales efforts. New entrants, on the other hand, may be forced to spend heavily to win customers and capture market share. Establishing a market presence in an industry with strong product differentiation can be both risky and expensive, thereby creating a strong barrier to entry.

Capital Requirements The capital investments required to compete in some industries can be prohibitive. For example, oil and gas, automotive, and airline industries necessitate larger upfront capital than most online service industries. Capital requirements, therefore, will serve as a barrier to entry to those firms that either cannot secure the funds or cannot bear the risk premiums charged. However, it is important to note that capital markets have become very efficient and effective at financing large-scale investments. Whereas at one time the sheer magnitude of an investment posed a barrier to entry, that is no longer the case.

Cost Disadvantages Potential entrants may face other cost disadvantages that serve as barriers to entry that are irrespective of scale. For example, established firms may benefit from longer learning curves, which reduce unit costs and allow for a cost advantage. Existing firms may also possess proprietary product technology, have secured favourable access to limited raw materials, or already captured the most favorable geographic locations in a market space. In multi-national settings especially, incumbents may also benefit from preferential government subsidies. These cost disadvantages may be sufficiently large to prevent potential new players from entering the industry.

Access to Distribution Channels In some industries, established distribution channels can also leave little room for new players to enter given the nature of the channel itself or due to established channel relationships. Barriers to entry are strong if new entrants face fierce competition for limited space or cannot break through long-standing partnerships. For example, a new producer of breakfast cereal will first have to pay large fees to have its product listed in a national supermarket chain, as well as convince the retailer that it will provide extensive support through advertising and promotion to ensure that the cereal generates sufficient sales for the channel. Difficulties and costs associated with securing the required distribution channels are therefore also a barrier to entry.

Government Policy Lastly, many industries such as liquor and tobacco retailing, mineral extraction, and air transportation are by nature highly regulated. Government policies can be impediments on their own, creating strong barriers to entry through legislation, the imposition of standards, lengthy approvals, monitoring or control processes, and licensing issues.

In summary, Porter argues that where there are high economies of scale, incumbents with a differentiated product or service, large capital requirements to enter, incumbents who have advantages other than size such as location or patents, difficult-to-access distribution channels, and prohibitive government policies, new entrants will be deterred from the industry by these very high barriers to entry. New players may also be deterred by the potential for retaliation by existing competitors should they decide to enter regardless of the barriers. Incumbents with substantial resources, entrenched commitments to the industry, and/or a history of retaliatory actions are more likely to respond forcefully to the threat of new entrants in order to protect their established profit margins.

Suppliers The second force affecting industry structure is the bargaining power of suppliers. Porter suggests that suppliers' power can impact industry profitability as they have the potential to place firms at the mercy of rising input costs or reduced quality of necessary products or services. For example, in the fall of 2007, a worldwide shortage of hops raised the cost of a key ingredient in the production of beer, placing many microbreweries dangerously close to extinction. What characteristics render suppliers particularly powerful? As in the case of hops growers, suppliers are more powerful if their industry is dominated by a few companies and are more concentrated than the industry to which they sell, if there are no other substitute products to be sold into the industry, or if the supplier's product is an important input to the buyer's business. Suppliers can also wield bargaining power if they sell to a number of different industries and their product is differentiated. Furthermore, if there are large switching costs in changing suppliers, then suppliers will have more bargaining power. Many of these elements explain why Microsoft has been a very powerful supplier to many industries.[5] Labour is another example of a particularly powerful supplier force, as the need for highly skilled labour and/or the presence of highly unionized employees can significantly influence an entire industry's profit structure.

Buyers The bargaining power of an industry's most important buyer groups—be they intermediaries or customers—can also alter the profitability of an entire industry. For example, companies that want to sell their products to major retailers, such as Wal-Mart (the buyer), are at the mercy of such large distributors. With similar attributes as supplier power, there are several circumstances that can affect a buyer group's overall bargaining power: Buyers are more powerful if they are concentrated or purchase in large volumes, if they have full information, if they face few switching costs (i.e., not locked in to a single supplier) and if they earn low profits. Furthermore, if the products being purchased represent a significant portion of the buyer's costs, they are more likely to shop around for the best deal, especially if the products themselves are standard or undifferentiated or are not important to the overall quality of the buyer's product or service. Lastly, if buyers pose a credible threat to backward integration they can also yield significant bargaining power. Where there are several downstream buyers, it is important to examine where the power lies. For example, "DuPont has created enormous clout by advertising its Stainmaster brand of carpet fibers not only to the carpet manufacturers that actually buy them but also to downstream consumers. Many consumers request Stainmaster carpet even though DuPont is not a carpet manufacturer".[6] Generally, individual consumers have little or no power as a buyer. Yes, individuals can buy from one firm over another, or not at all, but individual consumers are not usually organized to purchase in large volumes. As an airline passenger (a buyer of a flight), an individual consumer is relatively powerless to affect price or quality of service.

Substitute products Substitute products are products from outside the industry that can provide a similar package of benefits or otherwise perform the same function as the main product or service in the industry. Substitute products can reduce profitability in the industry as they place a new ceiling on the price that can be charged for the original product or service. Often, the assessment of threat by substitute products can be difficult and quite dynamic as there are a variety of forces that shape product features that can be 'replaced' by substitutes with superior cost competitiveness. For example, water is a substitute for cola, although in its traditional form, it did not provide the same package of benefits. However, branded bottled water was introduced with a different package of benefits and began to steal market share from the cola products. Similarly, video conferencing can be a substitute for business air travel, just as VoIP can be a substitute for more traditional telecommunications. Substitute products have the potential to alter significantly the structural dynamics of an industry.

Intensity of Competitive Rivalry Competitive rivalry is affected by the other forces, but also has a dynamic of its own that can be witnessed by advertising and price wars, escalating promotional tactics, and new product extensions or introductions. Some industries can be characterized by relatively moderate competitive rivalry, while others are described as very intense, where brands "battle it out for market share" in public confrontations. However, even in cases of very intense and public rivalry it is important to understand the basis for the rivalry and its impact on profitability. Rivalry is affected by the interaction of other structural forces as well as through the sheer number and nature of competitors in an industry. Where there are only a few large players, the balance of power can be easily observed and the extent to which these firms direct the competition on price, brand, or distribution, for example, is relatively transparent. Where there are many small firms, however, rogue behavior is more likely. Diverse competitors, especially foreign entrants, add complexity and create instability in the competitive landscape of the industry. Where strategic stakes are high, the nature of competitive activity can also be unpredictable.

The intensity of competitive rivalry is also affected by the rate of growth in the industry. The greater rate of growth, the less the competitive rivalry since all "boats rise with the tide." However, slow or no-growth industries and especially industries in decline can turn into bitter market share battles for the remaining pieces of the pie. In some cases, even despite negative returns, management may become unwilling to let go emotionally from the business or be prevented from disengaging by some other social or governmental restriction. Rather, stuck with specialized asset configurations, long-term fixed costs, and strategic partnerships which now act as barriers to *exit* from the industry, firms engage in desperate competitive tactics to stay afloat. Porter warns that it is competitive rivalry on the basis of price which may be the most dangerous since it transfers profitability from firms directly to customers in the form of increased value. As well, it is important to pay attention to the various dimensions on which firms compete since, if competitors are undifferentiated, it results in zero sum competition, whereas if they compete on different dimensions targeted to different customer segments then rivalry can actually increase industry profitability.[7]

How do you define your industry? Porter suggests using the five forces to determine whether the product market scope is similar for the various products, services, and geographic markets. The more they differ, the greater the likelihood that a firm may be operating in multiple industries and therefore it would be important to examine each industry using a five forces analysis. He offers the following common pitfalls:

- Defining the industry too broadly or too narrowly;
- Making lists instead of engaging in rigorous analysis;
- Paying equal attention to all of the forces rather than digging deeply into the most important ones;
- Confusing effect (price sensitivity) with cause (buyer economics);
- Using static analysis that ignores industry trends;
- Confusing cyclical or transient changes with true structural changes;
- Using the framework to declare an industry attractive or unattractive rather than using it to guide strategic choices.[8]

In summary, Porter views industries with low supplier power, low threat of entry, low buyer power, low threat of substitute products, and low competitive rivalry as five-star industries with a high level of expected profitability for firms within the industry. Once the strengths and weaknesses of the forces affecting the industry as a whole have been identified, the firm can then determine the strengths and weaknesses of its position relative to the industry to formulate its competitive strategy. Porter also cautions that industries are dynamic and while the structure of the industry shapes strategy, firms can also shape industry structure.

VALUE CHAIN

Porter also introduced value chain[9] analysis which we have represented as an organizational value chain in Figure 4.2 below. The organizational value chain is the primary activities selected from the industry's value chain (which includes all activities from raw materials to sale to the final consumer and disposal) that have been integrated into the structure of an organization. For example, an automobile manufacturer may make parts, assemble cars, and then market and distribute them. Yet the whole value chain would include, for example, mining iron ore, manufacturing paint, producing radial tires, and disposing of old vehicles. The organizational value chain model illustrates how any product or service could be described in terms of a set of primary activities and a set of supporting activities. Primary activities involve such things as inbound logistics, operations, outbound logistics, marketing and sales, and after-sale service. Support activities include firm infrastructure, human resource management, technology development, and procurement. The fundamental principle is that primary and support activities contribute to both a firm's costs as well as the ability for a firm to deliver value to its customers. The value created, less the costs, dictates the margin, or lack thereof, derived by each activity along the value chain.

The delivery of any product or service can be broken down into the activities that add value in the process. For example, an athletic shoe company can break down the price paid by the consumer for a particular pair of shoes into the cost of support activities such as technology development to research and design the shoe and primary activities such as operations and outbound logistics to manufacture and ship the product. At each step along the organizational value chain, firms will have direct product or service costs and an associated margin contributing to indirect costs and overall profit. As another example, consider the price you pay for a bottle of Coke or Pepsi. Very little of the cost, but much of the value or margin, is derived from the production of the actual concentrate used in the beverage. While bottling and distribution are of course essential in order for

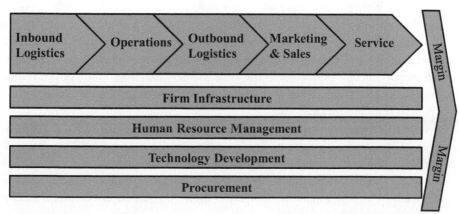

Figure 4.2 Value Chain

you to receive the finished product, the bottling technology is less proprietary than the concentrate and hence does not add as much value in the industry chain.

Companies seek to lower costs and increase a customer's willingness to pay (customer value) in order to generate economic value. One approach is to consider how supporting activities could help to increase margins. Technological applications have certainly helped create value all along the value chain. For example, Wal-Mart has been able to reduce costs through effective inventory management. Technology has enabled it to undertake sophisticated forecasting of customer needs, while providing real-time tracking of in-stock merchandise, a direct link to suppliers in order to replenish stock, and the capacity to manage its massive distribution centers effectively and deploy its fleet of trucks. Southwest and WestJet airlines have sought to add value and reduce costs through their human resource management strategy.

It is also helpful to consider what might increase a customer's willingness to pay. In the above example, Wal-Mart's inventory system ensures that product is always on the shelf when a customer needs it, thereby increasing revenues. Consider the differences that exist in both price and associated margin when you purchase a can of Coke or Pepsi from the grocery store versus a vending machine. We are willing to pay double, if not triple, the price to have the product cold and ready to consume where we need it and when we need it. Coke and Pepsi's strong international vending machine network allows them to extract value from distribution. Value chain analysis can also identify where and why customers may be willing to pay less, identifying where value is being eroded in an industry. For example, distribution of music through illegal, yet free, downloads has the effect of significantly reducing willingness of customers to purchase music, hence destroying economic value for music producers.

The value chain can be understood at both the firm and industry levels. Different firms competing in the same industry may choose to perform or outsource the different activities that constitute the industry's value chain. For example, Nike chooses to outsource the production of its athletic shoes, while New Balance performs this function internally. The bottling and distribution functions of the value chain are often contracted to third parties, which allows Coke and Pepsi to focus on the activities such as concentrate development and marketing where they have significant strength. Similarly, firms may choose to give more or less emphasis to the activities. Nike places great emphasis on marketing, New Balance much less so. As a result, the core activities component of the strategies of different businesses in the same industry may vary in important respects. Thinking deeply about such differences is critical to understanding how firms have chosen to compete in their industries.

Porter's value chain is stylized, containing discrete boxes encompassing many of the activities in a firm's value chain. This analytical tool can and should be modified to include the specific steps in a firm and industry's unique value chain. For example, a value chain for Pepsi and Coke would most likely separate marketing and sales since, aside from vending machines, these soft drink companies invest heavily in marketing, but do not retail their own products.

Porter's Five Forces Model can be used to understand where economic profit lies in the value chain for the industry. By understanding the power of suppliers and buyers across the chain, and the associated competitive rivalry, barriers to entry and substitute products at each stage, it is possible to identify which parts of the chain are more attractive. Collis and Montgomery provide the example of the Australian concrete industry to point out that most of the economic profit is captured in cement production and stone and sand quarrying. The actual concrete mixing and transportation generate less economic profit. Transportation accounts for almost 50 percent of the costs of a delivered ton of concrete, yet generates little economic return.[10]

COOPERATION AND COMPETITION: GAME THEORY

Game theory provides additional insight into the nature of competitive rivalry. In most jurisdictions around the world it is illegal to collude with competitors. As a result, competitors attempt to read and interpret the signals sent by one another to determine motivation and intent to cooperate or compete. This is tacit collusion. Barney suggests eight industry attributes that facilitate the development and mainte-nance of tacit collusion:[11]

1. Small number of firms enables monitoring

2. Product homogeneity focuses attention on price, which is more easily monitored

3. Cost homogeneity enables a common price structure and level of output

4. Price leaders provide order and discipline to the market

5. Industry social structure or recipe defines the standards of operating in the industry

6. High order frequency and small order size minimize the cost of losing an order and incentive to compete

7. Large inventories and order backlogs create buffers and reduce pressure to compete

8. Entry barriers as noted by Porter in his Five Forces Model.

Game theory is generally valid when there are few competitors, as the intent is to study the interactions among the players and the payoffs they receive. There are zero-sum games, in which one player's gain is exactly equal to the other player's losses, and non-zero-sum games that relax this constraint. The non-zero-sum game is reflective of most business situations since it offers the potential for both cooperation and competition.

Ghemawat suggests several conditions that make a game theoretic approach a valu-able analytic perspective.

Identifiable (rather than faceless) players, relatively clear-cut options for them, and good data sources all facilitate the task of mapping actions into payoffs. Players' familiarity with one another and their repeated interactions among them increase the likelihood that they will actually reason or grope their way to game-theoretic equilibrium, enhancing its usefulness as a reference point . . . Even when these conditions are generally satisfied, simplifications tend to be necessary—as in any model-building exercise—before we can apply game theory to a strategic issue.[12]

The simplifications Ghemawat proposes include reducing the number of players, or the number of iterations of the game, simplifying some of the parameters of the game, and suppressing uncertainties. The prisoner's dilemma is a simple exchange game between two individuals that is commonly associated with game theory. The idea of a prisoner's dilemma arises from the situation where two prisoners, who are being interrogated about a crime, face the choice of turning their partner in, or remaining silent. If both prisoners decide to turn each other in, they both go to jail. If only one turns the other in, one will go to jail, and one will go free. If they both remain silent they will be slightly better off than if they both confess, but not as good as the situation where only one confesses and is freed. The point of the prisoner's dilemma is that there is incentive to turn the partner in, however, if both prisoners act in this way, they will both suffer, hence the dilemma.

Applying the prisoner's dilemma concept to the situation of two firms, we generate a payoff matrix as presented in Figure 4.3. If both firms choose Strategy A they will receive $6,000. If both firms choose Strategy B they will only receive $2,000. However, if only one firm chooses Strategy B, they will receive the highest payout of $10,000 while the other firm receives nothing. As in the case of the prisoners, the firms may be motivated to receive the higher payout, but if they both act in this way, each will receive less than if they cooperated and both choose Strategy A with a payout of $6,000 each.

Barney argues that the decision to cooperate, compete, or cheat on a cooperative agreement depends on a number of factors. "For example, players are more likely to cooperate, and to continue cooperating, if (1) they can directly communicate with one another; (2) cheating does not lead to large payoffs; (3) cheating leads to costly sanctions; or (4) players are more interested in maximizing their payoffs than in beating the payoffs of other players (Fudenberg and Tirole, 1991). When these conditions do not exist, competition and cheating on cooperative agreements is more likely."[13]

| | | FIRM TWO | |
		STRATEGY A	STRATEGY B
FIRM ONE	STRATEGY A	I: $6,000 II: $6,000	I: $10,000 II: $0
	STRATEGY B	I: $0 II: $10,000	I: $2,000 II: $2,000

Figure 4.3 Prisoner's Dilemma Matrix

In spite of the promise of game theory, Coyne and Horn suggest that using game theory to predict competitor reaction is complex and often impractical in real life. Rather, they suggest three questions that help to predict competitor reaction: 1) will the competitor react? 2) what options will they consider? and 3) which option will they choose?[14]

MATH FOR STRATEGISTS

Khanna and Rivkin provide a terrific summary of the kind of tools you need to undertake the various types of strategic analysis.[15] For example, classic supply and demand curves from economics provide more rigour to understanding the relationship between supply demand and price. Even without specific numbers, understanding the logic associated with supply, demand, and price is critical. "Take, for instance, the worldwide market for construction material such as steel, cement, and plywood. In recent years, extremely rapid infrastructure growth in China has led to a tremendous surge in demand for these materials, and prices have soared accordingly, especially in Asia." Yet China's capacity to produce is also ramping up, thereby influencing supply. The expectation from this analysis is that the price of construction materials will rise with the increased demand and then fall with the increase in supply.

When it comes to pricing and competitive analysis, it is essential to understand fixed and marginal costs in relation to the decision being made. For example, in the airline industry, the marginal cost of filling an empty seat at the last minute is substantially lower than the marginal cost of adding an additional flight to the schedule, which would include all of the marginal costs for an additional flight, not just the marginal costs associated with the addition of a passenger on a flight. As well, break-even analysis is useful to determine what benefit would have to be achieved to justify an investment. Strategic decisions typically involve significant investment and therefore understanding the return on investment is critical. Building on the Five Forces Analysis and the Value Chain, it is important to understand the economics of value creation, capture, and distribution. When the Apple iPod was first introduced, analysts did a tear-down analysis of the product to examine the cost of its components and the associated suppliers who were going to benefit from the introduction of this new product that would change the industry.

Understanding competitor cost structure to the best that you can is an essential aspect of competitive analysis. As well, each competitor will command a different level of "willingness to pay" by the customer, often for products or services that do not seem differentiated on the surface. Exploring the differences in willingness to pay will no doubt reveal aspects of a competitor strategy or elements of the industry structure that may not have been immediately apparent. "Consider for instance an apparel maker who delivers clothes to a retailer with the clothes already on hangers and ready to display rather than folded. The apparel maker saves the retailer the labor cost associated with preparing the clothes for display as well as the costs of clothes hangers. If you understand the amount of time required to prepare the clothes, the wage rate of in-store labor, and the cost of a hanger, then you can estimate the incremental will-ingness to pay generated by this service".[16] Finally, tools such as game theory can be used to help identify the economics of competitive response including the likelihood and cost of retaliation.

PEST

PEST analysis stands for political, economic, social, and technological forces that impact the industry. These forces can be viewed as more macro in orientation than Porter's Five Forces, and in many respects are the early warning signals about changes in the industry. As depicted in Figure 4.4, the PEST forces impact supply, competition and demand. It might be helpful to think about how the PEST forces impact each element of the value chain. For example, demographics can be used to assess demand many years in advance, as in the case of planning for the construction of new schools. Prior to the commercialization and adoption of technology there is often a period of time, during which the technology is developed and tested, that provides advance notice of the commercialization. While firms may be blind-sided by sudden changes in the economy, such as devaluation of a currency, many economic trends have predictable impacts on an industry. For example, exchange rates, interest rates, and unemployment rates will all affect supply, demand, and competi-tion within an industry. Finally, regulatory changes are often years in the making, although the final outcome or vote on a particular regulation may be less predictable. These political forces often have a significant effect on who is allowed to compete in a given industry.

Overall, the PEST forces can provide a long lead time in their evolution or develop-ment. However, the final outcome or impact of the force may be less than precise. Often there are multiple paths and possible outcomes, which calls for scenario planning.

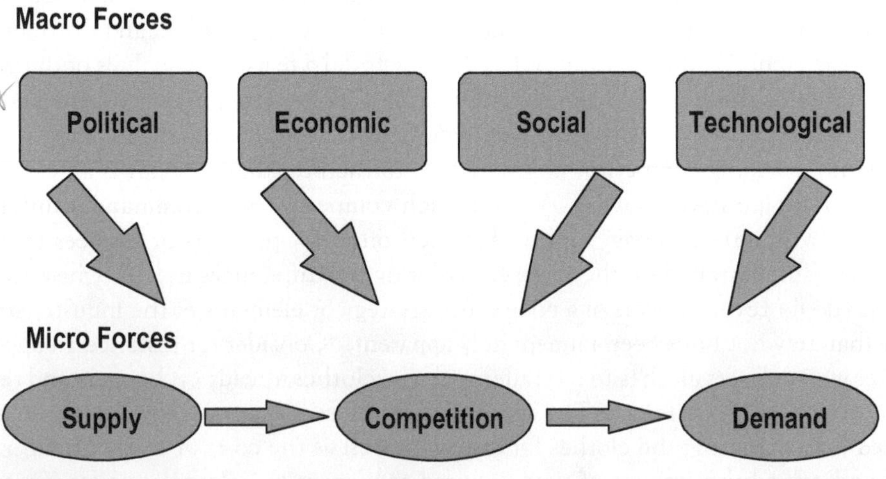

Macro Forces

Figure 4.4 PEST Forces

SCENARIO PLANNING

Scenario planning recognizes the potential for a significant amount of variability in industry analysis. Courtney, Kirkland and Viguerie suggest four levels of uncertainty, what can be known under each kind of uncertainty, the analytical tools that can be used, and some examples.[17] In situations where there is a clear enough future, the traditional strategy tool kit can be applied. When there are alternative futures with clear options, decision analysis, option valuation models, and game theory can be employed. When there is a range of futures, scenario planning is a key tool.

Schoemaker describes scenario planning as a tool for strategic thinking.[18] He outlines several steps for constructing scenarios as follows:

1. Define the time frame and scope of analysis
2. Identify the major stakeholders
3. Identify basic trends
4. Identify key uncertainties
5. Construct initial scenario themes
6. Check for consistency and plausibility
7. Develop learning scenarios of the strategically relevant groups
8. Identify further research needs
9. Develop quantitative models to examine the scenarios
10. Evolve toward decision scenarios.

Many of the steps suggested are consistent with strategic analysis in more predictable environments. The difference in scenario planning is that the variance, diversity, and uncertainty in the analysis are preserved until the final step when decisions need to be made. In doing so, firms understand the complexity, inter-relatedness, and risks associated with the various scenarios.

NEW ECONOMY MODELS

Porter argues that strategy in the internet environment is not fundamentally different from strategy in industries not dominated by the internet. The failure of many internet firms, he argues, can be attributed to their lack of attention to the fundamentals of strategy.[19] We concur with Porter, but suggest that there are ways of thinking about industry analysis in the new economy that can enhance current models.

New economy models recognize that technological change (the "T" of PEST) has had a fundamental and pervasive impact on industries. As a result, models have been developed to deal with the idiosyncrasies of the new economy, where technology and electronic commerce provide new challenges in industry analysis. These models do not negate the other models. Rather, they highlight particular issues associated with technology. As will be discussed, models like the value chain are required, yet firms need to think about how technology can transform the value chain in significant ways.

Disruptive Technologies Bower and Christensen discuss the impact of disruptive technologies. They suggest that many firms develop new technologies far in advance of customer acceptance, and risk dropping them as a result. Yet they suggest that "disruptive technologies introduce a very different package of attributes from the one mainstream customers historically value, and they often perform far worse along one or two dimensions that are particularly important to those customers."[20] They identify a transition period in which customers adopt the technology in new markets or new applications, after which the technology may be adopted more widely. The implication of this perspective for industry analysis is that the relationship between the value proposition offered by the firm, and the needs of the market, may not be that clear when dealing with disruptive technologies. As Bower and Christensen indicate, firms that leapfrog existing competitors may in fact have inferior technology. However, over time, the value proposition may shift away from traditional measures such as quality or performance, to new areas such as flexibility in application, as was the case with smaller disk drives.

Bower and Christensen point out that organizational issues are often the major impediments to assessing whether a technology is disruptive, and acting on that information. They suggest that the organizational discord can actually be an indicator of whether a technology is, in fact, disruptive. Finance and marketing managers have a vested interest in preserving the status quo and will rarely support disruptive technologies, while the technical personnel will persist even in the face of significant opposition.

New Economics of Information Evans and Wurster suggest that strategy is affected by the new economics of information and that the new economics can drastically change the competitive landscape. The rapid emergence of universal technical standards enables tremendous connectivity. The nature of the technology and the connectivity allow the simultaneous achievement of both richness and reach. In doing so, physical product flows and information flows can be separated, meaning that many businesses need not rely on their physical infrastructures, such as retail space or branch banking networks, to deliver products and services.

Evans and Wurster propose that "existing value chains will fragment into multiple businesses, each of which will have its own sources of competitive advantage. When individual functions having different economies of scale or scope are bundled together, the result is a compromise of each—an averaging of the effects. When the bundles of functions are free to re-form as separate businesses, however, each can exploit its own sources of competitive advantage to the fullest."[21] The implication of this perspective is that firms need to radically rethink their businesses given the opportunities and threats posed by the dramatic changes to the competitive landscape. A closer look at how technology impacts the industry value chain is critical.

Unbundling Hagel and Singer also suggest that firms need to rethink what business they are in. "The unbundling of the corporation into its three component businesses—customer relationship management, product innovation, and infrastructure management—is only the first step in the reshaping of organizations. The customer-relationship and infrastructure businesses can be expected to consolidate as companies pursue economies of scope and scale. The product business will likely remain fragmented, with many small, nimble companies competing on the basis of speed and creativity."[22] They see the competitive landscape shifting to include a powerful group of "infomediaries" who will control access to customers. The implication of this perspective is that there may be new roles in the value chain of industries for groups who control and manage information.

The Long Tail Chris Anderson argues that the impact of technology in new economy models has fundamentally changed the dynamics of the value chain and consequently the five forces of certain industries. He proposes that the new economy is not about scarcity, but rather about abundant choice; where a customer used to be limited to what was available on the local book store shelves, in the new economy, the selection of titles available for purchase is almost endless – a phenomenon he calls The Long Tail.[23] Other industries such as television, film, and music have seen similar shifts where the distribution of products to desktops is instantaneous, driving much of the profit out of the retail networks. The dynamics of The Long Tail also affect the suppliers and buyers in an industry. For example, recording artists no longer require the backing of major music studios to reach a wide audience, one that now also has the power to decide how much to pay for that product. Anderson labels this shift in power as the democratization of production and distribution through zero-cost information which extends traditional demand curves out to infinity.

The implication of this perspective is that it has the potential to change which industries are seen as 'attractive' or, at a minimum, significantly alter where the economic profit lies within an industry's value chain. To visualize Long Tail economics, consider the traditional 80/20 rule which has dominated the retail industry profit structure for decades (80% of sales are generated by 20% of products). A traditional music retailer will overstock on 'mega-hits' and 'chart-toppers' and minimize the inventory of lesser known talent to try to maximize its profits. For Wal-Mart, this might mean it stocks approximately 5,000 CDs which have already been pre-selected as 'best sellers' (the 20% that are more likely to sell) and yet it will still suffer from inventory turn issues. In contrast, iTunes can carry over one billion tracks of which even the one billionth track will be downloaded at a profit. The new economic model here has made even very niche products profitable.

BLUE OCEAN STRATEGY

As we discussed above, substitute products and services from outside the industry can pose a significant threat to industry profitability. Some firms within industries, however, are also able to position their offerings in such a way as to create value across the traditional barriers to competition, in effect offering substitute products from within the same industry. Firms employing a Blue Ocean Strategy are deliberately redefining existing industry boundaries and creating uncontested market spaces as a source of competitive advantage.[24] For example, the circus industry, which could easily be labelled as 'unattractive', with years of declining revenues, high supplier and buyer power, and multiple alternate entertainment options, was changed dramatically by the entrance of Cirque du Soleil. This company essentially made the competition irrelevant by creating and capturing new demand for a unique circus experience.

The Blue Ocean Strategy proposed by Kim and Mauborgne presents a view of strategy that differs from Porter's more static, deterministic view of industry analysis; instead they believe "there is scarcely any attractive or unattractive industry per se because the level of industry attractiveness can be altered through companies' conscientious efforts of reconstruction [of the industry]" (p. 211). They argue that Porter's 5 forces model limits managerial decision making to existing market spaces with limited consumer demand that reduces competition between rivals to a zero-sum game. Firms engaging in Blue Ocean Strategy, on the other hand, believe that the barriers to competition are not only surmountable, but present opportunities for untapped revenues. These two paradigms can be labelled Red Ocean vs. Blue Ocean Strategies and the key conceptual distinctions are (p. 18):

Red Ocean Strategy	Blue Ocean Strategy
- Compete in existing markets	- Create uncontested market spaces
- Beat the competition	- Make the competition irrelevant
- Focus on existing customers	- Focus on non-customers
- Exploit existing demand	- Create and capture new demand
- Make the value-cost tradeoff (create greater value to customers at a higher cost or create reasonable value at a lower cost)	- Break the value-cost tradeoff (seek greater value to customers *and* low cost simultaneously)
- Align the whole system of a firm's activities with its strategic choice of differentiation or low cost	- Align the whole system of a firm's activities in pursuit of differentiation *and* low cost

The implication of this alternative perspective to environment analysis rests with how you interpret industry forces—as changeable or not. As well, executing a Blue Ocean Strategy presupposes having the resources and organization to deliver on it, something that we will address in forthcoming chapters. Indeed, being able to reconfigure an industry with a Blue Ocean Strategy is largely a function of how you are able to organize and configure your resources. Even if you decide that industry forces can be reconstructed, successful execution of a Blue Ocean Strategy can be difficult as it necessarily entails all the risks inherent in creating new consumer demand and finding new markets.

GLOBAL INDUSTRY MODELS

Global industry models recognize the added complexity when moving from operating in one country to operating in many countries. One of the key challenges is assessing the need and opportunity for global integration across geographic contexts versus the need for local responsiveness. At the extremes, a high need for global integration leads to a global model, where there are economies of scale to keep prices low and customers accept standardized products; whereas, a high need for local responsiveness generates a multidomestic model, where the products are locally tailored and the benefits of being local outweigh the added costs for customers. Of course, many firms seek to have the benefits of both with a transnational model; however, such a model leads to many challenges in determining which aspects of the strategy and organization are global and which are customized to the local market.

Yip and Coundouriotis present a framework for analyzing the global nature of an industry.[25] They suggest that viewing industries as either global or not is an oversimplification. Their framework encourages examination of each aspect of an industry to assess its global orientation. For example, supply may be global, while marketing may be multilocal or multidomestic.

STAKEHOLDER ANALYSIS

As we will discuss in Chapter 5, analysis of customers and competitors is a critical element of environment analysis. However, there are many and varied stakeholders that warrant consideration, and often little guidance on how to carry out an analysis of stakeholder interests. Although not necessarily the case, stakeholder analysis is often associated with corporate social responsibility (CSR). Porter and Kramer argue that CSR can be a source of competitive advantage.[26] While we will revisit this topic in Chapter 7 when we discuss management preferences, in this chapter we present a basic framework for stakeholder analysis arising from the work of Mitchell, Agle, and Wood.[27] Before you can determine the roles that various stakeholders might play, it is important to identify them, define their interests, and understand how those interests may relate to your strategy.

Identify Stakeholders There are many possible stakeholders that need to be considered. Externally, stakeholders include customers, competitors, suppliers, the community, government, and a variety of interest groups. Internally, you need to consider employees, unions, the management team, investors, and shareholders. At the outset, stakeholders should be broadly defined to incorporate any individual or group who has an interest in the firm's strategy.

Define Stakeholder Interests For each stakeholder group, identify the particular needs of the group by addressing the following questions: What would be "best" for each stakeholder group? Could you possibly deliver this? At what expense?

Attempt to identify alliances and commonalities amongst the stakeholder groups. The following questions may be helpful: Do some stakeholder interests align? What are the dominant or recurring positions taken?

Porter and Kramer suggest using the value chain shown in Figure 4.2 to help identify stakeholder interests. For example, with respect to the support activities in the value chain, Procurement focuses attention on the supply chain practices that may reveal issues around child labour, bribery, utilization of natural resources or problems with materials such as lead paint. Human Resource Management focuses attention on employment practices and issues such as compensation, safe working conditions, and discrimination. Examining the primary activities such as Outbound Logistics may reveal issues with transportation and packaging whereas Service may point to issues with customer privacy or disposal of obsolete products.[28]

Keep in mind that your strategy may have many externalities, which are the spill-over effects of your strategy on society. It is these externalities that draw in many stakeholders who are affected by the spillover effects. Understanding the role of the organization in the overall ecosystem helps in identifying and defining stakeholder interests. "Given the gargantuan size of many of today's multinationals, even the smallest decision, or non-decisions, add up. UPS recently decided to stop printing paper labels and sticking them to packages; instead it designed a device to stamp shipping information directly on boxes. That will save at least 1,338 tons of paper per year".[29] Whereas once it was difficult to measure externalities, today the sophistication of doing so is staggering. Take, for example, scorecard.org in the United States. By inserting your zipcode you can identify the worst polluters in your area and are given options for taking actions such as sending a fax to the company.[30] There are an increasing number of measures and indexes of CSR that make it extremely difficult for firms to avoid facing the externalities of their strategies.

Compare Strategy to Stakeholders' Interests Having identified the stakeholders and their interests, compare the stakeholder interests to the strategy. The following questions may be helpful:

1. What are the likely consequences of your actions?
2. What reactions will the stakeholders have?
3. What is your personal feeling about the issue?
4. How do you weigh the positions of others?
5. How do you set priorities? What are the effects?
6. Are you prepared to defend your decision?
7. Can you justify your action to others?

Considering how stakeholder interests relate to the strategy may reveal important insights about how to better create, capture and distribute value. For example, Whole Foods has aligned its value proposition with customer needs in a socially desirable way. Many companies have realigned their core activities in ways that are both socially responsible and deliver better value.

Take Action to Align Strategy and Stakeholder Interests Given the previous analysis, assess whether the strategic choice benefits each stakeholder. If not, assess whether the stakeholder can be brought on side, and how. If it is not possible to align the stakeholder interests with the strategy, assess whether and how you can deal with it. Harrison and St. John provide a list of tactics for managing and partnering with external stakeholders.[31] Porter and Kramer suggest prioritizing social issues into three buckets: 1) Generic Social Issues that do not significantly affect a company's operations, 2) Value Chain Social Impacts that have a significant affect on a company, and 3) Social Dimensions of Competitive Context that have a significant impact on the underlying drivers of a company's competitiveness.[32] For example, they point out that supporting a dance company is likely a generic social issue of a utility company but may be central to the competitive context of a company like American Express, which is heavily invested in the entertainment sector. They conclude that no company can deal with all of the social issues it faces and therefore it is necessary to prioritize and address those that intersect most squarely with its strategy, thus making CSR more strategic than simply responsive.

Mitchell, Agle, and Wood provide a stakeholder typology based on three key attributes of the stakeholder: 1) the stakeholder's power to influence the firm, 2) the legitimacy of the stakeholder's relationship with the firm, and 3) the urgency of the stakeholder's claim on the firm, as depicted in Figure 4.5. In the long-standing debate about who should

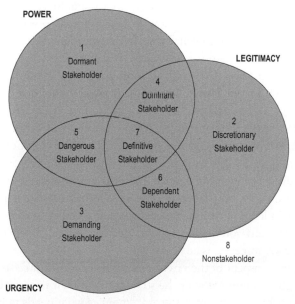

Figure 4.5 Stakeholder Typology

Source: Reprinted with the permission of *Academy of Management Review*. Mitchell, R.K.; Agle, B.R. and Donna J. Wood, "Toward a Theory of Stakeholder Identification and Salience: Defining the Principle of Who and What Really Counts" *The Academy of Management Review*, vol. 22, no. 4 1997, p. 874.

be considered a stakeholder, they clearly state that anyone without power, legitimacy, or urgency is not a stakeholder. Stakeholders possessing only one of the three attributes will have low salience with management, those possessing any two of the three will have moderate salience, and stakeholders possessing all three will have high salience.

We find their framework helpful in being able to classify stakeholders based on the three attributes, and in identifying implications for management. "Dormant stakeholders (1)", possessing only power as an attribute, have low salience but considerable potential to add to it with either legitimacy or urgency. Mitchell, Agle, and Wood provide the example of employees who have been fired or laid off and have exercised coercive power as in the case of the shootings by the ex-U.S. mail employee; utilitarian power in the case of wrongful dismissal suits; and symbolic power in the case of employees who have invoked the media to support their cause. Examples of "discretionary stakeholders (2)" are beneficiaries of corporate philanthropy. They have neither power nor urgency, but invoke legitimacy. In contrast, "demanding stakeholders (3)" present a sense of urgency through their demands, but have no legitimacy or power. They present more of a nuisance or bother to management, but are not particularly dangerous unless they gain power or legitimacy.

Stakeholders who possess two of the three attributes fall into a class of "expectant stakeholders". "Dominant stakeholders (4)" have both legitimacy and power and tend to have formal mechanisms to exercise them such as corporate boards of directors and public affairs departments. "Dangerous stakeholders (5)" have power and urgency but no legitimacy. Often desperate moves such as wildcat strikes, employee sabotage, and political terrorism are characteristic of their position. While "dependent stakeholders (6)" do not possess power, they have legitimacy and urgency as was found in the case of the oil spill from the Exxon Valdez.

"Definitive stakeholders (7)" possess all three attributes. When dominant stakeholders press an urgent claim, they move into the definitive stakeholder category, which is often seen when significant shareholders demand action to rectify a situation.

It may also be important for firm managers to consider a stakeholder's influence with another stakeholder. For example, a demanding stakeholder (high urgency, low power, and legitimacy) may not be able to influence the firm directly, but may be able to influence the firm indirectly by acting against the firm's customers or by lobbying regulators who then act directly on the firm. When environmentalists began acting against MacMillan Bloedel's logging operations in British Columbia, senior managers ignored them. When the same environmentalists boycotted MacMillan Bloedel's customers, however, the company was forced to take action to respond to their demands.

In summary, a key aspect of the environment analysis is to take stock of stakeholder interests to assess their alignment with the strategy. Overall, it is critical to assess whether the strategy is the right strategy given the assessment of what needs to be done, and what the company can do. Few strategies achieve a perfect or comfortable alignment. When stakeholder interests cannot be fully aligned, the critical question is whether the firm can live with the choice and manage stakeholders in the process.

SUMMARY: COMPARING AND CONTRASTING INDUSTRY ANALYSIS FRAMEWORKS

The frameworks and approaches presented in this section are not mutually exclusive. In fact, they are quite complementary, each providing a somewhat different focus and orientation. The Five Forces framework is helpful in understanding the competitive rivalry in an industry, and ultimately the overall industry attractiveness. The value chain complements the Five Forces analysis, and at an industry level, it is possible to link several Five Forces frameworks to understand why one aspect of the industry value chain may be more profitable than another, such as, in the soft drink industry, the concentrate producers sell to bottlers. A Five Forces analysis examining the competitive rivalry of concentrate producers can be linked to a Five Forces analysis examining the competitive rivalry of bottlers. The buyer power for the concentrate producer fits into the supplier power component of the bottlers.

The discussion of competition and cooperation hones in on the area of competitive rivalry and suggests game theory as an approach for dealing with some aspects of competitive analysis. It also suggests that focusing solely on competition is limiting as more and more industry players rely on cooperative approaches.

PEST takes a very macro approach, focusing on the early warning signals that impact industries. Applying the foregoing models to any industry will likely lead to a great deal of variability and uncertainty. It is important not to ignore or remove that uncertainty, but rather to incorporate it into the analysis. Scenario planning acknowledges the potential for significant variability and uncertainty associated with the industry analysis and suggests approaches for dealing with the uncertainty.

New economy models do not replace other models. The newer models place more emphasis on the implications of two areas: the impact of technology, and the reconfiguration of company and industry value chains. The global industry models overlay another level of complexity on the industry analysis by focusing attention on the considerations in operating in multiple geographic, cultural, and political jurisdictions. Finally, the framework for stakeholder analysis helps to identify and categorize the various stakeholders in relation to the firm. Some of these stakeholders are explicitly recognized in other models including suppliers and customers.

While we have suggested that many of these tools are complementary, there are those who advocate extreme caution in using them. For example, Jacobides suggests that "Traditional strategy tools carefully organize data about the competitive landscape, but they create static categories and visual representations. For instance, the frameworks used by industry analysis (the five forces and maps) and the tools of blue ocean thinking (value maps and comparative value curves) help managers better understand the environment in which they operate. However, these devices reduce complexity by creating stationary maps and projecting the landscape onto two-dimensional graphs—approaches that offer reliable guidance only when the environment isn't changing rapidly."[33] We do not agree that these tools of environmental analysis are necessarily static, but agree with the warning that they are a simplification of a complex reality. Jacobides advocates a deeper examination of the underlying logic, story lines, decisions, and motives of the various players in an industry, much like a playscript. The point is that these are all tools and the aim is to generate insight.

In carrying out an environment analysis, you are not expected to apply every model presented here. Rather the models provide a point of departure to think about the key aspects of the industry. The models operate as a mental checklist to assess whether their application yields any important insights. Ultimately, it is important to recognize that the environment analysis needs to address five key tasks:

1. Identify the underlying industry economics and drivers of profitability

2. Understand the industry value chain

3. Assess the attractiveness of the industry for future investment

4. Identify the key success factors—what it takes to win in the industry

5. Make preliminary assessments of how environment analysis will impact strategic options.

In the next chapter we will present an approach to applying environment analysis to strategic choices.

Notes

1. Kim, W. Chan, and Renée Mauborgne. "How Strategy Shapes Structure." *Harvard Business Review* 87.9 (2009): 72–80. *Business Source Complete, EBSCO.* Web. 15 Aug. 2011.

2. Porter, Michael E. "How Competitive Forces Shape Strategy." *Harvard Business Review* 57 (March–April 1979): 137. Print.

3. Porter, Michael E. "The Five Competitive Forces That Shape Strategy." *Harvard Business Review* 86.1 (2008): 78–93. *Business Source Complete, EBSCO.* Web. 16 Aug. 2011.

4. Porter, Michael E. "The Five Competitive Forces That Shape Strategy." *Harvard Business Review* 86.1 (2008): 78–93. *Business Source Complete, EBSCO.* Web. 16 Aug. 2011.

5. Porter, Michael E. "The Five Competitive Forces That Shape Strategy." *Harvard Business Review* 86.1 (2008): 78–93. *Business Source Complete, EBSCO.* Web. 16 Aug. 2011.

6. Porter, Michael E. "The Five Competitive Forces That Shape Strategy." *Harvard Business Review* 86.1 (2008): 78–93. *Business Source Complete, EBSCO.* Web. 16 Aug. 2011.

7. Porter, Michael E. "The Five Competitive Forces That Shape Strategy." *Harvard Business Review* 86.1 (2008): 78–93. *Business Source Complete, EBSCO.* Web. 16 Aug. 2011.

8. Porter, Michael E. "The Five Competitive Forces That Shape Strategy." *Harvard Business Review* 86.1 (2008): 78–93. *Business Source Complete, EBSCO.* Web. 16 Aug. 2011.

9. Porter, Michael E. *Competitive Advantage: Creating and Sustaining Superior Performance.* New York: Free Press, 1985. Print.

10. Barney, Jay B. *Gaining and Sustaining Competitive Advantage*. Reading, Mass.: Addison-Wesley Publishing Company, 1997. Print.

11. Barney, Jay B., *Gaining and Sustaining Competitive Advantage*. Reading, Mass.: Addison-Wesley Publishing Company, 1997. Print.

12. Ghemawat, Pankaj et al. *Strategy and the Business Landscape: Text and Cases*. Reading, Mass.: Addison-Wesley Publishing Company, 1999. 79. Print.

13. Barney, Jay B. *Gaining and Sustaining Competitive Advantage*. Reading, Mass.: Addison-Wesley Publishing Company, 1997. 257. Print.

14. Coyne, Kevin P., and John Horn. "Predicting Your Competitor's Reaction." *Harvard Business Review* 87.4 (2009): 90–97. *Business Source Complete, EBSCO*. Web. 17 Aug. 2011.

15. Khanna, Tarun, and Jan W. Rivkin. "Math for Strategists." Harvard Business School Note 705-433. Boston, MA: Harvard Business School Publishing, 2004. Print.

16. Khanna, Taru,n and Jan W. Rivkin. "Math for Strategists." Harvard Business School Note 705-433. Boston, MA: Harvard Business School Publishing, 2004. 8. Print.

17. Courtney, Hugh, Jane Kirkland, and Patrick Viguerie. "Strategy Under Uncertainty." *Harvard Business Review* 75 (November–December 1997): 66–79. Print.

18. Schoemaker, Paul J. H. "Scenario Planning: A Tool for Strategic Thinking." *Sloan Management Review* 36 (Winter 1995): 25. Print.

19. Porter, Michael E., "Strategy and the Internet," *Harvard Business Review* 79 (March 2001): 62–78. Print.

20. Bower, Joseph L., and Clayton M. Christensen. "Disruptive Technologies: Catching the Wave." *Harvard Business Review* 73 (January 1995): 43, 45. Print.

21. Evans, Philip B., and Thomas S. Wurster. "Strategy and the New Economics of Information." *Harvard Business Review* 75 (September–October 1997): 70–82. Print.

22. Hagel, John III, and Marc Singer. "Unbundling the Corporation." *Harvard Business Review* 77 (March–April 1999): 133–141. Print.

23. Anderson, Chris. *The Long Tail: Why the Future of Business is Selling Less of More*. NY, NY: Hyperion, 2006. Print.

24. Kim, W. Chan, and Renée Mauborgne. *Blue Ocean Strategy: How to Create Uncontested Market Space and Make the Competition Irrelevant*. Boston, Mass.: Harvard Business School Press, 2005. Print.

25. Yip, George S., and George A. Coundouriotis. "Diagnosing Global Strategy Potential: The World Chocolate Confectionery Industry." *Planning Review* 19 (January–February 1991): 4-15. Print.

26. Porter, Michael E., and Mark R. Kramer. "Strategy & Society: The Link Between Competitive Advantage and Corporate Social Responsibility." *Harvard Business Review* 84.12 (2006): 78–92. *Business Source Complete, EBSCO*. Web. 16 Aug. 2011.

27. Mitchell, Ronald K., Bradley R. Agle, and Donna J. Wood. "Toward a Theory of Stakeholder Identification and Salience: Defining the Principle of Who and What Really Counts." *The Academy of Management Review* 22, (1997): 853–886. Print.

28. Porter, Michael E., and Mark R. Kramer. "Strategy & Society: The Link Between Competitive Advantage and Corporate Social Responsibility." *Harvard Business Review* 84.12 (2006): 78–92. *Business Source Complete, EBSCO.* Web. 16 Aug. 2011.

29. Meyer, Christopher, and Julia Kirby. "Leadership in the Age of Transparency." *Harvard Business Review* 88.4 (2010): 38–46. *Business Source Complete, EBSCO.* Web. 15 Aug. 2011.

30. Meyer, Christopher, and Julia Kirby. "Leadership in the Age of Transparency." *Harvard Business Review* 88.4 (2010): 38–46. *Business Source Complete, EBSCO.* Web. 15 Aug. 2011.

31. Harrison, Jeffrey S., and Caron H. St. John. "Managing and Partnering with External Stakeholders." *The Academy of Management Executive* 10 (May 1996): 46–60.

32. Porter, Michael E., and Mark R. Kramer. "Strategy & Society: The Link Between Competitive Advantage and Corporate Social Responsibility." *Harvard Business Review* 84.12 (2006): 78–92. *Business Source Complete, EBSCO.* Web. 16 Aug. 2011.

33. Jacobides, Michael G. "Strategy Tools for a Shifting Landscape." *Harvard Business Review* 88.1/2 (2010): 76–84. *Business Source Complete, EBSCO.* Web. 16 Aug. 2011.

Chapter 5
Environment Analysis: The Strategy-Environment Linkage

Your job in the crucial early phases of building and evaluating a strategic proposal is to look ahead and to evaluate the fit of your strategy with a changing environment and to forecast its performance if adopted.

CONDUCTING ENVIRONMENT ANALYSIS

The primary obstacle that you will face is the sheer complexity of the forces at work and their interaction and change over time. To cut through this complexity, we have set out a series of procedural steps (see Figure 5.1) that will help you to focus your analysis on the critical environmental forces and to make more robust predictions about the success of the strategy under study. The steps tie directly into the broader processes of the Diamond-E and strategic analysis that we described in Chapter 3 and the tools for environment analysis presented in Chapter 4. However, as we have noted before, procedural steps are not intended to lock you into a rigid approach; they are created for clarity of exposition and to represent a general progression of analysis. Your actual analysis will undoubtedly be much more spontaneous and iterative.

Our discussion of the strategy-environment linkage will follow the proposed analytic steps. The first task is one of preparation, of isolating the questions and the forces that are of greatest importance and of doing the background work on this subset of variables to ensure that you understand their implications. The analysis then moves to a second phase of increasingly rigorous tests of the strategy and to forecasts of its performance if adopted. The final step is one of deciding whether there is justification to carry forward the proposal, as now understood, to further phases of the Diamond-E analysis.

STEP 1: FOCUS THE ENVIRONMENT ANALYSIS

In Chapter 4 we presented many tools for environment analysis. While you are not expected to apply all of these tools, we suggested that you can use them as a mental checklist to identify those tools which are particularly salient to your situation. The initial challenge in environment analysis is to find and to focus on the major forces that will affect the success of your strategic proposal. This begins by establishing the rough boundaries of

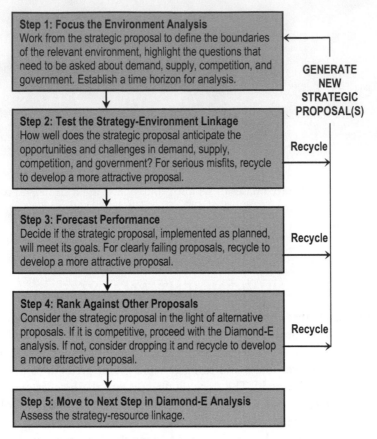

Step 1: Focus the Environment Analysis
Work from the strategic proposal to define the boundaries of the relevant environment, highlight the questions that need to be asked about demand, supply, competition, and government. Establish a time horizon for analysis.

Step 2: Test the Strategy-Environment Linkage
How well does the strategic proposal anticipate the opportunities and challenges in demand, supply, competition, and government? For serious misfits, recycle to develop a more attractive proposal.

Step 3: Forecast Performance
Decide if the strategic proposal, implemented as planned, will meet its goals. For clearly failing proposals, recycle to develop a more attractive proposal.

Step 4: Rank Against Other Proposals
Consider the strategic proposal in the light of alternative proposals. If it is competitive, proceed with the Diamond-E analysis. If not, consider dropping it and recycle to develop a more attractive proposal.

Step 5: Move to Next Step in Diamond-E Analysis
Assess the strategy-resource linkage.

GENERATE NEW STRATEGIC PROPOSAL(S)

Recycle

Recycle

Recycle

Figure 5.1 Environment Analysis

the targeted environment (e.g., the industry or market segments); these boundaries represent what we call the *relevant environment* for the strategic proposal. Then, within this limited environment, you will need to establish a time horizon for analysis and to isolate the specific forces of demand, supply, competition, and government policy that have the greatest impact on the strategy under consideration.

Focus is critical to understanding the prospects of a strategy. Without focus it is all too easy to get lost in reams of data and long lists of possibilities, and then to become frustrated because your observations turn out to be of little use. Naturally, there is a risk that the pursuit of focus can go too far, to the point where you might miss important external facts and forces. But we believe that this is an acceptable risk, provided you are sensitive to it and employ the safeguards that we suggest for avoiding too limited an analysis.

Three tools will be particularly useful in achieving a focused and properly timed environment analysis: your assessment of the performance of the business, the strategic proposal itself, and the profit model underlying the business and the specific proposal. These tools overlap in their application, in the sense that performance assessment links to strategic goals and the profit model links to core activities, but each can make a distinct contribution to the process of focusing your analysis. We will discuss them in turn below.

Performance Assessment as a Focusing Tool

As we discussed earlier, the ongoing performance of a business sets a general context for the process of strategic analysis. As a focusing tool, your performance assessment can help you to set an appropriate time horizon for environment analysis and to indicate the range, detail, and depth of study that suits the situation at hand. Consider, for example, the differences in focus implied for a base case analysis of the strategy of a healthy business versus the strategy of one in crisis.

The first task in the base case analysis (see Chapter 3 for a description of base case analysis) of a healthy business is one of projecting how long you expect the good times to last. A strong performance record suggests a good fit between strategy and environment. The forecasts of future performance will likely have to stretch well into the future and uncover and examine very fundamental trends. If you were involved in a base case study of the drug giant Pfizer, for example, an appreciation of the company's impressive financial performance would prompt you to look well down the road for potential opportunities in its new drug pipeline and for potential challenges such as the revenue impact from the expiry of patent protection on its blockbuster drugs such as Lipitor and the downward pressure on prices from generic intruders and government drug price controls. This analysis would tie naturally into an equivalently long-term exploration of strategic intentions, such as Pfizer's use of acquisitions to replace revenue lost due to the expiry of patent protection. Here the healthy past performance of Pfizer would give you some confidence that the company knows what it needs to do and help you to focus your analysis on their chances of doing it successfully.

A business in crisis, on the other hand, is on a very short fuse. The base case questions go to the feasibility of a rescue effort. How much time do you have? What are the most significant problems that you have to resolve right away? Your environment analysis will have to be as immediate, tangible, and detailed as possible. For example, BP, the international oil and gas company, found the events surrounding the 2010 Deepwater Horizon oil spill in the Gulf of Mexico were quickly getting out of control. What had started out as an, albeit serious, accident and a small spill, a controllable situation, was spiraling into one of largest oil spills to date. The spill had the potential to cause massive environmental damage, the financial and public relationship costs of which threatened the very existence of BP as an independent company. Quick decisions were required on how to manage the spill and relationships with various stakeholders including the public and federal and local government entities. The required environment analysis was immediate and to the point. How could BP support the local communities that had suffered economic and environmental losses due to the spill? What could be done to minimize the environmental impact of the spill? How would competitors react to BP's recently weakened state? Would customers boycott its products? How would large shareholders, such as pension funds, react to the possibility of dividend cuts required to fund the costs of the cleanup? Time horizons were short and the priority for analysis was on isolating the most immediate and critical environmental forces.

The Strategic Proposal as a Focusing Tool

By its very nature, the strategic proposal that you are considering helps to identify the relevant business environment and the specific conditions on which the analysis should focus. Each of the strategy components we described in Chapter 2 has a role to play in this process:

1. Strategic goals establish the performance priorities and expectations that need to be evaluated in your environment analysis. The implications of high revenue growth targets, for example, are that you would have to ask pointed questions about the growth potential in the served market and the possibilities of increasing market share. Alternatively, a commitment to high, short-term profits would direct your attention to equivalently short-term market conditions and possibilities.

2. Product market focus sets up a bounded environment for the analysis of demand, competition, and so on. A proposal to enter a new geographic territory, for example, gives you a specific target area for pursuing questions of demand and competition.

3. A proposal's value proposition—the very core of strategy—defines a tangible benchmark for testing customer appeal and competitive differentiation. If your business chooses to emphasize price, for example, you would have to estimate the price sensitivity in the market and the capability and willingness of competitors to match or better your pricing initiatives.

4. The nature and structure of a proposal's core activities provide a basis for identifying the cost, control, and flexibility trade-offs that would be sensitive to external trends and developments. If your proposal is based on a fully integrated activity system, for example, you will carefully have to examine the potential for demand surges or setbacks since these will have a major impact on the economics of the system.

The short case study of Jantzen Technologies that follows illustrates further the role of the strategic proposal in focusing the strategy-environment analysis. Please follow this example carefully, as we will be returning to it throughout this chapter and in later parts of the book.

Jantzen Technologies: A Case Study

Jantzen Technologies is a major supplier of an important component system to personal computer manufacturers. The company was started in the mid-1980s by Harry Jantzen, an electronics engineer. Jantzen had worked for several years for a large computer company, but had become disenchanted by large company procedures and decided to strike out on his own. He had always thought there were opportunities for small companies to do a better job by out-servicing their larger rivals, and from the beginning he focused his new business on building very close technical relationships with customers, followed up by continually developing new product features. The company had grown rapidly and now had production facilities in the United States, Taiwan, and Ireland to serve customers based in these areas.

By staying at the forefront of product development in a market with fast-changing requirements, and by meeting the sometimes idiosyncratic demands of its customers, Jantzen had historically enjoyed reasonable flexibility in pricing and very good profit margins. In recent months, however, negotiations with customers had become increasingly difficult. Price was becoming a much bigger factor, to the point where a major order had just been lost to an emerging competitor. There were clearly some significant changes taking place in Jantzen's business environment.

The strategic goals for Jantzen Technologies were very much a reflection of Harry Jantzen, although ownership was now substantially dispersed to the public market and employees. Growth and comfortable profit margins were paramount, not just as a matter of financial return, but to keep up the level of excitement in the company and provide the funds for continuing product development. Harry Jantzen was well known for his commitment to innovative design and for making sure that the company's development engineering staff was well taken care of. The emerging question was whether these goals were sustainable into the future.

Jantzen Technologies had taken a very deliberate approach to its product market opportunities. It had focused on a single component system, although it had always been willing to modify it, or add custom features as requested by customers. On the customer side, Jantzen had always concentrated on direct sales to what Harry Jantzen called the "customers who mattered," a list of a dozen or so businesses around the world, which varied somewhat with the ebb and flow of the computer business. Almost as an afterthought, Jantzen sold a fairly standardized line through a major components supply house.

Jantzen's position as the leading global supplier in its field relied on innovation in product features and a willingness to work closely with individual customers and build systems customized to their particular technical specifications. Maintaining this position was a never-ending race to convert a changing basic technology into commercial systems, then to move on to the next generation of systems to stay abreast of the technology and ahead of competitors. The relationships that Jantzen's sales engineers and design teams had built with customer design teams had proved to be a major asset.

Jantzen had chosen to build a comprehensive and integrated system of core activities ranging from design through manufacturing to direct sale. This system had served to maintain close relationships with customers, proprietary control on innovations for as long as possible, and internal control over critical outputs such as quality and delivery. Plant operations in general were set up for flexibility to accommodate a high variety of custom requirements.

Jantzen's Strategy as a Focusing Tool A base case analysis of Jantzen's prospects would rely heavily on the company's past and current strategy to provide direction on the environmental questions and conditions to explore. Here is a sampling:

1. Jantzen's growth and profit *goals* are ambitious. Is there enough growth potential and competitive room in the market to support these goals even in the short term?

2. Jantzen's *product market focus* is very narrow. With such a high reliance on a single component system and relatively few customers, it is essential to understand them thoroughly, not just in terms of their technical needs but also in terms of the economic pressures they are coming under in their marketplace. This understanding will help to build a better basis for dealing with the new negotiating pressures, and a convincing forecast based on individual customer potential and buying requirements.

3. Jantzen's *value proposition* is based on superior technical features and individual customization. This suggests two critical areas for analysis. First, will the basic technology continue to generate opportunities for product innovation? If this window is closing, what are the competitive consequences for Jantzen? Second, will the trend towards price sensitivity continue and will this introduce new influencers and new agendas into the purchasing process?

4. Jantzen's *core activities* are highly integrated. Will this system remain cost effective in the light of possible changes in customer purchasing criteria, and the potential development of greater competence among competitors and sub-component suppliers?

The Profit Model as a Focusing Tool

Underlying every strategy is a profit model that consists of the structure of revenues, costs, profits, and investment associated with it. You can develop the profit model for a current strategy from the actual performance records of the business. For new proposals you can develop a profit model out of the substance of the proposal, and particularly from the structure of goals and core activities. In both cases it is important to distinguish between variable costs (which vary with volume) and fixed costs (which do not vary with volume). The utility of this effort is illustrated in the following examples.

High Fixed Cost Structures If you find that a high proportion of the costs at expected operating volumes are fixed, some special care should be given to assessing the prospects for price stability in the market. Consider the situation that prevails in the airline industry. Once an airline has set its schedule for a season, its costs are largely fixed and the battle is on to maximize total contribution. Since variable costs are quite low in airline operation, there is a strong temptation in this structure to cut price to capture additional volume. Unfortunately, this structure leads to fierce price wars and serious profitability problems for the industry as a whole.

High Variable Cost Structures If a high proportion of the costs at expected operating volumes are variable, however, you should take care to assess the accuracy of the assumptions about the significant input costs. Consider the problems that a large agrochemicals company has with one of its ammonia plants. The plant has a high variable cost structure and a large part of these costs are for the natural gas used in the conversion process. So much so, in fact, that the profitability of the plant hinges directly on access to natural gas at prices that are competitive with other regional producers. Some miscalculations at the time of proposing the plant about continuing political support for advantageous gas supply, however, have left this company with a major investment that simply cannot make money.

High Break-Even Points If the break-even point of your proposal is high relative to the size of the target market, you need to make a very careful assessment of your ability to achieve the required share position. You should also weigh the possibility that if you do achieve the high share position, you may have established a significant barrier to new competition.

High Up-Front Investment The timing of the investment commitments anticipated in a strategic proposal relative to the development, introduction, and market acceptance of a product will create different levels of risk. In the pharmaceutical industry, for example, much of the investment behind a new product is committed before a single dollar of revenue is received. Proposals with high up-front investment require a *very* careful assessment of market potential. In addition, the inescapable risk of such proposals suggests the need for ample supplies of risk capital. This is an argument that pharmaceutical companies use in support of patent protection—that the high returns on successful products provide the needed capital funding for the development of new products.

In the plastics products industry, on the other hand, all that may be necessary to support a proposal to introduce a new product line may be a relatively modest investment in the design and fabrication of new moulds. Often manufacturing capacity can be built as the product succeeds in the market. Operating in this type of environment should certainly not be taken as an opportunity for sloppy market assessment, but in these circumstances there is less pressure for accuracy. The relative ease of entry, on the other hand, suggests that you must look closely at potential competitive developments.

Inflexible Investment Structures In some cases, you will find that the nature of the investment required by a strategic proposal is such that there will be little salvage value if things do not work out. The impact of such investments on the availability and cost of capital needs to be carefully considered. A small winery that intended to age all of its products, for example, had to revise its proposal because its bankers were not prepared to finance the inventory. Similarly, a group with a uniquely designed restaurant had difficulty raising money from lenders who were concerned about the fact that the building had no alternative uses if the restaurant failed. In circumstances such as these you should carefully explore the probabilities of external forces that would lead to such "worst case" scenarios.

The Profit Model as a Focusing Tool: The Jantzen Example The Jantzen activity system, as we noted earlier, was highly integrated from design through manufacture to direct sale, and the manufacturing process itself relied on a heavy investment in specialized, computer-controlled tools to produce sub-components. The result was a fixed cost structure that could become a serious problem if the environment became more hostile. This means that some very careful analysis must be done on the stability of market prices. What effect will maturing demand and competitive pressure have on prices? Jantzen may well have to modify its strategy to accommodate these emerging realities.

Defining the Right Time Horizon

So far, we have concentrated on picking the right questions to ask in an environment analysis. A parallel job is that of setting a time horizon for the pursuit of these questions. You will clearly have to project into the future, but how far? Earlier we mentioned the role of your performance assessment in establishing time horizons. There are three additional factors that will help: (1) the pace of change in competitive and other industry forces; (2) the flexibility of the strategic commitment under consideration; and (3) the time required to implement the new strategy.

Pace of External Change Life cycles for products and technologies are becoming shorter and shorter, compressing the time horizons that are relevant for environment analysis. Increasingly shorter gaps between the introduction of new versions and speed levels of microprocessor chips are a telling example of this phenomenon. Each generation of chip development changes the environment for computer builders, microprocessor suppliers, and other industry participants and each generation imposes new and ever-shorter time horizons on strategic proposals in the industry.

But the pace of change varies widely from one situation to another, so gauging the speed with which major changes are likely to occur is a critical first step in setting the time horizon for analysis. In some markets, like personal computers, the time horizon may be measured in months. In other markets, such as commercial aircraft, the time horizon for fundamental change stretches far off into the future.

Anticipating the pace of change in a market should be integral to your study of demand trends, competitive developments, and so forth. However, you should also be thinking hard about the period of continuity for which the strategic proposal will be valid.

Flexibility of Commitment By definition, a strategic proposal involves a commitment that is hard to reverse. But the flexibility or reversibility of proposals does vary. The less flexible the strategic commitment, the further ahead you must look. For example, a consumer packaged-goods company may be able to introduce a new product on a limited basis, in test areas, thereby reducing the scale of the required initial investment. However, if a resource company is considering the development of a new mine, there are no half measures. The company will have to make the whole investment, and it may not earn returns for several years. In such cases the time horizon for analysis is correspondingly extended.

Implementation Horizon Some strategic ventures, like the mining example just mentioned and other major capital projects, require years of planning and construction to complete. In such cases these logistical realities determine the relevant period for environment analysis.

Setting a time horizon is more subtle for strategic initiatives that count on major organizational change to support them. Organizations have great inertia. If you want to be ahead of, or at least ready for, new developments, you have to look quite a distance down the road. In later chapters we develop the topics of strategic and organizational change and these will give you the base for making judgments about necessary and required time horizons from an implementation standpoint.

Defining the Right Time Horizon: The Jantzen Example The Jantzen example calls for a base case analysis of a very successful business strategy. The crucial question is its sustainability—will the strategy continue to produce excellent results? The outcome of recent sales negotiations suggests that Jantzen's business environment is changing; customers are putting a new emphasis on price and competitors are meeting these demands. In this context, the time horizon for analysis is immediate. The changes are already under way that will create a substantially new set of environment conditions.

Minimizing the Risks of Focus

We have gone to some lengths to emphasize the importance of focus in your environment analysis. This makes for an efficient process and provides specific, in-depth results. It is important for you to recognize that these benefits are possible only at the risk of what we call *strategic myopia*. If your focus is too specific, you might miss the emergence of a new market opportunity, or the arrival of unconventional competition. Similarly, if you concentrate overly on a particular time horizon, you may get blindsided by events that lie just beyond the limit.

The risks of focus can be reduced, however, by ensuring that your analysis is accompanied by continuous macroenvironment scanning, and that the analysis is recycled as it proceeds, to incorporate the redefinition, as necessary, of both the relevant environment and questions being addressed. With these precautions, the practical advantages of concentrated analysis far outweigh the risks and disadvantages of missing something.

Macroenvironment Scanning A sensible hedge against the risks of focus is to maintain a concurrent awareness of the events and institutions surrounding the relevant business environment—what is called *macroenvironment scanning*. The chief differences between the focused environment analysis that we have been talking about and macroenvironment scanning are summarized in Table 5.1. Macroenvironment scanning is essentially an issue-seeking process. It is an ongoing search for basic developments that may offer a firm brand new opportunities or present unconventional threats to its continuing performance.

Table 5.1 Comparison of Focused Environment Analysis and Macroenvironment Scanning

	Key Characteristics	Primary Subjects	Output
Focused Environment Analysis	Driven by strategic proposal Relatively formal	Analysis of fit with forces in defined environment	Forecast of performance Decision to proceed
Macro-Environment Scanning	Issue-seeking Continuous, informal process	Fundamental social, economic, and technical trends	Identify events of potential impact on the business

As we discussed in Chapter 4, PEST is a popular model for macroenvironment scanning. The aim in reviewing the PEST trends is to identify broad forces and basic changes in the total environment of a business. A broadly based assessment is particularly useful when the uncertainty in the environment is very high. In Chapter 4, we presented tools for scenario planning, which are particularly helpful in uncertain environments.[1] But you need to be careful here; the aim is to look wide, but avoid aimlessness. A useful approach is to take analytic expeditions that work outward from your defined business environment. Used this way, macroenvironment scanning and the PEST model become an extension of your basic strategy-environment analysis. The underlying guidelines are set by your understanding of your business strategy and its environment. From this base you can screen the many events that occur on the fringe of the business environment and isolate those that have a potential impact on the business.

Identifying Market Intrusions A second way to minimize the risks of focus is to keep your eyes open for newcomers into your industry. Trucks and aircraft have taken business that historically belonged to the railroads. Upstart "low fare" airlines are challenging the traditional hub and spoke network airlines. Plastics have replaced wood, paper, and metals in numerous applications. The development of new technology is often the edge that allows outsiders to break into an industry and successfully penetrate its markets—witness the move by cable companies to enter the household phone market by way of voice over internet telephony. In Chapter 4, the value chain tools and new economy models help you to consider how the boundaries of the industry might change, and whether there is opportunity for new competitive entry. You do not need incredible foresight to recognize these developments; you simply need to keep watch on patent registrations, technical reports, and products or processes already in use in other industries that may be applicable in your own situation. Given the time lags associated with truly novel commercial development and market diffusion, there will be enough time to respond, as long as a clear and imaginative view is taken of the potential of the innovation and the intentions of its sponsors.

Recycling A third hedge against the risks of focus is to ensure that the analytic process stays open—that you are prepared to incorporate new information and to double back or recycle your work as the need arises. This proposition is easy to agree with in the abstract, but difficult to follow in practice. Recycling breaks the momentum of a proposal and may require substantial additional analysis. You may be reluctant, particularly in ambiguous situations, to go back a step, perhaps to the beginning, and redefine and reassess the situation. Fight this tendency or you will lose the important benefits of learning about new possibilities as the work develops.

Naturally, there is a limit to recycling. You must be careful to avoid the extreme of "analysis paralysis." At some point risks must be taken and decisions must be made. The art of good analysis is the ability to balance the need for additional study with the need to take action. You should be fully aware of this balance at all stages of your strategic work.

STEP 2: TEST THE STRATEGY-ENVIRONMENT LINKAGE

We now turn to the task of testing how well a strategic proposal addresses the opportunities, challenges, and timing requirements of the environment. To help organize this process we have classified environmental forces into four basic categories: demand, supply, competition, and government. The elements of this model are portrayed in Figure 5.2. In the following sections we will review each of the environment

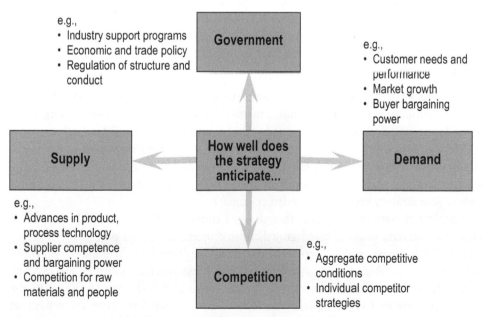

Figure 5.2 Testing the Strategy-Environment Linkage Business Environment Analysis Model (BEAM)

categories and present several concepts that will help you to pursue your analysis. This model is not intended to supplant the models previously presented. Rather it is intended as a starting point to conduct your environment analysis. It is helpful to mentally review the other models to assess whether they might provide some insight into the situation at hand.

The four components we identify are quite consistent with the models presented in Chapter 4. As noted in the discussion of the value chain and Porter's Five Forces, understanding supply, demand, and competition is critical. We add government to the list since in many economies the regulatory environment has a direct impact on the industry. Simply examining the political factors that affect the industry, as in the PEST model, does not adequately capture the microprocesses of industry analysis. In the following sections we develop each component of the model in further detail.

As the process of questioning and testing proceeds, you will develop a better understanding of environment conditions and an accumulating evaluation of the strategy-environment fit. These may lead to an early conclusion that the strategic proposal is inadequate, in which case you should recycle the analysis, as indicated in Figure 5.1, to develop a better proposal that incorporates your findings.

Demand

The test of the linkage of your proposal and demand is whether it anticipates opportunities and creates advantages in the way that it addresses customer requirements and trends in the market. Is the strategy aimed at growing market segments? Does the strategy tap into new customer needs? In this process it is particularly important for you to gauge the degree to which a strategic proposal incorporates (1) the needs and preferences of current and potential customers; (2) the scale and timing of market development; and (3) the bargaining power of customers.

Needs and Preferences It is surprising and discomforting to observe the degree to which companies will sometimes commit themselves to strategies without pinning down the fundamentals of anticipated demand. The literature on new product development is full of warnings on this account and of examples of setbacks in companies that ought to have known better, such as Microsoft with Microsoft Bob and IBM with OS/2.[2] The lesson is that you simply should not feel comfortable unless you understand the links between your strategy and your intended customers.

Consider the strategic change that drove a turnaround at the Blockbuster Video chain. After several years of rapid growth, Blockbuster's sales and profitability faltered in the mid-90s. Some analysts explained the slump by pointing to the increasing popularity of new technologies such as video on demand, but the real source of the problem was utterly prosaic. Customer service levels at Blockbuster had been sacrificed to the point where one in five shoppers went home empty-handed or went away without the exact video that they wanted.[3] How could a company like Blockbuster underestimate the importance of having available the videos that customers wanted when they visited the store? It was partially out of arrogance, no doubt, but beneath this there was a strategy and profit model under which Blockbuster purchased tapes outright from the movie studios, making a fully adequate inventory a very expensive proposition. As a result, now that dissatisfaction was showing up in deteriorating performance, it had become commonplace at Blockbuster to manage dissatisfaction rather than to deal with the basic customer service issue. The habits of the past were so ingrained, moreover, that it took a new and forceful CEO to highlight the importance of customer service and to work out a solution to the problem. This was not easy; to support new higher service levels, Blockbuster had to overhaul its profit model completely. It did so by negotiating a new deal with the studios under which revenue-sharing arrangements were used to reduce substantially the fixed purchase cost of tapes. This made adequate inventories feasible, at the penalty, of course, of unit profit margins. The result was an immediate improvement in business.

Then Blockbuster once again missed a change in customer preferences as customers moved towards digital downloads such as NetFlix and low cost rentals at kiosks such as Redbox. Blockbuster's large brick and mortar operation became an anchor on its business, In 2010 it filed for bankruptcy protection in the US to re-invent itself to focus on digital download offerings.

The problem in such instances is not that managers are unaware of the importance of customer needs and preferences. It is that other priorities get in the way. Blockbuster is a case in point. Another classic example is the belated recognition by Levi Strauss & Co. that its basic North American blue jeans business was in trouble. Changing demographics and tastes had been leaving Levi's traditionally dominant jeans behind and creating opportunities for new competitors such as Tommy Hilfiger, Calvin Klein, The Gap, JNCO, and others. But Levi was slow to take note, in good part because its design, marketing, and merchandising units operated quite autonomously, to the point, even, of working from separate office buildings.[4] Structure and politics were getting in the way of timely focus and market response. Levi ultimately moved to streamline its organization and get on with a push into new fashion concepts.

A major benefit of periodic strategic reviews is that they give you the opportunity to stand back and make sure that customer needs and preferences are being effectively addressed by your organization.

Scale and Timing of Market Development The goals of a strategic proposal set out performance expectations. A critical test of these promises is whether the revenue projections are reasonably consistent with the anticipated scale and pace of market development. The uncertainties that you will need to address in this test will vary across the product market life cycle. In the early stages of the cycle, the major concern is timing: When and at what rate will the market develop? Later, with growth established, the key question is one of ultimate potential: Where is the ceiling? Even later, in maturity, the worry is vulnerability: How will substitutes affect future demand?

Timing is thus a particularly crucial issue in many strategic proposals. The questions that you will face are often not so much whether a market exists, but how fast it will develop and how long it will last. Think of the timing question facing Cinram International in

2003 as it considered the acquisition of AOL Time Warner's DVD and CD manufacturing operations. The $1 billion deal would make Cinram the world's largest DVD and CD producer. CD demand was in decline and manufacturing contracts were becoming increasingly competitive. DVD was on the rise, but to what heights and for how long before capacity increases squeezed pricing, and new formats such as video on demand and personal DVD recorders cut into the market? While initially the purchase contributed to Cinram's bottom line, by 2007 the DVD industry had matured and Cinram took a $314m write down primarily related to this business. It took a further write down in 2010 when Warner House Entertainment cancelled its agreement to purchase DVDs from Cinram.

Customer Bargaining Power In Porter's Five Forces Model, the thrust of the analysis focuses on the bargaining power of the buyer. Porter contends that the higher the bargaining power of the buyer, the lower the industry attractiveness. However, it is helpful to pursue the issue of bargaining power beyond the issue of industry attractiveness. In consumer goods and services, customer buying power is an aggregate phenomenon, summarizing the collective ability and willingness of buyers to influence prices and volumes. A significant question in the analysis of the fit of a strategy with demand forces is whether the strategy properly anticipates the timing and degree of change in buying power that will occur as a result of industry disruptions, such as the advent of new technology. The internet, for example, is fundamentally changing the role of store-based retailers by providing consumers with a competitive place to make a purchase, or, at a minimum, with powerful tools to "pre-shop" for price and product features before visiting a store.

In industrial goods, demand is shaped more directly by the bargaining power of individual customers. For example, the automakers usually have a high degree of bargaining power because (1) they buy goods in quantities that represent important volumes to their suppliers; (2) they have a choice of suppliers from which to buy; and (3) they have the capability, should they choose to exercise it, of integrating backward into production for themselves. As a consequence, the supplier firms in the industry are frequently caught in tough bargaining situations in which their customers have a distinct advantage. To counter such circumstances, suppliers build strategies to link their customers into their unique capabilities and to spread the risk of individual projects by maintaining a broad portfolio of contracts and customers.

There are, of course, many aspects of demand that you will need to consider as you review the prospects of your strategy. The key is to stay on track and stick to fundamental issues such as we have illustrated with the foregoing examples.

Supply

A further test of the linkage between your strategic ideas and the environment lies in the potential for advantage and disadvantage in supply conditions and trends, as Porter identified in the Five Forces Model. Consider, for example, the possibilities in the matching or mismatching of strategy with (1) technology, (2) supplier competence and bargaining power, and (3) competition for raw materials and people.

Technology If your strategy anticipates developments in technology, it might give you a head start on your rivals and an opportunity for industry leadership. The pioneer internet retailer Amazon.com, for example, took early advantage of the new possibilities in electronic commerce to challenge the conventional booksellers Barnes & Noble Inc. and Borders Group Inc. Then, as the internet bubble burst, Amazon was widely thought to be heading for the scrap heap. Not so. With a singular attention to the possibilities of technology in supply and delivery as well as in internet selling, Amazon.com bounced back as a dominant and increasingly broader-based retailer. As CEO Jeff Bezos says, "The three most important things to us are technology, technology, technology."[5]

On the other hand, if your strategies fail to anticipate and respond to technical change you might quickly become the laggard in the industry. Research in Motion, for example, suffered serious consequences to its corporate performance and reputation when it underestimated the speed of technological change in smartphones by companies such as Apple, LG and HTC, and overestimated the protection that its traditional enterprise business would offer. As in the estimation of demand forces, the issue with technology is often one of timing; it is critical that you keep your strategic reviews up to date on the pace of new developments.

Supplier Competence and Bargaining Power Another area of potential strategic advantage or constraint that you need to consider is in the linkage of strategies to the competence and bargaining power of suppliers. The issue of supplier power is a primary focus in Porter's model. However, as in the case of the bargaining power of the buyer, it is helpful to look beyond industry attractiveness to assess the implications of supplier power. The ability of strategies to create marketplace advantages, for example, will often depend on high levels of supplier competence. Retailers such as Home Depot and Canadian Tire are a case in point: their ability to deliver superior prices and in-stock reliability relies heavily on their programs to develop supplier competence, to the point of virtual integration through electronic data interchange. Their considerable bargaining power relative to most suppliers helps expedite the process of development and integration. When the reverse is true, however, supplier capabilities and bargaining power can be a significant problem. Wal-Mart's expansion in Brazil, Argentina, and other developing countries, for example, has been delayed by both the reluctance and the limited competence of local suppliers, and their superior bargaining power relative to the Wal-Mart start-up business.

If you face powerful suppliers that can influence the cost, quality, and delivery of essential inputs, you need to account for this in the development of your strategic proposal. Fabricators of steel products, for example, try to reduce their reliance on powerful raw steel suppliers by seeking product markets where they can incorporate value-added services in design and installation, and reduce their reliance on raw steel supplies.

Competition for Raw Materials and People In many industries, the most significant strategic opportunities lie in the ability to achieve an advantage in raw materials and people. You will need to be particularly careful in these instances to check that your strategic proposals have fully considered these possibilities. In resources, for example, the quantity and relative cost of gas, oil, timber rights, mineral deposits, and so forth go a long way towards defining the position and future possibilities for the companies in their respective industries. The critical strategic test in these industries lies in how well the businesses develop and sustain their raw materials positions. Consider the fall over the last few years in the cost of production of natural gas with development of shale gas production techniques in North America. The cheaper recovery costs and widespread availability of shale gas threaten to undermine the viability of conventional natural gas plays. In response to these changes, Exxon Mobil acquired XTO Energy and thus provided itself access to significant unconventional natural gas reserves along with the technology and knowledge that XTO brought on exploiting unconventional natural gas fields.

In skill- and service-intensive industries, businesses vie to become the "best company to work for." W.L. Gore, for example, focuses on innovation (Gore-Tex, vascular graft materials, guitar strings, etc.) and attributes much of its success to empowerment policies such as letting employees find out what they want to do. New project champions must recruit "volunteers." As one such champion said with respect to his project, "If you can't find enough people to work on it, maybe it's not a good idea."[6] In the service-intensive airline industry, Southwest Airlines in the United States and WestJet Airlines in Canada translate their capacity to hire flexible and energetic people into customer service advantages over their traditional airline competitors.

Competition

The test of the linkage of a strategic proposal and competition is in whether it pursues competitive opportunities and offsets competitive challenges and vulnerabilities. Consider, for example, the development and appraisal of a strategy relative to (1) aggregate competitive conditions and their impact on market attractiveness, and (2) the specific strategies of individual competitors.

Aggregate Competitive Conditions You will need to check product market entry strategies, in particular, against an assessment of the attractiveness of the market as determined by aggregate competitive conditions. In this process, Porter's model provides a useful vehicle to gauge rivalry and the resulting attractiveness of industries and market segments.[7]

Consider the industry-level opportunities and obstacles faced by a privately held manufacturer of plastic drainage products. The company's early growth had been based on an innovative application of extrusion technology to the fabrication of corrugated plastic pipe for agricultural and industrial drainage. In many applications, the new plastic pipe provided significant advantages in cost and ease of installation over existing clay, steel, and concrete products. After a very profitable ten-year period, however, a number of changes in the industry were squeezing growth and profitability. Product and process technologies for existing applications had matured and were readily available to competitors and new entrants. Large installation contractors were bargaining successfully for very significant price and delivery concessions. Resin suppliers had consolidated and accumulated significant bargaining power relative to users. Substitute product producers in steel and concrete had redesigned their product lines to compete vigorously with the plastic contender. Together these forces were creating an unattractive market for the industry. The company's response to such a challenging environment, after an appreciable delay in recognizing what was happening, was to shift its product market focus to very large diameter applications that had not been developed because of technical obstacles, and to invest heavily in a risky process development program. As it turned out, the development efforts were successful. The resulting proprietary technology allowed the company to repeat its earlier success, only now in a new and, for a time at least, more attractive industry segment.

Individual Competitor Strategies In many markets competition boils down to a handful of readily identifiable competitors. In these situations it is imperative for you to look at the competitors individually, study their strategies, and determine the potential impacts on your strategic intentions. More specifically, you should be trying to determine (1) how capable each competitor is, and how steadfast it will be in pursuing its strategic course; (2) how your strategic proposal might affect the competitor's prospects; and (3) how motivated and capable each competitor is to react to your strategic initiative, and how it might go about doing so. These results, in turn, will condition your expectations for your own strategic proposal.

At times, the strategies of close competitors are reasonably easy to figure out. Monsanto has long been developing its capabilities in the growing crop biotechnology industry. When rival Dupont spent nearly $3 billion on acquisitions and partnerships in the industry, its underlying strategy was quite apparent. Dupont was intent on weaving together a formidable competitive position by integrating the core activities of crop biotechnology, from basic science to farm distribution. Monsanto had little choice but to respond in kind if it intended to be a long-run contender in the industry. Accordingly, a year later Monsanto was in the process of bolstering its position through over $5 billion in acquisitions including DeKalb Genetics Corp., Delta and Pine Land, and Cargill Inc.'s international seed operations.

At other times it is more difficult to pin down what your competitors are up to. Consider the consternation at Coke when PepsiCo announced in 2009 its intention to purchase the two largest bottlers of the PepsiCo products. Coke and PepsiCo dominate soft drinks and know virtually every step and misstep the other makes. Their bottlers had traditionally been independent entities that, in addition to bottling activities, handled packaging, promotion, and distribution. Coke must have been concerned. What was PepsiCo up to? How would the acquisition impact PepsiCo's distribution capability and supply management system? Would this become an additional cost and competitive threat to Coke? These were important questions to answer. Then in February 2010 Coke announced that it would purchase its largest Coke bottler. The acquisition was completed in October 2010 just a few months after the completion of PepsiCo's acquisition. These examples underline a key point. However obvious or obscure the situation, it is only at your peril that you ignore or underestimate competitors or the potential for competition.

Knowing your competitors, like knowing your customers, is a central law of survival and success.

Government

Government involvement is a pervasive aspect of the business environment and is expected to play an even greater role after the massive failure of world economies in 2008.[8] Not only has government stepped up its regulatory oversight, it has also become financially invested in a variety of industries. In addition, as the externalities or spillover effects of a firm's operations on the environment have become easier to detect, the visibility and enforcement associated with environmental and social issues is increasing.[9] Whether we like it or not, governments play many roles—from framing and implementing the basic legal framework for business conduct, to establishing taxes, incentives, and supports, to being customers and even competitors. The scope and importance of government activity in the economy is enormous, creating a complex context of opportunities and constraints for businesses. It is vitally important that you train a clear eye on these realities as you create and test strategic proposals. Consider, for example, the importance for strategy of correctly anticipating (1) government support; (2) changing trade policy; and (3) regulatory compliance.

Government Support Many businesses and industries operate with a level of government support that goes well beyond that normally available to everyone. Some of this support is direct, for example, in the form of grants and subsidies for research or plant location. Some is indirect, for example, where an industry may be given preferential legislation that provides protection from foreign competition. You need to weigh carefully your strategy in terms of its ability to create advantage from government support and to offset any potential changes in support activities. Some film production companies, for example, seek cost advantages by working in locations where generous government incentives are available. The large automobile companies pit governments in various jurisdictions against each other as they search for the most attractive subsidies for their plant construction and modernization programs. Pharmaceutical companies throughout the world use their considerable research and development spending as a bargaining chip in lobbying for the maintenance of patent protection.

Some companies leverage their strategies on close government ties. Consider the way in which Bombardier, for example, has used its considerable skills in government relations to help build its various businesses. Bombardier's market entry and expansion activities have often been driven by opportunities to assist governments who have become embroiled in troubled transport and aerospace facilities. Some examples are the acquisition of rail transit and rolling stock assets in Canada and Mexico respectively, and of aircraft assets in Canada and Ireland. In these and other circumstances, Bombardier has demonstrated a capacity to acquire technology and plant facilities on advantageous terms, and to integrate these advantages into its total operations. On another front, Bombardier has also been very aggressive and skilful in developing a government customer base for its transportation projects. The company's willingness to target government and its effectiveness in sorting its way through complex economic and political considerations has given it significant advantages over more conventional competitors. Finally, Bombardier has been very successful in obtaining government loans to the customers of its aircraft division; so much so, in fact, that there is considerable controversy over the fact that over $5 billion of Export Development Canada's $20 billion plus portfolio was committed to Bombardier's airline customers, who, being airlines, are not the soundest credit risks in the world.[10]

Changes in Trade Policy In the past 20 years or so, governments have been backing away from regulation and protectionism. Overall, the aim is to improve economic efficiency by increasing the opportunities open to businesses and with this, the competition that they face. As deregulation and trade liberalization proceed, albeit in fits and starts at times, it is crucially important that you develop strategies that anticipate the freedoms created by the changing circumstances and the challenges of new competition.

Consider, for example, the advent of the North American Free Trade Agreement (NAFTA) and the fortunes of the Canadian furniture industry, whose sales to the United States have grown fourfold in the past decade. The early years were tough as companies that could not adapt went out of business; over 15 companies and hundreds of jobs were lost in Ontario alone. But those who did adapt prospered, selling into the United States because they could, and because they had to. The garment industry was one of the industries that went through a major re-structuring. A company like the Montreal-based Gilden Activewear could now manufacture garments in Mexico at a lower cost and ship the finished products into the United States without attracting any custom duties. Gilden's moves to even lower cost jurisdiction in the Caribbean Basin and Central America were helped with the implementation of the Trade Enhancement Act in the early 2000s that gave these countries benefits similar to those enjoyed by Mexico under NAFTA. More recently, Gilden is also expected to reap benefits as a result of the 2011 Free Trade Agreement that Canada signed with Honduras, a country where Gilden had substantial manufacturing facilities and was its largest private sector employer

Regulatory Compliance The matter of compliance is often straightforward—the rules are clear and the actions anticipated in your strategic proposal either comply or they do not. At times, however, compliance is not nearly so easy as it sounds. Some policies are vague, requiring judgments by the business, regulatory authorities, or even in the courts. Some policies are administered inconsistently, and some are changed in midstream. In these murkier circumstances you will need to take great care in identifying the regulatory sensitivities in your strategic plans and in working out an action plan to deal with them.

In order to increase competition in the cellular wireless market, the Canadian government auctioned wireless spectrum in 2008. Globalive Wireless was the winner of $442 million of the auctioned licenses and got permission from Industry Canada to launch its wireless services. However in 2011 the Canadian Radio-television Telecommunication Commission (CRTC), responsible for regulating broadcasting and telecommunication systems, rejected Globalive Wireless' application for a carrier license on the grounds that Globalive Wireless violated foreign ownership limit rules. But then seven weeks later the then industry minister Tony Clement over turned the CRTC ruling and approved the license application. But this was not the end of the matter! The issue ended up in court and in February 2011 a Federal court passed judgment reversing the minister's decision. Imagine the uncertainties faced by potential entrants as they make their plans to enter the Canadian cellular wireless market.

Many organizations are doing a better job at anticipating regulatory pressures, which are often associated with trying to control the externalities, or unwanted spillover effects, of an organization's strategy on society. "When Kraft, Nabisco, and Nestlé decided to reformulate their recipes, and national restaurant chains such as Wendy's and Burger King switched to less artery-choking fats in their fry-o-laters, they were choosing to internalize an externality. They were taking ownership of an issue that they could, by law, have continued to say was not their problem. Yes, they did so under some activist pressure, and yes, they could still do more. But unlike tobacco companies in the 1980s, the food companies didn't wait for regulation or lawsuits. They acted."[11]

Testing the Strategy-Environment Linkage: The Jantzen Example How well does Jantzen's existing strategy fit its environment? The answer, unfortunately, is not very well at all. The strategy does not fit with the environment of maturing demand and competition. The inconsistencies are so great, in fact, that even with this first set of qualitative tests it is clear that a complete reformulation of Jantzen's business strategy is badly overdue.

A major problem facing Jantzen was the changing nature of market requirements for its component product. In earlier years its customers were very receptive to the custom design support and technical liaison that Jantzen provided so well. Now, these same PC manufacturers were facing fierce competition in their own markets and looking for ways to reduce their product costs. One route was to standardize components, develop alternative suppliers, and press for low prices. This was diluting Jantzen's competitive edge in custom design and its traditional strength in customer relationships, since engineers were now being displaced on buying teams by purchasing and manufacturing executives. With the standardization of products increasing, independent distributors, which Jantzen had chosen largely to ignore, were starting to take a greater position in the market by servicing the many smaller, local, PC assemblers.

As if demand shifts were not enough, a number of well-qualified competitors were now operating in the market. These competitors had mastered the basic technology, erasing much of Jantzen's competitive lead. Within the established technology, however, there were still rapid changes in product speed and capacity, which left competitors leapfrogging each other to deliver the best performance for a price. In spite of the pace of product change, some of the new competitors had chosen to operate as designers and assemblers and rely quite heavily on a rapidly developing and very competitive, global sub-component supply industry. These competitors had been foremost in cutting prices in recent months. A further and quite disturbing development for Jantzen was the announced plans of two of the largest PC manufacturers to enter the open market as merchant suppliers, both of whom had previously produced the component solely to meet a portion of their own needs.

Jantzen's strategy was being eclipsed by demand and competitive developments. There might be room in the industry for it to continue as a specialist supplier, but this would cap its ability to grow. If Jantzen wants to grow it has to radically change its value proposition and core activities to conform with new industry realities. At this point of analysis it would be appropriate to recycle and create a new strategy for the company.

First Check for Fit or Recycle

You have now completed an initial assessment of how well your strategic proposal anticipates and addresses demand, supply, competition, and government. If some serious questions have come up in the course of this analysis, now is the time to stop and reshape the proposal or build a substantially new proposal that incorporates the accumulated understanding of the environment. There is nothing to be gained from spending more time on a strategic proposal that obviously does not fit with the environment. On the other hand, if the proposal seems reasonable in most respects (not perfect, because perfect does not happen in such complex considerations), the analysis should move on to a forecast of performance to see if the proposal will meet its goals.

STEP 3: FORECAST PERFORMANCE

As you move to forecasting the expected performance of your strategic proposal, it is important to recall a beginning assumption in the strategy-environment analysis—that the strategic proposal, by and large, will be implemented as planned. In other words, you are assuming that the business has the will and the capabilities to put the strategy into place. These additional issues of will and capability come later in the analysis, after there is some assurance that you are working with a proposal that suits the environmental realities. It would be an obvious waste of time to go into the other considerations if the proposal cannot pass this first test!

The goals incorporated in the strategic proposal provide a useful reference point for the performance forecast. The question that you want to answer is whether the strategic proposal, implemented as planned, will meet these goals.

By this stage in the analysis you will have already weeded out the proposals that clearly do not fit with the environment. Now, you must focus on those that remain. Work systematically through the strategic goals for each proposal (for example, the revenue, cost, return, and investment goals) and use what you have learned about the environment to draw conclusions about the likelihood of achieving them.

While this is being done it is useful to identify and note the primary risks entailed. These points of risk are helpful to focus the immediate analysis as well as the subsequent comparison of the current proposal with competing alternatives. We will illustrate the process with respect to the two most tangible goal dimensions: revenues and costs.

The strategic goals for revenue growth and their underlying components of price and unit volume need to be evaluated in terms of how the strategic proposal addresses expected developments in the environment. Is the strategy powerful enough to deliver the promise? Watch out for questionable assumptions about market growth and the impact of competitive activity. A fault that we often see in strategic proposals in large companies is overly ambitious revenue goals, which are made without sufficient thought or are biased to justify the project that is being proposed. Were the Jantzen strategy pushed to this point, the issue would be whether the company could sustain prices and increase volumes at over 20 percent in the next few years. While the *overall growth* in demand for PCs might support this expectation, the changing *nature* of demand has diluted Jantzen's value proposition and the advent of aggressive competition suggests severe pricing pressures in the market.

Cost performance goals require just as critical an eye. First, you want to ensure that the projected operating costs incorporate anticipated supply developments and the possibilities of government regulatory or tax action. This is relatively straightforward. A more difficult task is to evaluate the cost goals that hinge on competitive conditions. What are the promotional costs, for example, that will be required to introduce a new product? Further, what is the possibility of competitively induced cost changes as time goes by in such areas as distribution margins, credit allowances, transportation arrangements, advertising and promotion spending, and so on?

As you continue to test performance forecasts against strategic goals, you may begin to question the goals or the other supporting elements of the strategic proposal. Here again it is time to recycle the proposal using the new information to revise the strategy where appropriate. This time, try to use the analysis to improve the proposal; abandonment should come only after some good creative effort has failed to address your concerns.

STEP 4: RANK AGAINST OTHER PROPOSALS

At this point the strategic proposal is considered to be compatible with the environment. Subject to some understood risks, it is expected to achieve its goals. The only question before going on to other steps of the Diamond-E analysis is whether it is competitive with other proposals you are considering. A definitive answer is impossible until the whole analysis has been completed, but a preliminary screen can weed out proposals that promise less or have higher risks, or in some other way are not competitive with others in the running. If the proposal is clearly not competitive, then shift your attention to the superior options. Otherwise, it is time to move on and examine the strategy-resource linkage.

SUMMARY

This chapter has presented the basic steps for analyzing the links between strategy and environment. The early priority in this process is to focus the analysis, and we demonstrated the utility of performance assessment, the strategic proposal, and the business profit model in pursuing this task. We acknowledged the potential risks of overfocusing the analysis, but argued that there are sufficient safeguards in a careful process of analysis that the merits of focus well exceed the risks involved.

The next step of analysis is to examine the substance of the strategic proposal in the light of current and anticipated demand, supply, competition, and government policy. For demonstrably poor fits we suggested developing a more attractive proposal that incorporated the insights gained in the analysis.

After assessing the fit between the strategic proposal and the environment, the next step is to forecast the performance of the strategic proposal. If the forecast turns out to be consistent with the strategy's goals, the next steps are to compare it with alternatives and then move on to further stages of the Diamond-E analysis. If the forecast is not consistent with its goals, the remedy, again, is to recycle and improve the proposition.

Now, armed with a proposal that fits with the environment, we turn our attention to its execution. The first topic to address is whether the resources needed to support the proposal are available or can be readily acquired or developed by the business.

Notes

1. For an elaboration of this theme, see Courtney, Hugh, Jane Kirkland, and Patrick Viguerie. "Strategy Under Uncertainty." *Harvard Business Review* 75 (November–December 1997): 67–79. Print.

2. For an instructive example of reading demand in high technology markets, see Tabrizi, Benham, and Rick Walleigh. "Defining Next-Generation Products: An Inside Look." *Harvard Business Review* 75 (November–December 1997): 116–124. Print.

3. Kadlec, Daniel. "How Blockbuster Changed the Rules." *Time* 152 (August 3, 1998): 48–49. Print.

4. "Levi's Decides It's Time to 'Break Rules'." *Wall Street Journal* [New York] August 4, 1998. Print.

5. Vogelstein, Fred. "Mighty Amazon." *Fortune* 147 (May 26, 2003): 62–74. Print.

6. Harrington, Ann. "Who's Afraid of a New Product." *Fortune* 148 (November 10, 2003): 189–192. Print.

7. Porter, Michael E. "How Competitive Forces Shape Strategy," *Harvard Business Review* 57 (March–April 1979): 137. Print.

8. Reich, Robert B. "Government in Your Business." *Harvard Business Review* 87.7/8 (2009): 94–99. *Business Source Complete, EBSCO*. Web. 15 Aug. 2011.

9. Meyer, Christopher, and Julia Kirby. "Leadership in the Age of Transparency." *Harvard Business Review* 88.4 (2010): 38–46. *Business Source Complete, EBSCO.* Web. 15 Aug. 2011.

10. McLearn, Matthew. "Bombardier's Bank." *Canadian Business* 77 (March 29, 2004): 20–22. Print.

11. Meyer, Christopher, and Julia Kirby. "Leadership in the Age of Transparency." *Harvard Business Review* 88.4 (2010): 38–46. *Business Source Complete, EBSCO.* Web. 15 Aug. 2011.

Additional Readings

1. Bower, Joseph L., and Clayton M. Christenson. "Disruptive Technologies: Catching the Wave." *Harvard Business Review* 73 (January–February 1995): 43–54. Print.

2. Porter, Michael E. *Competitive Strategy: Techniques for Analyzing Industries and Competitors*. New York: Free Press, 1985. Print.

Chapter 6
Resource Analysis: The Strategy-Resource Linkage

If you have worked through the analysis outlined in the previous chapter, you now have a strategic proposal that fits well with the external environment. Your analysis has shown that the proposal is likely to generate the kind of results that you want—if you can execute it!

The first implementation questions that are addressed in this chapter have to do with resources. What resources will you need to execute the proposal? What gaps are there between the resources required by the proposal and the resources that your business has on hand or readily available? What are the possibilities of closing the most important gaps? If the gaps are modest, or can be bridged at acceptable cost and risk, you can move to further steps of the Diamond-E analysis. If the gaps are sizeable, however, and the risks of closing them are high, you will need to recycle to develop a more viable proposition.

This chapter discusses the nature and role of resources in the strategic process and sets out an analytic process to deal with the questions implicit in the strategy-resource linkage in the Diamond-E framework.

THE NATURE OF RESOURCES

Resources provide your business with the potential to act. To execute a strategic proposal you will need to draw on financial resources for the required investment, operating resources to supply the product or service, marketing resources for promotion and sales, and so on. In Table 6.1 we classify the many and varied resources to which you might refer as you consider implementation and provide some examples of particular resources in each category.

Three important points need to be made about the nature of resources as they relate to strategic choice. The first is that the adequacy of a resource is relative to the demands of your strategic proposal. Absolutes in terms of size or depth or scope may or may not be important. Chrysler, for example, was a very large firm with very significant marketing, development, and financial resources, but in management's judgment these were insufficient to implement a strategy aimed at global scope, setting the stage for a merger with Daimler-Benz.

However, the merger did not achieve the desired benefits and a troubled Daimler-Chrysler opted for a new strategy.

> In a shift that has attracted little attention, Chrysler is transforming itself into Chrysler Lite. Instead of developing cars from scratch . . . it is leaning on partners . . . to provide everything from intellectual capital to assembly-plant paint shops. If Chrysler can make the new formula work, it will spend less money, employ fewer workers, and reduce the amount of assets devoted to engineering and building cars. That would give it a huge advantage. . . . Lots can go wrong. Coordinating the engineering and manufacturing done by outsiders adds another layer of complexity to what is already a very complicated business. Chrysler will have to manage a multicultural communications and data network that stretches around the world. At the same time it must avoid alienating its unionized workforce. . . .

Finally, Chrysler must ensure that it doesn't erode the distinctive character of brands like Jeep by mixing in too many parts from other models.[1]

This suggests caution about some approaches to strategic analysis that start from an absolute or internally referenced review of resources (such as the strengths and weaknesses component of a SWOT analysis—strengths, weaknesses, opportunities, and threats). You need to cast resources in the context of their intended utilization before they can be said to be adequate or otherwise. That means considering how your resources compare to your competitors.

A second noteworthy characteristic is that certain resources are more or less easy to augment or to adapt to meet the requirements of a proposal. If plant capacity is an issue, for example, it may be fairly simple to reallocate it, or to expand as necessary through investment. But if critical workforce skills are the issue, it may take substantial time to hire and train the needed people and in some circumstances this may not be a practical possibility at all. Thus, as your analysis proceeds and you perceive gaps, you will have to be sensitive to the particular issues of expanding the specific resource to meet the strategic needs.

A final notable characteristic is that the value of particular resources tends to be context specific and, additionally, is more or less transferable to new applications. Resources have primary as well as other uses. It is this use-value that is consequential. Suppose you have a production line, a piece of equipment that in essence makes aluminum cans for the beverage industry. Its primary use is, of course, producing aluminum cans. What is its next best use? Its next best use may well be scrap metal. In the context of an aluminum tin can manufacturing company, then, a production line has a high value. That same resource in a context other than a specialized use (i.e., as scrap metal) has a value approaching zero. A computer, on the other hand, likely has a market value impacted by supply and demand pricing. Computers are more generalized assets. They are not specialized assets in quite the same way that specialized equipment, a patent, or a highly trained expert might be.

Some resources are more easily transferable. A brand name might easily transfer to a new product line. A computer can be put to a wide range of uses. Management skills developed in a particular market, say Canada, may not easily transfer, however, into, say, Mexico. Again, the caution is to be sensitive to the potential issues in your particular proposal of transferring what are otherwise good and solid resources.

OTHER CHARACTERIZATIONS OF RESOURCES

We have characterized resources in specific terms to keep the analysis of your strategic proposal as tangible and as operational as possible. In wider ranging discussions about the future direction of your business, however, such as in the development of vision, mission, and very broad strategic thrusts, you may find it useful to work with more broadly based conceptions of resources.

In the late 1950s Selznick[2] and Ansoff[3] used the term *distinctive competence* to highlight the core activities that a business can perform better than its competitors. Thus, Dow Chemical might be said to have a distinctive competence in the low-cost production of commodity chemicals. The implications of this concept for strategy formulation are clear cut, in that distinctive competencies translate, in effect, into competitive advantages. In their strategies, businesses should seek to exploit their distinctive competencies and to avoid initiatives which hold no relationship to what the organization is good at doing.

In the early 1970s, Wrigley[4] introduced the term *core skills* to describe the collective skills accumulated by a management or professional team as they worked together over time in a common pursuit. Thus, Merck might be said to have developed core skills in the process of bringing a drug product from discovery through commercialization. The core skills possessed by businesses represent potentially valuable resources in that they are not easy to develop—and hence are hard for competitors to copy. The implications for strategy are that a business ought carefully to identify and nourish its core skills and then use them as reference points in creating or evaluating new initiatives.

In the 1990s Prahalad and Hamel[5] further developed the notion of competing on the basis of unique resources by introducing the concept of *core competencies*. Core competencies are the skills possessed by corporations that underlie a whole range of products and business units, such as miniaturization in the case of Sony and materials coating in the case of 3M. Although the various resource concepts are now becoming somewhat redundant, the particular spins that the authors put on them can add value to your analysis. Thus, core competencies, conceived of as corporate resources, provide a focal point for strategy at the corporate level and give direction to corporate management in the integration of the efforts of the various parts of the corporation.

The advantages of summary conceptions of resources, such as those of distinctive competence, core skills, and core competence, lie in the facility they provide for informal and open-ended explorations of strategic direction. We find the notion of distinctive competence, in particular, a quick and easy reference point in creating and sorting through ideas and in raising questions for subsequent, more detailed analysis. The disadvantages of these concepts, however, lie in their high level of abstraction, which creates difficulties pinning down whether they really do exist in a particular business and subsequently in testing the validity of specific strategic ideas. We are aware, for example, of businesses that have become very frustrated trying to pin down their core competencies and in this respect Collis and Montgomery criticize the search for core competencies as too often becoming "a feel good exercise that no one fails."[6] Perhaps more dangerously, these concepts might build a false confidence that they provide a sufficient basis for actual decisions, and lead to ignoring or slighting the many other resources that are critical to any undertaking.

Our advice is simply to proceed with an understanding that there are natural phases of exploration and analysis. In early exploratory work the broad concepts are useful. But as the analysis proceeds it is critically important that you move to an operational definition of your strategic proposal and to the consideration of specific, tangible resource requirements.

RESOURCES AND COMPETITIVE ADVANTAGE

Barney suggests that for a resource to offer a competitive advantage it must be valuable, rare, inimitable, and organized appropriately. The model is called VRIO (valuable, rare, inimitable, organization). The following questions can be used to assess whether a firm's resources contribute to competitive advantage.[7] In responding to the questions it is critical to keep in mind how the resource provides competitive advantage given the strategy the firm is pursuing or intends to pursue. In the abstract a resource does not provide a competitive advantage. The resource needs to be considered in a strategic context.

1. The Question of Value: Do a firm's resources and capabilities enable the firm to respond to environmental threats or opportunities?

2. The Question of Rareness: How many competing firms already possess specific, valuable resources and capabilities?

3. The Question of Imitability: Do firms without a resource or capability face a cost disadvantage in obtaining it compared to firms that already possess it?

4. The Question of Organization: Is a firm organized to exploit the full competitive potential of its resources and capabilities?

Barney sees the questions building on one another. For example, a response to the first question that a resource is valuable and enables a firm to respond to environmental threats and opportunities is not sufficient to provide a competitive advantage. Such a resource only has the potential to generate competitive parity. To provide at least a temporary advantage, the resource must be comparatively rare amongst the competing firms. For the competitive advantage to endure and to have the potential for competitive advantage, it must be difficult for other firms to imitate the resource or to utilize substitute resources. Finally, to have the potential to generate sustainable competitive advantage from the resource, the firm needs to be organized to leverage to exploit it. The question Barney poses around organization will be addressed in Chapter 8. In the Diamond-E framework, organization is explicitly identified as a key component that needs to be assessed. While a firm may possess the appropriate resources, it may not be able to leverage the resources if it is not organized in a manner to do so. It is the organization that transforms a resource into a capability.

The question of inimitability and the sustainability of competitive advantage has been central to strategic analysis. Barney suggests four key aspects or components of imitability. First, unique historical conditions may create the opportunity to acquire or to develop a particular resource, as for example some companies were able to do during the Second World War. Caterpillar was chosen as the single supplier of construction equipment to military bases around the world at a time when no supplier had global presence. Coca-Cola also developed much of its global distribution network at that time. These historical conditions are not likely to be recreated and hence make the resources difficult to imitate. Unique historical conditions may also arise when one firm pre-empts competitive investment by being the first to market in an arena where subsequent investors will yield below average returns. History may be viewed as creating a path-dependency, so that the development of the resource arises from a series of events occurring over time that would be difficult to replicate. Collis and Montgomery offer the example of the Gerber Products Company whose reputation in baby food was developed over many years. Even though a competitor might be able to imitate or copy the Gerber food products, the Gerber brand itself would be extremely difficult to copy.

The second aspect of inimitability is causal ambiguity. It occurs when the conditions or the nature of the competitive advantage is ambiguous. While one firm may attempt to disguise or to hide the nature of its advantage, causal ambiguity often arises because even the firm that possesses the advantage may have difficulty understanding the underlying causes. As Barney points out, sometimes sources of advantage are taken for granted because they may be tacit, there may be competing claims by managers within the firm on the source of the advantage, or there may be thousands of highly inter-connected organizational attributes, creating a level of complexity that defies understanding. For example, Lincoln Electric's success in manufacturing welding equipment has often focused solely on the piece-rate compensation system. A closer look reveals, however, a complex web of inter-related functions and factors that make the overall system very difficult to replicate. Southwest Airlines is arguably one of the most analyzed and discussed business models. It has been the subject of numerous attempts at replication by US competitors and others around the world. Yet few if any (Canada's WestJet perhaps comes closest) have been able to replicate Southwest Airlines' success. One key reason? Former Southwest CEO, James Parker, says that Southwest Airlines' culture of fun, family, frugality, and focus is difficult for competitors to imitate.[8]

Barney points to social complexity as a third aspect of inimitability. He suggests that social complexity arises from the interpersonal relations among managers, firm culture, relationship with suppliers, and relationship with customers. A socially complex organization need not be inherently positive. Social complexity is both difficult to imitate, and difficult to change. The Disney theme parks are an example of social complexity. There is a strong underlying culture in the Disney organization that enables its members to deliver a unique experience to the customer. In our view, social complexity and causal ambiguity are closely related, as often socially complex phenomena have a great deal of causal ambiguity—Southwest Airlines' culture, for example, is socially complex and ambiguous.

Finally, although patents appear to be an obvious aspect of inimitability, Barney points out that while in some cases they are, at other times, patents accelerate the diffusion process, and make imitation more likely.

Collis and Montgomery point out that a test of competitive advantage is the durability of the resource. Although this could be adopted under several of the headings posed by Barney, it is important to consider the durability of a resource, such as brand or a natural resource. Brands like Coke and Nike may be extremely durable, creating a competitive advantage that sustains itself over a period of time, even without high levels of investment. Collis and Montgomery also introduce the test of "appropriability," suggesting that it is important to know whether an advantage accrues to a firm, or to individuals, such

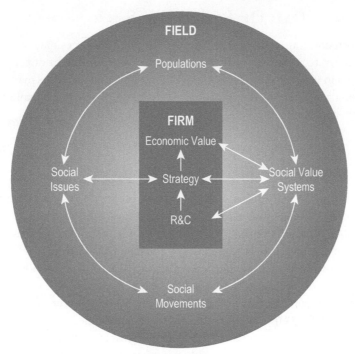

Figure 6.1 Culturally Informed RBV (CRBV)

as in investment banking or professional sports teams where the superstars appropriate disproportionate value for themselves.

However, Maurer, Bansal and Crossan[9] advance a culturally based view of RBV, which they refer to as CRBV. They argue that resources cannot be understood independent of the social context in which the firm is housed. There are social values, social issues, and social movements that can enhance or undermine a firm's resources. And it is the firm's resources and associated strategy that activate these social dimensions as depicted in Figure 6.1. Take, for example, TD Bank's approach to human resources and in particular its approach to diversity. TD Bank has been publicly supportive of the gay, lesbian, bisexual, and transgendered (GLBT) community and did not back down in face of opposition, whereas Wal-Mart did. TD Bank positioned its strategy as a push for human rights, which was consistent with its diversity programs and policies. Paul Douglas, the Executive Vice President of Commercial Banking for TD Bank Financial Group, stated that:

> Genuine diversity isn't about token gestures or lip service. It's not about filling quotas, labeling people, or grudgingly complying with the federal government's employment equity requirements. Nor is it about political correctness or "pseudo diversity." There has to be a deep-seated commitment to and understanding of diversity and groups such as the GLBT community. And concrete actions have to back up the rhetoric.[10]

THE DUAL ROLE OF RESOURCES

Resources both constrain and drive strategy. Inadequate resources may prevent you from implementing strategic proposals that otherwise make sense in light of the opportunities and challenges in your firm's external environment. Powerful resources may drive strategy if they represent a potential for competitive advantage that can be exploited with the right strategic approach.

The Constraining Role of Resources

Most managers are all too familiar with the powerful role that resources can play in constraining strategy. Often, a strategic proposal promises to take the business into growing markets with good profit potential, but a look at its resources suggests that the firm does not really have the resources that it needs to implement the strategy. How long would it take to develop or acquire the needed resources? Is it possible to modify the strategy to take advantage of the resources that are available? On one hand, you do not want to overstretch your resources; on the other, you cannot afford to enter into the new market too late, or risk making customer promises that you cannot meet.

Consider the situation facing Steve Jobs when he reassumed control of Apple Computer in 1997. Apple's resources had been ravished by years of unsettled management—among other things, finances were stretched, market share was down to around three percent, many program developers had stopped producing for the Apple line, and customers were questioning the credibility of the business as an ongoing proposition. In the face of this, Apple was compounding its problems by stretching its remaining resources across 15 different computer products. With an understanding that Apple would surely fail if it continued to try to operate beyond its resource constraints, Jobs pressed for simplification of the product line to focus on just two market categories and four new products. This move had its own risks, as Jobs acknowledged: "We're the last company left that can bet a company on a new idea—this is Apple's future."[11] But these were necessary risks given the company's need to work within its resource limitations. As Jobs reflected on the turnaround in 2001, he said, "I'm actually just as proud of what Apple hasn't done as what it has done, because it hasn't squandered resources since I've been back. And that's really easy to do in our industry."[12]

The Driving Role of Resources

On the other hand, resources can be an extremely important driving force, underlying the creation of new strategic proposals. Even in the case of Apple Computer, the company's powerful G3 microprocessor and loyal (if dwindling) customer base provided the seeds for the first products of the turnaround endeavour—the Power Mac G3 and PowerBook G3 for the professional market and the iMac for the consumer market. From this platform

Apple then ventured out into digital devices producing the iPod, which is a tiny device that can store thousands of songs as well as podcasts, photos, and video. Apple also developed its own on-line music store, iTunes. It is important to recognize the serendipity in some of these moves. For example, the iPod was developed after Apple realized its oversight in not having CD burners on its Macs.

Further, strategy may be driven by attempts to build and reinforce a resource advantage. First mover advantages may disappear if they are not pursued to their limit. Consider the case of Amazon.com. From selling its first book in 1995 to revenues of $5.3 billion in 2003, Amazon only turned its first real profit in 2004. It has remained profitable ever since and its revenues (in 2006) have grown to US$10.7 billion. Massive investment was required to build the scale of technological and warehousing operations to run the global business. As an early entrant into online book sales, Amazon.com knew that its real asset was its customers. Whatever its ambitions, from a strategic standpoint, Amazon had to continue to press for growth in books, in product lines such as CDs and airline tickets, and in any other ways that would add utility to its customers, otherwise the resource represented by its leading customer list would dissipate and with this, Amazon's fortunes.

As you consider resource-pushed strategies it is vitally important not to lose sight of your customers. The trick is to identify, develop, and take advantage of your unique resources without getting too inwardly focused. You may, for example, conceive an extremely innovative strategic proposal built on a unique resource, but you must ensure that this does not lead you to develop products or services that customers simply do not care about. For example, the New Product Showcase and Learning Center in Ithaca, New York, has a library of thousands of failed products launched by companies that thought it would be all too easy to extend a product line, to transfer a brand name, or otherwise to try to leverage off existing resources.[13]

RESOURCE ANALYSIS

We now turn to the process of testing your strategic proposal against your firm's resources. The logical flow of this process is presented in Figure 6.1. In this process we concentrate on the constraining role of resources because this phase of the Diamond-E analysis ultimately boils down to whether you have, or can develop, the resources needed to support your strategic proposal. If the immediate answer is no, you may turn to an examination of your existing resource base for inspiration regarding new strategic ideas. Then, any resulting proposal will still have to be recycled through the Diamond-E analysis. The fact that a particular proposal was inspired by the identification of a unique resource is no guarantee that the business will have the full set of resources required for its successful execution.

The process outlined in Figure 6.2 takes you through three phases of analysis to (1) determine the resource requirements of the strategic proposal; (2) identify gaps between the required and available resources; and (3) evaluate the risks associated with closing the gaps.

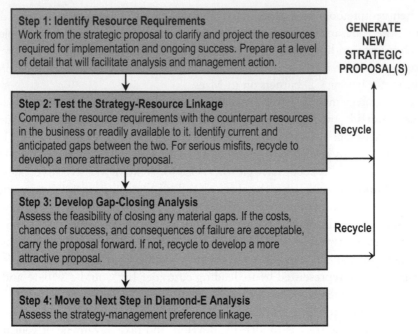

Step 1: Identify Resource Requirements
Work from the strategic proposal to clarify and project the resources required for implementation and ongoing success. Prepare at a level of detail that will facilitate analysis and management action.

GENERATE NEW STRATEGIC PROPOSAL(S)

Step 2: Test the Strategy-Resource Linkage
Compare the resource requirements with the counterpart resources in the business or readily available to it. Identify current and anticipated gaps between the two. For serious misfits, recycle to develop a more attractive proposal.

Recycle

Step 3: Develop Gap-Closing Analysis
Assess the feasibility of closing any material gaps. If the costs, chances of success, and consequences of failure are acceptable, carry the proposal forward. If not, recycle to develop a more attractive proposal.

Recycle

Step 4: Move to Next Step in Diamond-E Analysis
Assess the strategy-management preference linkage.

Figure 6.2 Resource Analysis

There are two subsidiary formats that you will find helpful in working through the analytic process. The first format, presented in Table 6.2, focuses on the use of the proposed strategy to identify and describe the relevant resource considerations. The second format, which is intended for concurrent use and ultimately as a summary document, is illustrated in Table 6.3. It helps you to highlight the resource categories in which there are going to be bottlenecks and reflects your assessment of the likelihood of solving the problem.

STEP 1: IDENTIFY RESOURCE REQUIREMENTS

The starting point for your analysis is to determine the resources that are most critical to the successful execution of your strategic proposal. To facilitate this, key in on the strategic proposal and work back to the various resource areas in a systematic way. In particular, focus on the elements of your strategic proposal that represent a change from the status quo. If Jantzen Technologies, the personal computer component supplier described in Chapter 5, needs to begin to compete on price, for example, Harry Jantzen should focus on the resource implications of that particular change. He will, for instance, need a marketing system tuned to the needs of an increasingly commodity-like product, product designers with an ability to create products that are simple to manufacture, manufacturing managers and facilities suited to longer runs of standardized products, demanding purchasing agents, and so on.

Table 6.2 Resource Analysis by Strategy Component

Strategic Proposal	Required	Available	Gaps	Risks
Goals	What are the most critical resources required by the goals of the strategic proposal (e.g., for growth, risk, market dominance); what are the gaps between these requirements and available resources; and what are the risks and consequences of not being able to close these gaps in a timely way?			
Product/ Market Focus	What are the most critical resources required by the product market focus of the strategic proposal (e.g., for a specific market focus, diversification); what are the gaps between these requirements and available resources; and what are the risks and consequences of not being able to close these gaps in a timely way?			
Value Proposition	What are the most critical resources required by the value proposition of the strategic proposal (e.g., for price, features, execution); what are the gaps between these requirements and available resources; and what are the risks and consequences of not being able to close these gaps in a timely way?			
Core Activities	What are the most critical resources required by the core activities of the strategic proposal (e.g., for activities to internalize, degree of integration); what are the gaps between these requirements and observed resources; and what are the risks and consequences of not being able to close these gaps in a timely way?			

Table 6.3 Resource Analysis by Resource Category

Resource Category	Required Resources	Available Resources	Major Gaps	Gap-Closing Analysis
Marketing				
Operations				
Development				
Financial				
Human Resources				
Reputation				
Other				

Some resource requirements are reasonably easy to predict. The financial requirements for a strategic proposal, for example, can be worked out as a matter of straightforward logic from the substance and performance forecasts of the proposal. When it comes to qualitative resources and particularly those of management skills, however, the resource requirements may be harder to pin down. In its early steps to enter South American markets, for example, Wal-Mart seemed to assume that the required leadership skills would be largely the same as those in the United States, making the requirements essentially a quantitative matter. This was far from the truth, however, as evidenced by Wal-Mart's early difficulties in these markets.[14] Wal-Mart's response was to the point, including, for them, the unprecedented step of hiring a senior manager from outside the firm to lead its international operations. The caution here is to be very careful about qualitative resource requirements because it is all too easy to assume that new requirements are just an extension of old requirements. This is where the quality of your understanding of your strategy and its environment linkages really comes under test.

Finally, as a matter of focus, concentrate your work on the resources that seem most critical to the execution of the strategy. The key to this is to understand what is unique about your strategy and, in particular, what competitive advantage it seeks to create or to exploit. A strategy based on superior product features, for example, pushes you immediately to focus on the required development and commercialization resources.

STEP 2: TEST THE STRATEGY-RESOURCE LINKAGE

Once you have identified the most critical resources for implementing your strategic proposal, it should not take long to match them against the firm's existing resources. The advantage of determining the required resources first is that you now have a list that allows you to examine your existing resources in a focused way, and to avoid a "laundry list" approach. You know the resources that you need. The first task is to determine whether you have them, or can readily develop them. The second is to clarify the gaps that remain. If these gaps are truly formidable, it makes sense to drop the proposal and recycle the analysis to generate better ideas. If there is some hope, however, that extraordinary action might address the gaps, you pass to a third phase for an analysis of the practicality of the correction and risks involved. The following paragraphs provide some examples of linking strategy to resource requirements and availabilities in selected resource categories.

Marketing Resources When Terry Semel became CEO of Yahoo! Inc. in 2001, he faced significant challenges. The dot-com bubble had burst and half of Yahoo!'s advertising revenue disappeared. Yahoo! had lost $100 million on revenues of $717 million. Semel looked for new ways to diversify revenue; however, Yahoo!'s salesforce was ill-prepared. They did not have the capabilities or the contacts to drive new business. Prior to the bubble bursting, they had simply been order takers as most of the advertising business was unsolicited. Semel gutted Yahoo!'s salesforce, brought in new leadership to run it, and refocused Yahoo!'s efforts on direct personal selling.

Operations Resources Having enjoyed the position as the largest commercial aircraft producer in the world for its eighty-nine year history, Boeing yielded that position to Airbus Industrie in 2003. Boeing's operational deficiencies became clearly evident in the mid-1990s when the aircraft industry moved into a period of surging demand. Boeing adopted an aggressive strategy of maintaining share in the face of growing price and delivery pressure from the major airlines and the increasing capabilities of its key competitor, Airbus. New orders were booked at an unprecedented pace, which, if filled, would require the company to double its production output in two years. Not a big deal, you might think, for a progressive aerospace company. The problem, however, as *Fortune* reported it, was that, "Boeing executives have known for years—for decades even—that their factories were inefficient, their supply chains tangled, their computer systems outmoded. Ever since the 1970s they have tried, in a piecemeal fashion, to fix these problems. But they never took the issues seriously."[15] The Boeing culture was one of excellence in design and the tailoring of design to individual customers. In this, the urgency for simplification and efficiency in manufacturing was difficult to grasp. The result was a serious strategy-resource mismatch. Boeing's plants were overwhelmed to the point that they were actually shut down for a month to try to recover order; Boeing absorbed losses estimated at $3 billion in 1998 and faced a serious loss of credibility with customers and investors. It is quite possible that Boeing did not have much choice on the strategic front—giving up market share and follow-on business would probably have been prohibitively expensive. But management's insensitivity over time to the resource implications of foreseeable changes in environment and strategy surely cost the company dearly.

Financial Resources Balancing the requirements of strategic ambitions against the financial capacity of the business is a critical senior management responsibility. As Kodak assessed its financial resources to invest in digital cameras and accessories, it realized it would have to divert investment from its core film business to the new business. In addition, Kodak had to cut its dividend by 72 percent to meet the financial requirements.

Amazon.com's initial decision to become the biggest internet bookstore, locating in Seattle for its pool of engineers and proximity to the largest book distribution warehouse in the world, turned out to be short-sighted. They discovered they were not able to provide the level of service required without their own warehousing capability. Short of the financial resources to invest in this key strategic asset, they had to issue $2 billion in bonds.

Human Resources Ensuring you have the right people with the right capabilities may seem obvious, but it is surprisingly difficult in practice. With $240 billion in sales in 2003 and 1.3 million associates, Wal-Mart needed to manage its human resources carefully. In 2003 it was projecting the need to hire 40,000 managers in the next few years. Cole Peterson, Wal-Mart's top HR executive, stated that "we never want it to be said that we were unable to expand our business around the world because we didn't have the people to do it. We look at the growth of the organization and understand that we've entered diverse markets across the country and around the world. Our work force has grown to reflect the diversity of the communities we serve."[16] Wal-Mart has a three-pronged strategy: keep, grow, and get. They have been actively working to retain top talent, develop the talent they have, and actively recruit the best people they can.

Table 6.4 Options For Leveraging Resources

	Other Fiction	Trade/ Reference Books	Magazines	Movies	Greeting Cards	Geographic Expansion	Forward Integration
Author							
Editor							
Production							
Marketing							
Distribution							

We have found it helpful to compare the key success factors across the industry value chain with the resources of the firm across its own core activities. This can be carried out for the existing business as well as for each strategic option to identify areas of strength and weakness. For example, Harlequin, the world's leading publisher of romance novels, was assessing how to leverage its resources against several strategic options including developing movies, greeting cards, other book lines such as science fiction, and publishing magazines. One way to examine the options is to array Harlequin's core activities against each strategic option to determine what resources each activity leverages. Table 6.4 provides an example.

It is important to recognize that each strategic option has its own set of core activities, value chain, or business system. Therefore, while the analysis provided above may suggest that Harlequin could leverage several resources in pursuit of a strategic option, it does not identify resources Harlequin may be lacking in pursuit of that option. Ultimately, a comparison needs to be made between the resources of the firm and the required resources for each option.

Recycling

Returning to the analytic flow, as your work proceeds you will find yourself in one of three positions. In the first of these the required and available resources will match up in a reasonable way, with the result that you can expect to sail through the next step of gap-closing analysis very quickly. The second outcome is that there are significant but potentially addressable gaps between required and available resources. In the Jantzen case, for example, a proposed transition to a low price strategy might result in cash flow requirements that are beyond the company's immediate capacity. So a key question is whether financing can be found to cover the shortfall. This is what the gap analysis process is all about.

The third outcome of testing the resource-strategy linkage is that you identify resource gaps that you know immediately you cannot close. Say, for example, that your comparison of required research and development strength with current strength suggests that you need to increase the staff by 50 percent. You may know that for financial reasons this is absolutely not feasible. An alternative may be to focus your research spending on fewer projects, but this, in effect, creates a new strategic proposal involving changes in product market focus, and logically this proposal needs to be taken through the Diamond-E analysis from the beginning. So the result, one way or another in the case of obvious misfits, is to drop the proposal in hand and to recycle for the generation of new proposals.

STEP 3: DEVELOP GAP-CLOSING ANALYSIS

As we mentioned above, a well-matched strategy will pass easily through this step and should be carried on to further stages of the Diamond-E analysis. The issue for discussion is whether it makes sense for you to stick with a strategy that creates some significant but potentially addressable gaps. The primary matters to consider here are additional costs that you will incur in the attempt to close the gap, the probability that your efforts will be successful, and the consequences of going ahead with the strategy but failing to close the gap in a sufficient and timely way.

Additional Costs In all likelihood the costs of extraordinary efforts to close resource gaps will not have been taken into consideration in formulating the strategic proposal and in preparing performance forecasts. These now need to be factored into your assessment of the strategy. For example, when John Labatt Limited, a Canadian brewer, purchased a 22 percent stake of the Mexican brewer FEMSA Cerveza for $720 million, it should have subtracted the cost of hedging its currency exposure from the returns expected from the investment. If your strategy cannot stand up to these new costs (as probably would have been the case in the Labatt investment) then it should be abandoned and steps taken to generate new proposals.

The Probability of Success You may recognize a resource gap, you may take extraordinary action to address it, and you may still fail to close the gap and provide the strategy with the support that you were counting on. Consider Seagram Co.'s high profile $10 billion acquisition of PolyGram, which was aimed at creating a global giant in rock, pop, and classical music. The acquisition price assumed significant operating savings through the merger of PolyGram and Seagram's existing Universal Music Group. It was no secret that both companies were short on the required people, disciplines, and procedures to achieve these efficiencies. Seagram took extraordinary steps to close this management gap by bringing in an "army" of consultants.[17] But this had the side effect of upsetting the creative executives who were at the heart of both of the businesses, creating the potential for serious operating problems. There was, in short, a good chance that the efforts to fill the management gaps would fall short in the early going and put the economic justification of the transaction at risk. In 2000, Edgar Bronfman Jr., the CEO of Seagram's, made the decision to sell Seagram's to Vivendi for $34 billion in stock. Bronfman, a third generation Seagram CEO, felt the sale was the best way to preserve the value of the company for the next generation. However, the deal turned out to be a disaster. The plan had been to build a media giant through the marriage of Seagram's

Universal Studios and Universal Music Group with Vivendi's internet, cable television, and wireless divisions. However, Vivendi's CEO, Jean-Marie Messier, drove the company to the brink of insolvency through a series of deals racking up $19 billion in debt.[18]

A high proportion of gap-closing initiatives will depend on some form of organizational change. In the case of Boeing, the chances of it closing its manufacturing productivity gaps and containing its losses to those originally estimated will depend on how fast it can implement some fundamental changes in the way that it operates. Later chapters in this book are intended to help you to analyze and to plan organizational changes, and to assess the likelihood of success where the closing of resource gaps is an issue.

The Costs of Failure The failure to close a critical resource gap will handicap a strategy and perhaps cause it to fail outright. The consequences of this need to be identified and weighed in the context of other strategic options and the impact of failure on the company as a whole. You need to ask, "what happens if we can't implement the strategy?"

If the potential consequences of not being able to implement a strategy add up to a "bet the company" situation, for example, you obviously need to do a very searching review of the strategy, of the implementation issues, and of the rationale for assuming that level of risk. In most cases this review will result in a decision to move on and search for a better way.

In some cases, however, such as when a company is already in crisis, the possibility of drastic downside consequences may be acceptable if the strategy offers a better future than doing nothing! Consider, for example, the circumstances of Canadian Airlines in 1995. The airline was facing accumulating losses and predictable failure if it carried on as it was. Management was considering two strategic options, which they had labeled Plan A and Plan B. Plan A was based on seeking concessions from the company's unions to improve efficiencies significantly, enabling the airline to increase capacity and flight frequencies with minimal increases in cost. The added capacity would then be deployed in an attempt to increase revenues, particularly in the more lucrative business traveler market. There was a serious environmental risk in this strategy, of course, in that Air Canada, Canadian's arch rival, would respond in kind, starting a war of escalating commitment. With this possibility in mind, the internal risks of Plan A were that the concessions and productivity gains might not be achieved and that even if they were, the company would not have the financial capacity to survive a price and capacity building war. Plan B, on the other hand, called for shrinking the airline to a defensible core through major reductions in people, fleet, and routes. The risks with Plan B were that once a retreat was started competitors would step in and make the situation increasingly untenable and that this process would be accelerated internally by the departure of good people and the evaporation of financial support. Faced with the dilemma of an unacceptable current strategy and two problematic future choices, management moved in the direction of Plan A. In an absolute sense this was a "bet the company" proposition, but in the crisis context at the time it might also be seen as the choice of probable death over certain death.

In less dramatic circumstances the inability to implement a strategic proposal properly may add up to substantial but affordable penalties in cost, market position, reputation, and so on. Here the issue is whether the strategy still makes sense relative to other possibilities. Given the overall competitive imperatives driving the strategy, the consequences of stumbling might well be accepted as part of a risk that needs to be taken. At Seagram, the chain of events following the PolyGram acquisition have cost the company dearly. The scale of consequences and the likelihood of management miscues surely raise questions about whether there were not better alternatives available for the investment of $10 billion.

STEP 4: MOVE TO THE NEXT STEP IN THE DIAMOND-E ANALYSIS

You now have a strategy that links well with the environment and with resources. The next step is to consider the strategy-management preferences linkage. But first, we will recap the benefits of the resource analysis. First, it should have helped you discard any highly inappropriate strategic proposals, saving you the task of taking them further through the Diamond-E analysis. Second, you may have created a new strategic proposal or two, based on unique resources that you identified in the course of your analysis. Third, you may have identified certain resource categories that need development and investment—if some of your otherwise good ideas are being rejected for reasons of resource gaps, maybe it is time to work on the missing ingredients.

DYNAMIC RESOURCES

One of the challenges posed by the resource-based view of the firm is whether a firm should continue to rely on current resources and capabilities, or attempt to develop new ones. In a rapidly changing environment, the concern is that firms need flexible resources in order to respond. There are suggestions that there is a meta competence that enables firms to be adaptive. As Arie De Geus, a former strategic planner for Royal Dutch Shell suggested, the only sustainable competitive advantage may be a firm's ability to learn faster than its competitors.[19] We will address this more dynamic view of strategy in Chapter 10. However, for the purpose of this analysis, we will suggest that firms should attempt to leverage their current competencies as much as possible. Simply worrying that something is going to change, without any foundation for the worry, is not sufficient to warrant a move away from a current base of competitive advantage. It is critical that firms continue to assess the environment for threats and opportunities that signal the need for change. The dynamic nature of industries suggests that firms need to think about ways to configure and re-configure resources and capabilities. As we discuss in Chapter 8, strategic alliances are often employed to complement the resources of the organization. In doing so, however, the actual boundaries of the organization become less clear.

RESOURCES AND THE SCOPE OF THE FIRM

Traditionally the question of firm scope was related to choices about product market, geography, and vertical integration. Product market scope captures the position a firm takes with respect to its product and geographic markets. The question of vertical integration relates to the core activities required to support the overall strategy. The assumption made in early studies of strategic analysis was that vertical and horizontal integration entailed diversification. However, the resource-based view of the firm suggests a different perspective. The question of whether a firm is in fact diversifying can be addressed by assessing whether it is able to leverage current resources in the process.

Decisions about the scope of the firm, the boundaries of the organization, and the need for alliances span both the internal and external analysis. Firms need to have a clear understanding of how the environment is unfolding to assess the threats and opportunities, and identify what they "need" to do to compete, and where value can be generated and captured. As well, firms need to assess their organization, resources, and capabilities to determine what they "can" do. Since the competitive landscape may shift rapidly, firms often need to fill the gaps quickly. Alliances, joint ventures, and acquisitions may be a means to that end.

SUMMARY

Resource analysis is a critical step in the Diamond-E analysis. This analysis acts as a filter, culling out inappropriate strategic proposals, and as a generator of new proposals, based on unique resources identified in the course of the analysis. If a proposal makes it through the resource analysis it means that you either already have the resources required to implement it, or that you believe you can develop the required resources in the time available. Successful proposals should now be taken forward for a test of their fit with the preferences of the managers in your business. This process is described in the following chapter.

Notes

1. Taylor III, Alex., "Just another sexy sports car? Sure. But it's also a whole new way of doing business at Chrysler." *Fortune*, vol. 147, Mar. 17, 2003, pp. 76-80.

2. Selznick, P., *Leadership in Administration: A Sociological Interpretation*. New York: Harper & Row, 1957.

3. Ansoff, Igor. *Corporate Strategy: An Analytic Approach to Business Policy for Growth and Expansion*. Harmondsworth, U.K.: Penguin, 1965. Print.

4. Wrigley, Leonard. "Divisional Autonomy and Diversification." Diss. Harvard Business School, 1970. Print.

5. Hamel, Gary, and C. K. Prahalad. "The Core Competence of the Corporation." *Harvard Business Review* 68 (May–June 1990): 79–91. Print.

6. Collis, David J., and Cynthia Montgomery. "Competing on Resources: Strategy in the 1990s." *Harvard Business Review* 73 (July–August 1995): 118–128. Print.

7. Barney, Jay B. *Gaining and Sustaining Competitive Advantage*. Reading, Mass.: Addison-Wesley, 1995. 145. Print.

8. Parker, James F. *Do The Right Thing: How Dedicated Employees Create Loyal Customers and Large Profits*. Reading, Mass.: Pearson Education, 2008. Print.

9. Maurer, Cara, Pratima Bansal, and Mary Crossan. "Creating Economic Value Through Social Values: Introducing a Culturally Informed Resource-Based View." *Organization Science* 22 (March–April 2011): 432–448. Print.

10. Douglas, Paul. "Diversity and the Gay and Lesbian Community: More than Chasing the Pink Dollar." *Ivey Business Journal Online* (September–October 2007), Web. 29 Sept. 2011. <www.iveybusinessjournal.com>.

11. Jackson, David S. "Apple's New Crop." *Time* (May 18, 1998). Web. 29 Sept. 2011. <www.time.com/time/magazine/article/0,9171,988346-1,00.html>.

12. Schlender, Brent, and Lenore Schiff. "Steve Jobs: The Graying Prince of a Shrinking Kingdom." *Fortune* (May 14, 2001). Web. 29 Sept. 2011. <http://money.cnn.com/magazines/fortune/fortune_archive/2001/05/14/302936/index.htm>.

13. Lukas, Paul. "The Ghastliest Product Launches." *Fortune* (March 16, 1998). Web. 29 Sept. 2011. <http://money.cnn.com/magazines/fortune/fortune_archive/1998/03/16/239261/index.htm>.

14. Friedland, Jonathan, and Louise Lee. "When the Wal-Mart Way Doesn't Play." *Wall Street Journal* [New York], October 8, 1997. Print.

15. Henkoff, Ronald. "Boeing's Big Problem." *Fortune* (January 12, 1998). Web. 29 Sept. 2011. <http://money.cnn.com/magazines/fortune/fortune_archive/1998/01/12/236418/index.htm>.

16. Janoff, Barr. "Strength in Numbers." *Progressive Grocer* 79 (December 2000): 39–42. Print.

17. "Corporate Focus: Seagram-PolyGram Duo: Off Key?" *Wall Street Journal* [New York] 25 September 1998: B1. Print.

18. Leonard, David. "The Bronfman Saga From Rags to Riches To . . . " *Fortune* 146 (November 25, 2002): 108–116. Print.

19. De Geus, Arie P. "Planning as Learning." *Harvard Business Review* 66 (March–April 1988): 70–74. Print.

Additional Readings

1. Bleeke, Joel, and David Ernst, *Collaborating to Compete: Using Strategic Alliances and Acquisitions in the Global Market Place*. New York: John Wiley and Sons, 1993. Print.

2. Collis, David J., and Cynthia A. Montgomery. "Creating Corporate Advantage," *Harvard Business Review* 76 (May–June 1998): 70–83. Print.

3. Ghemawat, Pankaj. "Sustainable Advantage." *Harvard Business Review* 64 (September–October 1986). Print.

4. Stalk Jr., George. "Time: The Next Source of Competitive Advantage." *Harvard Business Review* 66 (July–August 1988). Print.

5. Stalk Jr., George, Philip Evans, and Lawrence Shulman. "Competing on Capabilities: The New Rules of Corporate Strategy." *Harvard Business Review* 70 (March–April 1992): 57–69. Print.

Chapter 7

Management Preference Analysis: The Strategy-Management Preference Linkage

As noted in Chapter 3, strategy choices resolve the tension between what firms "need" to do, what they "can" do, and what they "want" to do. Different models of strategic analysis treat the area of "want" quite differently. Some ignore it all together. Others view it as a negative or unwelcome aspect of strategic analysis and attempt to minimize it. We argue that it is an essential aspect of strategic analysis that must be taken into consideration. As Andrews writes, "to be implemented successfully over time, any strategy must command the creativity, energy, and desire of the company's members. Strategic decisions that are economically or ethically unsound will not long sustain such commitment."[1]

There are many facets to the analysis of management preferences. Central questions that need to be addressed include: In whose interest is management acting? What is management's central responsibility? What factors need to be considered in understanding management preferences? The first two questions are addressed by examining management's role in value creation, capture, and distribution. In doing so, we incorporate a discussion of corporate governance and corporate social responsibility (CSR). To address other factors that need to be considered we examine the roots of management preferences, by examining the role of basic needs, beliefs, and job context.

VALUE CREATION, CAPTURE, AND DISTRIBUTION

In assessing the link between management preferences and strategy, we need to address on what basis management can and should prefer a particular strategy. In whose interest are they acting? Ultimately, the general manager's role is to create, capture, and distribute value. The preceding chapters speak to the various ways in which value is created and captured; however, they do not address the fundamental question of value for whom, and how it should be distributed. Understanding the needs and preferences of the various stakeholders reveals the alignment, or lack thereof, between strategy and stakeholder interests. Companies that embrace stakeholders, rather than just shareholders, perform better.[2] However, we need to determine how to reconcile the various stakeholder interests.

In Chapter 4 we presented an approach to stakeholder analysis. In this chapter we address how management perceives and reconciles stakeholder interests. As Mitchell, Agle, and Wood state, "it is the firm's managers who determine which stakeholders are salient and therefore will receive management attention. In short, one can identify a firm's stakeholders based on attributes, but managers may or may not perceive the stakeholder field correctly. The stakeholders winning management's attention will be only those the managers perceive to be highly salient."[3]

Reconciling Stakeholder Interests

Typically, the discussion of reconciling stakeholder interests with respect to the creation and distribution of value centers on employees, customers, and shareholders. Shareholders invest in the corporation and expect a fair, if not exceptional, return on their investment. Customers delight in products and services that have the desired features at the lowest possible price. Employees want a fair, if not exceptional, wage for their efforts. Some argue that these interests are in conflict. For example, a lower price to customers translates into a lower wage for employees, or perhaps lower profits and hence returns to shareholders. Extreme imbalances between the interests of employees, customers, and shareholders may exist in the short term. However, in the long term, extreme imbalances are not sustainable: if shareholders do not perceive they are receiving a fair return on their investment, sources of capital dry up; if employees do not perceive themselves to receive a fair wage, they leave to pursue employment elsewhere. If customers believe that prices are too high, they will seek products and services from competitors. Without any one of the three key stakeholders, the firm will not survive. The management challenge is to reconcile the stakeholder interests.

There is no simple formula that determines the balance of stakeholder interests. The stakeholder analysis presented in Chapter 4 serves to identify the various stakeholder interests to achieve better alignment with the strategy. However, practical matters exist such as the degree to which a stakeholder holds a significant position of power vis-à-vis the firm. For example, venture capitalists typically demand a higher return on investment, in part because of the risk associated with the investment, but in part because the company requesting the funds may have few alternative sources of capital. Employees with rare and valuable skills may demand higher salaries. Companies who rely on a limited set of customers may find themselves vulnerable to escalating demands in terms of lower prices or more features.

Assuming that managers can assess the appropriate balance, the concern remains that they may act in a self-interested fashion, essentially tipping the balance in favour of their own interests. How does the firm ensure this does not happen? Although there should be many checks and balances in the operations of the firm, the ultimate responsibility for the direction and performance of the organization rests with the board of directors whose mandate is corporate governance. Contrary to popular belief, the mandate of the board of directors in most legal jurisdictions is to act in the best interest of the corporation, not simply the shareholders. For example, the Business Corporations Act of Ontario states that "every director and officer of a corporation in exercising his or her powers and discharging his or her duties shall, (a) act honestly and in good faith with a view to the best interests of the corporation; and (b) exercise the care, diligence and skill that a reasonably prudent person would exercise in comparable circumstances."[4] In the following section we discuss the critical issues associated with corporate governance.

Corporate Governance

Corporate governance "covers all the mechanisms that govern the managers' behavior and delineates their discretionary latitude."[5] The need for such mechanisms stems from the separation of ownership of the firm by shareholders and control of the firm by management. However, it runs more deeply than this, and ultimately resides in the concern that any manager may make decisions and take actions that are in his or her own interest with no regard for the interests of others.

Many mechanisms contribute to corporate governance, including firm-specific processes of checks and balances, and ultimately the board of directors; external mechanisms such as regulatory constraints; and the market itself which exerts pressures on firms to achieve their potential—underperforming firms become takeover targets. The seriousness and importance of corporate governance mechanisms became all too apparent amid one corporate crisis after another that revealed the shortcomings of those mechanisms. In early 2004 Economist.com stated that "a new mood of austerity appears to reign in America's boardrooms. The Sarbanes-Oxley Act of 2002, the most radical reform of corporate governance since the Great Depression of the 1930s, imposed tough new rules on companies—and harsh new penalties on wrongdoers. After a tumultuous few years in which a series of corporate America's best-known names admitted to wrongdoing of one sort or another—the roll-call includes Enron, WorldCom, Qwest, Adelphia, Rite Aid, Tyco and Xerox—the focus shifted to Wall Street's banks and fund managers, giving industrial companies some breathing space."[6]

Enron's collapse was dramatic, and a prime example of corporate governance failure. Once the darling of Wall Street, in 2001 *Fortune* stated that

> Right now, the title of "It Stock" belongs to Enron, the Houston energy giant. While tech stocks were bombing at the box office last year, fans could not get enough of Enron, whose shares returned 89%. By almost every measure, the company turned in a virtuoso performance: Earnings increased 25%, and revenues more than doubled, to over $100 billion. Not surprisingly, the critics are gushing. But for all the attention that is lavished on Enron, the company remains largely impenetrable to outsiders, as even some of its admirers are quick to admit. To skeptics, the lack of clarity raises a red flag about Enron's pricey stock.[7]

The red flag loomed larger as analysts began to uncover what lay behind the Enron numbers. By mid-August, 2001 the stock had fallen from $80 at the beginning of the year to the low $40s and CEO Jeff Skilling announced that he was leaving Enron. Skilling was replaced by Ken Lay, who had been Enron's former CEO, and who had a high level of credibility on Wall Street. Lay assured the public that there were no "accounting issues, trading issues, or reserve issues at Enron."[8] However, this was not the case. In an October press release Enron announced a $618 million loss. It had also written down shareholders' equity by $1.2 billion. On December 2, 2001 Enron filed for bankruptcy. Enron's auditor, Arthur Andersen, was drawn into the scandal and subsequently collapsed.

John Zimmerman of *USA Today* summarized the key learnings from the Enron debacle.

> Reviewing the entire nasty scene reveals at least three conclusions. First the breakdowns were internal and caused by ignored or flawed ethics and beliefs at the highest personal and corporate levels. Second, many parties beyond senior executives and their greed contributed to the mess. Boards of directors failed their governance and, in some instances, they shared in the gains; the giant accounting firm Arthur Andersen forgot what auditing and fiscal responsibility was all about and was found guilty; middle managers down through the financial and legal departments knew something serious was amiss, but remained silent; Wall Street became enamored with growth and stock value regardless of reality; and banks provided unlimited capital with little due diligence or even concern for repayment potential. Third, most of the corrective action is external [which] can be helpful, but ethical behavior can't be legislated. It has to come from within.[9]

Boards of directors have been a prime target for reform. Although the board of directors must ensure that the strategic direction of the organization is in the best interest of the corporation and in particular the shareholders, there have been many criticisms about its effectiveness in achieving this mandate. One of the primary criticisms is that the board tends to be dominated by internal management, or friends of management, rather than individuals who operate at arms-length. On the other hand, individuals with an arms-length relationship may not have sufficient understanding of the business to intervene in discussions of strategic direction. There have been numerous prescriptions to remedy the situation. A set of prescriptions revolve around the structure of the board: separating the roles of CEO and chairman of the board, and appointing more outside directors and directors with greater diversity to increase the representativeness of the board and enhance its objectivity. Another mechanism has been to manage executive compensation to better align the interests of management with those of shareholders through stock option plans.

Although these mechanisms have focused on tightening control over wayward managers whose management preferences may be out of line with what is in the best interest of the corporation, John Pound argues that these mechanisms "do not address the fundamental problems in corporate governance, which stem not from power imbalances but from failures in the corporate decision making process. . . .The goal should be to prevent significant mistakes in corporate strategy and to ensure that the mistakes that do occur can be corrected easily."[10] Pound argues that most performance crises are not because of incompetence or wayward managers, but because of failures of judgment. This is a critical point. Although there are blatant breaches of ethics, many unethical decisions are revealed more clearly with hindsight. In the midst of conversations and ultimately decisions, the ethical dilemmas may not be so apparent. In a recent study entitled "Leadership on Trial" it was deficiency in leadership character—wisdom, courage, justice, temperance, humanity, and transcendence—that was identified time and again by senior leaders as a major factor[11] contributing to the economic crisis. In Chapter 9 we outline a number of cognitive biases that lead to these failures of judgment. However, it is important to note that boards of directors are not immune to these biases.

In addition to the cognitive biases that managers face, boards also suffer from several other decision-making shortcomings. They often lack the expertise to question management, and when a director does have the expertise, he or she often feels like a lone wolf in questioning the direction posed by management. Furthermore, board members lack the time and information resources to collect evidence that would counter that presented by management. As a result, it is extremely difficult for board members to counter errors of judgment by management.

Pound offers five recommendations: 1) Board members must be expert; 2) Board meeting procedures should focus on debating new decisions, strategies, and policies, not just on reviewing past performance; 3) Directors need better access to information; 4) Directors should be required to devote a substantial portion of their professional time to the corporation; and 5) Board members must have the right incentives.

Ensuring strong corporate governance is essential to restoring confidence and trust in a capitalist system. "Trust reduces monitoring and transaction costs in companies and in the wider economy. At the most basic level . . . ethics are a low-cost substitute for internal control and external regulation."[12] Furthermore, evidence shows that the best companies worry about governance and integrity. In a *Financial Times* survey, the top 20 most respected companies (global operators with distinctive brands, strong leadership internally and in the market place, long-term track record of growth, financial performance, and delivering shareholder value) were also the top 20 demonstrating the most integrity.[13] In addition, "a study of 725 U.S. large capitalization domestic equity funds found that portfolios heavily weighted in companies with above-average corporate governance scores reported better performance over three and five year periods."[14]

There has been a wave of reform in corporate governance since Enron. A major study undertaken in 2002 revealed significant reforms in the boardrooms of Canada's public companies including an increase in corporate governance committees, formal systems for director recruitment, voluntary publication of corporate governance issues including how much a company's auditors are paid for non-audit work, the number of board meetings held, and the attendance records of directors. The study also found increasing independence of key board committees (e.g. no management on the audit committee), but a surprising decline in overall board independence. This may be due to a tighter definition of independence.[15]

The foregoing has focused on the tension in balancing interests of customers, employees, and shareholders. In a general sense, we can extend the list to include suppliers and other partners associated with the business. However, there is considerable pressure to expand the domain of stakeholders to include society at large. To understand this perspective we examine corporate social responsibility (CSR).

Corporate Social Responsibility

Carroll suggests that the socially responsible firm should "strive to make a profit, obey the law, be ethical and be a good corporate citizen."[16] However, he does not indicate how the firm balances these competing demands. Although the answer has proved elusive, the attempts to address the issue are enlightening.

Margolis and Walsh articulate the challenge clearly:

> The repeated calls for corporate action to ameliorate social ills reflect an underlying tension. On the one hand, misery loves companies. The sheer magnitude of problems, from malnutrition and HIV to illiteracy and homelessness, inspires a turn toward all available sources of aid, most notably corporations. Especially when those problems are juxtaposed to the wealth-creation capabilities of firms—or to the ills that firms may have helped to create—firms become an understandable target of appeal. On the other hand, a sturdy and persistent theoretical argument in economics suggests that such corporate involvement is misguided.[17]

The economic argument against CSR is that social welfare is maximized when firms are guided by the single objective function of wealth creation. Friedman argued that the social responsibility of business is to increase profits.[18] Social responsibility and the goodwill it may generate is justified if it is a by-product of expenditures that further a firm's own self-interests.

Proponents of CSR suggest that the firm serves more than its shareholders, customers, and employees; it serves society at large. Furthermore, many have argued that it is in the best interest of the company to be socially responsible, as doing so enhances financial performance. In reviewing the extensive literature reporting on the relationship between corporate social performance and corporate financial performance, Margolis and Walsh found that the 127 studies provide a clear indication of the positive association between a company's social performance and its financial performance and very little evidence of a negative association. However, they express serious reservations about interpreting those findings given the vast differences in how the studies were constructed and executed. They conclude that the studies raise more questions than they answer.

Margolis and Walsh point to three economic arguments against CSR. The first concern is "misappropriation" of the assets: using them for purposes other than which investors had intended. The second is "misallocation": the inefficient use of resources when employed for other purposes. The final concern is one of "due process": ensuring the firm is transparent and accountable in its actions. However, they also point to three counter-arguments. In many cases firms have a "duty to respond" if they have, in some manner, contributed to the condition that calls for a response. This is often the case with environmental impact. Even if the firm has not contributed, if the "company benefits" from a harmful or unjust situation, such as is the case with cheap labour in low-wage countries, it has a duty to compensate for the benefit received. The final argument is a "duty of benevolence," which many fear has no limit to its attainment.

In summary, when the economic and social objectives intersect, there is no conflict. However, the situation becomes murky when the objectives deviate. The foregoing has suggested that there are situations when the firm may have an obligation and duty to respond. A first step in understanding whether the objectives intersect is to conduct a stakeholder analysis to determine the cost and benefits of various strategic options. We view stakeholder analysis as a central aspect of strategic choice. As the boundaries of the firm become less distinguishable, and alliances and partnerships more commonplace, it is critical to consider stakeholder interests. Although there are many and varied stakeholders including employees, managers, shareholders, lenders, customers, suppliers, and the government, managers are the primary means through which the broader set of stakeholder preferences are understood. In particular, management is a key stakeholder that influences both choice and execution of strategy. In entrepreneurial firms where the owners and managers are the same, what management wants to do may in fact be the driving force behind strategic choice. Even in cases where ownership and management do not coincide, failing to gain management buy-in to strategic choices will likely lead to poor execution. We are not suggesting that what managers want to do should govern strategic choices. We are suggesting it is a major element that needs to be analyzed and managed.

MANAGEMENT AS A KEY STAKEHOLDER

In this section we hone in on management as a key stakeholder group. Given its role in both the formulation and execution of strategy, management is a critical stakeholder group. We will outline how to ensure that the skills and the energy of management are matched with attractive strategies for their businesses. Typically, there are two sources of conflict or inconsistency—inconsistency between the proposed and preferred strategy, and inconsistency between the preferred strategy and other realities. We consider each in turn.

Inconsistency Between Proposed and Preferred Strategy

The first type of conflict occurs when a strategic proposal is inconsistent with the preferences of one or more of the influential managers in your business. We described this situation in our discussion of the Diamond-E analysis in Chapter 3.

Every strategic proposal implies a set of strategic preferences, which may or may not conform with the personal preferences of managers in the firm. These conflicts need to be identified and corrected or the pursuit of the strategy could be hamstrung by management indifference or outright opposition.

Sometimes you can resolve these conflicts by modifying the strategic proposal, but this tactic is limited by the need for the proposal to remain consistent with the other elements of the Diamond-E. More often than not you will need to work with the managers involved to bring their preferences into line with the strategic requirements. Persuasion and training may suffice for relatively simple problems, but more significant system and structural changes will be needed in more difficult situations. As a last resort, you may have to replace the managers.

As the severity of the actions escalate, so, too, do the demands on you and on the underlying organizational capabilities in the business. These requirements need to be considered as part of a subsequent organization analysis before the matter can be closed and a final decision made on the strategic proposal under study.

Inconsistency Between Preferred Strategy and Other Realities

Another and more complex conflict occurs when management preferences are actually consistent with a strategic proposal, but the proposal itself is inconsistent with external forces or business capabilities. There are two quite different manifestations of this problem. In the first, some managers become committed to a new strategic proposal that is otherwise inconsistent with business conditions. In the second, some managers want to persevere with a strategy that is becoming obsolete in the face of changing conditions. In these cases the preference-strategy linkage is strong, but the strategy will not work. Any suggestions for change come into conflict with the preferences and momentum of some influential people. This takes you back to the beginning and puts you into the situation of dealing with preferences that conflict with otherwise sensible strategic ideas.

A serious difficulty arises when you (or other "objective" analysts) identify either of the conflicts noted above, but find yourself in a weak position to influence the other managers. The result, all too often, is another opportunity lost, or of a business driven into crisis because management preferences were frozen on inappropriate strategies. In the following sections we take a closer look at the role and the roots of strategic preferences. We then elaborate on the analytic and action steps required to focus, first, on conflicts associated with individual managers, and then on the difficulties created by different preferences within a single management group. Finally, we discuss the utility of the concept of management preferences in analyzing competitive behaviour.

THE ROLE OF MANAGEMENT PREFERENCES

You and your management colleagues drive strategy. Your analytic work shapes the strategic direction of your businesses and your actions put it into place. In this, your personal preferences—what you want the business to accomplish and how you think this should be done—play an inevitable and critical role. To suggest that managers should operate (or do operate) according to some impersonal dictate is a convenient simplification in some of the more abstract work on business strategy, but it flies in the face of reality. This reality, as Andrews puts it, is that "there is no way to divorce the decision determining the most sensible economic strategy for a company from the personal values of those who make the choice."[19]

Consider the role of management preferences as they have influenced the fortunes of Magna International Inc., the auto parts manufacturer whose revenues exceeded $24 billion in 2006. Magna's founder, Frank Stronach, was a classic entrepreneur with a strong appetite for growth, a willingness to take risks, and an unshakable confidence in his demonstrably impressive business skills. Stronach had built Magna into a strong and growing auto parts supplier by the mid-1980s when his eye started to wander. He took Magna into restaurant, publishing, and real estate ventures, went heavily into debt to fund the core business, and entered politics as a candidate for member of parliament. When an industry downturn struck in 1990, Magna was hit hard and its shares fell from over $20 to $2. While Stronach disagrees with criticisms that the side ventures were of any significance,[20] Magna quickly reverted to its base business. Magna rebounded and grew rapidly in the 1990s, focusing on auto parts and exploiting a clever combination of internal development and acquisitions. By the fall of 1997, Magna's shares were trading at over $100. Shortly afterward, they fell $20 on news that Stronach was planning to take the company into eight non-automotive ventures including an $800 million theme park near Vienna, an executive airline, and real estate development.[21] Investors were only partly reassured when Stronach wrote a special letter to shareholders vowing that the focus of the company would be on auto parts (and in this respect his personal vision for the company was to more than triple revenues to $30 billion), and further, that unrelated ventures would be held separate in a venture capital division.[22] While the Magna board approved the establishment of a new company "Ventures" to hold its non-automotive assets, Magna's share price started to slide on the announcement in early March 1999. Analysts suggested that the spin-off plan "failed to ease concerns about the company diverting assets from its auto parts business into other ventures such as race tracks, theme parks and airlines. In other words, many shareholders do not believe company founder Frank Stronach has finished investing in projects they dub too risky and not necessary for Magna to stay profitable."[23] Stronach's most recent foray under Magna Entertainment Inc. (controlled by Magna) is to become the world's biggest horse betting operation, with a longer-term vision to become the world's largest lottery corporation.

Management preferences clearly cut two ways. On the positive side, preferences serve to focus and motivate the efforts of the firm. The realities of the external environment and of internal circumstances seldom determine a single feasible course of action. Rather, they present a set of opportunities and constraints from which can develop a variety of feasible strategic options. Within these boundaries there is a need for a driving force to take hold of the situation and press for choices and performance.

On the negative side, management preferences may lead to pressures for inappropriate ventures, potential inflexibility, a focus on personal versus shareholder interests, and so on. In extreme cases, these circumstances may put you and your business at risk.

THE ROOTS OF STRATEGIC PREFERENCE

Strategic preferences of managers have their roots in the personal attributes of managers and in their job contexts. Personal attributes generate tendencies towards certain types of action; the job context adds a web of behavioural incentives and constraints. Together, these characteristics influence how managers perceive business situations, explore strategic possibilities, and evaluate options. The result for any specific manager is a set of strategic preferences regarding the nature and aggressiveness of the goals for the business, the product markets in which it should operate, the value proposition it should put forward, and the core activities of its operations. In the following paragraphs we will discuss how the basic needs, beliefs, and job contexts of managers shape their strategic preferences.

Basic Needs

Basic needs refer to central aspects of a manager's personality. They include the need for achievement, power, security, and recognition. These needs operate as fundamental influences on strategic preferences. Managers with a strong need for achievement or power will likely favour expansionary programs and accept the risks they may imply. Managers with a strong need for security and order will favour more cautious and methodical strategic development.

A manager's basic needs are fairly stable and enduring, and support a consistent approach to strategic decisions. This consistency can be valuable, but it can also pose problems if managers persist in the face of conflict between their preferences and other strategic determinants. It is not likely that basic needs can be materially changed. Your only practical options in these circumstances may be changing the nature of the job or changing the manager on the job.

Prescriptions like this may sound more severe than they are. Moving managers to improve the match between personal needs and strategic requirements may be practical for both the managers and the business. There is little point in shouldering aggressive

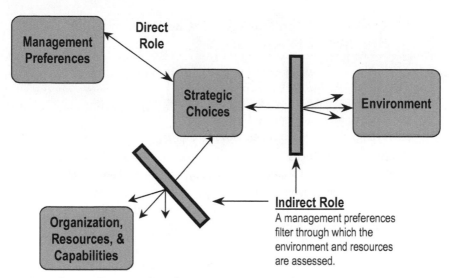

Figure 7.1 The Indirect Role of Management Preferences

and risk-oriented managers with the task of maintaining a mature, stable business, or asking careful and methodical managers to lead a risky project. As Harry Levinson points out: "It's like trying to put your best guard into a quarterback's slot—it just can't work."[24]

It is important to note that management preferences not only shape strategic choices, but they also act as a filter through which management interprets the other two components of the strategic analysis triangle: what they need to do, and what they can do. This dual role is illustrated in Figure 7.1.

Beliefs

Over the years, managers build up beliefs about their own competences, about the capabilities of their colleagues, and about the right way to handle strategic issues. These beliefs are not independent of personality; neither are they direct extensions of it. Accordingly, the degree to which managers are attached to their beliefs may vary from deep and emotional conviction to rather casual endorsement, and the degree to which you can influence and change their beliefs will range from extreme difficulty to relative ease, a factor which can be important when we come to questions of modifying strategic preferences.

Beliefs direct management preferences towards particular strategic initiatives and responses. The strategic direction given to a firm will be heavily influenced by the fields in which top management feels competent and comfortable. Consider, for example, the claim of Hayes and Abernathy that the wheeling and dealing in acquisitions and mergers that preoccupy top managers in some companies can be related to their legal and financial backgrounds. They are doing what they think is important and what they feel competent

Table 7.1 Examples of Top Management Beliefs Regarding Strategy

Goals

We must grow in volume and ROI.

We must maintain a conservative financial structure.

We must be measured against the best.

Stable employment is a basic employee right.

Product Market Focus

Don't diversify except where our technology can be applied.

We must not be dependent on one single product line.

We can't run a lot of businesses we don't know anything about.

We can manage a range of industries.

Value Proposition

Market share comes through technically superior products.

It is important to have a known brand name.

Quality of our product is our number one concern.

We must compete on innovation in processes and basic products, not price.

Core Activities

We must be a leader in manufacturing to keep costs down and quality up.

We need to control every input to our product.

Our abilities in marketing will make the difference in the future.

We are prepared to pay a price to remain flexible.

to do, often at the expense, the authors contend, of the more fundamental development of their companies.[25]

Table 7.1 demonstrates how some common managerial beliefs fit into our strategy format. It is pretty clear that beliefs like these, held by powerful managers, would significantly influence the development of strategy.

Job Context

Job assignments define the scope and nature of a manager's responsibilities, the manner in which performance will be measured and assessed, and the principles on which rewards are allocated. Further, each job is set within a context of formal and informal relationships, and of expectations from bosses, peers, and subordinates. The job context also determines the type of stakeholders the manager will encounter. Managers in sales are likely to learn more about the customer, while managers in finance are likely to be more familiar with lenders or analysts. As well, the pressures of the job context may help explain a condition we call frozen preference, in which a manager, having openly endorsed a strategic option, will find it difficult or virtually impossible to change.

Job Definition The status and responsibilities of their jobs affect the way managers look at strategic issues. In the Magna case just cited, for example, Frank Stronach was clearly in favour of moving the company into very significant non-automotive ventures. He planned to put his European finance director, Robert Gruber, in charge of the projects. But Gruber disagreed with the non-automotive thrust and with the supposed potential of the new projects. He resigned rather than take on the responsibility for them.[26] These were clear-cut differences of opinion, generated in part by the different needs and beliefs of the two managers, and in part by the job perspectives from which they viewed the situation.

Most strategic proposals will have different consequences for managers in different job positions. Strategic changes usually create winners and losers. For example, a shift from an emphasis on differentiation to a reliance on low relative price will change the budgets and status of several functional positions. It is only reasonable, then, for you to expect that job-related filters and biases will be imposed on strategic assessments. It is simple realities like this that help to explain why firms tend to like growth strategies and dislike retrenchment—the former offer the best prospects of making the most managers into winners.

The manner in which job responsibilities are specified and performance is measured and rewarded will also influence strategic preferences. A manager who is charged with producing maximum short-term profit from a business, and whose performance is measured and rewarded accordingly, will understandably emphasize short-term tactics. Alternatively, a manager with a compensation package that depends on growth can be expected to press for volume building and investment initiatives. It follows that the design and specification of job responsibilities, measures, and rewards is a major tool that you can use for shaping and changing strategic preferences.

Job Relations The expectations of bosses, peers, and subordinates may be less visible than formal job characteristics, but they are no less forceful. The expectations conveyed in subtle and not so subtle ways from board to chief executive, from chief executive to president, and from president to general or functional managers will have a significant effect on a manager's approach to strategic questions. A particular attitude to risk might be conveyed in a business, for example, that cues a manager to the kind of projects that will likely be given support and those that might be rejected out of hand.

Most managers need the cooperation and support of their colleagues to execute their programs. But they also compete with these same colleagues for status, resources, and jobs. As a consequence, managers tend to assess strategic initiatives with an eye to their impact on the balance of relationships and status among their peers.

The reliance of managers on their subordinates can also influence their strategic preferences. Subordinates have expectations of what their boss should provide: security, opportunity, and an interesting job, for example. To ensure employee cooperation, you have to respond in some degree to these expectations and include them among the now complex balances that influence strategic direction.

Frozen Preference

For an organization to function effectively, superiors, peers, and subordinates alike must be able to count on a manager's reliability and determination. If a manager changes positions after taking an open and firm stance on a strategic issue, except in the case of quite overwhelming evidence, he or she may be seen as poorly prepared, weak, or lacking sufficient power and influence to prevail. Any of these factors will damage a manager's credibility.

As management preferences are expressed in budgets, personnel changes, and investments, the firm's commitment to a position increases and it becomes more and more difficult to change direction. Fresh analysis or evidence may indicate that the position is questionable, and that it should be abandoned, with accumulated expenditures simply regarded as "sunk cost." This, however, is not how accountants will report the situation, nor necessarily how the various parties to it will react. There may be strong pressures to continue and these pressures will feed on the normally ambiguous circumstances that a manager faces. Managers may find themselves facing a dilemma in which a change of position that makes sense in the abstract could result in substantial personal loss.

Watch for instances of creeping commitment and for circumstances in which frozen preferences are distorting strategic choices. If you can address the problems before people have made a large and visible investment in a position, you may be able to change the direction without great disruption. Otherwise, you may be forced to make changes through radical alteration of the job context or the reassignment of the managers involved.

Implications

Management preferences are formed by the interaction of needs, beliefs, and situational pressures. These preferences have meaningful implications for strategic choice, whether they operate for the betterment of the organization or to its detriment. They should not be treated as unchanging or unchangeable. If the core influences change (if, for example, experience brings about a change in the beliefs of a manager) or are changed (for instance, if a manager's compensation package is altered), then preferences can be expected to change as well.

Managers' preferences are specific to their individual personalities, experiences, and situations. Differences in these factors among managers will lead to differences in their strategic preferences, which adds an extra dimension to your analysis. You must identify differences in preferences among the key managers, assess the implications of the differences, and, where necessary, find grounds for their reconciliation.

MATCHING PREFERENCES AND STRATEGY

A particularly challenging aspect of management preference analysis is that the task often calls for managers to reflect on their *own* values and attitudes. As Guth and Tagiuri note: "Few of us make the effort of studying our own values to the point of being able to be explicit and articulate about them. The busy executive is no exception. . . . Many top-level managers do not have an explicit and useful way of thinking about personal values and about the influences these have on the strategic choice processes of the company. As a result, this important element is often left unexamined."[27]

In spite of the difficulties of candid introspection, good managers appreciate that personal preferences enter into strategic decisions. They try to capture the benefits of serving these preferences while avoiding distortions that may be created by them. They also appreciate that no amount of introspection, analysis, and advice will help managers who refuse to be flexible and who insist on imposing their fixed preferences on a situation.

For the moment we will deal with the consistency of the preferences of an individual manager with other strategic determinants. We will work through the analytic steps presented in Figure 7.2 from your perspective and from that of an external advisor. Later, we will discuss the complications created when there are different strategic preferences among the group of managers running a given business.

As in Chapter 6, there are two subsidiary formats that you will find helpful in working through the analytic process. The first format, presented in Table 7.2, focuses on the use

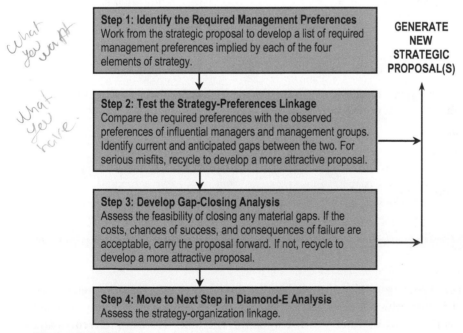

Figure 7.2 Management Preference Analysis

Table 7.2 Management Preference Analysis by Strategy Component

STRATEGIC PROPOSAL

Goals

What are the most critical goal preferences (e.g. for growth, risk, market dominance) required by the strategic proposal under consideration; what are the gaps between these requirements and observed preferences; and what are the risks and consequences of not being able to close these gaps in a timely way?

Product/Market Focus

What are the most critical product/market preferences (e.g. for a specific market focus, diversification) required by the strategic proposal under consideration; what are the gaps between these requirements and observed preferences; and what are the risks and consequences of not being able to close these gaps in a timely way?

Value Proposition

What are the most critical value proposition preferences (e.g. for price, features, execution) required by the strategic proposal under consideration; what are the gaps between these requirements and observed preferences; and what are the risks and consequences of not being able to close these gaps in a timely way?

Core Activities

What are the most critical value proposition preferences (e.g. for activities to internalize, degree of integration) required by the strategic proposal under consideration; what are the gaps between these requirements and observed preferences; and what are the risks and consequences of not being able to close these gaps in a timely way?

Table 7.3 Management Preference Analysis by Manager

Management Subject	Required Preferences	Observed Preferences	Major Gaps	Gap-Closing Analysis
Manager 1				
Manager 2				
Etc.				
Group 1				
Group 2				
Etc.				

of the proposed strategy to identify and describe the relevant management preferences. The second format, which is intended for concurrent use and ultimately as a summary document, is illustrated in Table 7.3. It emphasizes the links between preferences and specific managers or management groups.

STEP 1: IDENTIFY THE REQUIRED MANAGEMENT PREFERENCES

The logical flow for identifying the management preferences that count is from the proposed strategy to the required preferences. We use the term "required" to indicate the preferences that are implied by the stated strategy. That is, they are the preferences that would be required if the strategy were pursued. Work from your understanding of each element of the proposed strategy, as illustrated in Table 7.2. As you do this, try to focus your analysis or your list will rapidly become cluttered and unworkable. Concentrate on the strategic features that you know are (1) new and different, and (2) most likely to be controversial. Strategic proposals that are essentially extensions or variants on the current strategy are unlikely to generate serious conflicts with existing management preferences. But if your strategy calls for new ways of thinking and behaving in the management team and/or changes of management status and power, it is likely to run into some very definite preference issues. The new and contentious elements have to be carefully mapped into new required preferences. Clearly, the greater the skill with which you can pin down the sensitive areas of strategy and preference, the faster you will get to the preference gaps that really matter.

A second approach for isolating important preference dimensions is to work from your knowledge of the managers that will be involved in the execution of the strategy. Start by listing these individuals or groups as suggested by the Table 7.3 format. Then you can work from the demands of the strategy as it affects these particular managers and your knowledge of the managers to isolate the elements of management preference that are going to be of greatest importance. To some degree this overlaps the gap analysis to follow, though this is not an issue since we are not trying to draw lines between the suggested phases of analysis.

STEP 2: TEST THE STRATEGY-PREFERENCES LINKAGE

Your aim in this step of preference analysis is to identify the important gaps between the required and observed preferences. If your Step 1 work has been effective this will be a relatively straightforward task. We return now to the sample case of Jantzen Technologies, which we introduced in Chapter 5.

Harry Jantzen, the company founder, built a successful business by focusing on a narrow product range and pursuing continuous product innovation through close technical relationships with selected customers. The company has grown to the point where it has a global production base, but future growth and profitability are threatened by a maturing technical and market environment. Nothing is ever a given, but the Jantzen situation seems to call for major strategic changes. In particular, Jantzen must consider (1) broadening its market, in terms of the number and type of customers, and broadening its contacts within these customer organizations to encompass purchasing and manufacturing personnel; (2) improving its capacity to compete on price through design, purchasing, and manufacturing development and rationalization; and (3) reducing its insistence on total integration to take advantage of technical and cost innovation among sub-component manufacturers and distributors.

There are some far-reaching implications in these strategic proposals for the leadership role of Harry Jantzen. He must be, and be seen to be, enthusiastic about a new and very commercial approach to the market and to operations, under which customers are selected, products are designed, and manufacturing is driven on the basis of market and profit potential. These requirements are at odds with Harry Jantzen's experience and with his beliefs about how to run a business. He would much prefer the technology-driven success formula of the past. The obvious, but vital, question for the business is whether Jantzen is now prepared to change his thinking and to significantly reorient his efforts and those of the business.

As the areas of congruence and conflict between required and observed preferences are identified, you can start to consider the action that will be necessary to deal with the situation. In the case of gaps that you think will be irreconcilable, there is no option but to recycle and start to work on new proposals. This will not be a happy decision and will certainly be a last resort since the proposal that you have in hand looks attractive from the point of view of your environmental and resource analysis. In the more likely circumstance of significant but potentially workable preference gaps, you need to carry on to consider the feasibility of steps to bring about consistency.

STEP 3: DEVELOP GAP-CLOSING ANALYSIS

In this section we will deal first with the relatively straightforward, but by no means simple, process of gap-closing analysis with respect to an individual manager. Then we will proceed to the more complex issues involving groups of managers.

Framing the Gap-Closing Issues— Individual Managers

In the paragraphs below we classify potential conflicts by order of severity and discuss the diagnostic implications that arise from them.

Minimal Conflict This is a fortunate situation in which there appears to be only minor discrepancies between required and observed preferences of the manager in question. Even so, these differences should be carefully considered. One tool that you might use in this respect is to forecast the firm's performance assuming that the observed differences persist. Will the performance of the business under the strategic proposal be affected by the conflicts observed? This is the ultimate test of how seriously the conflicts should be taken and the lengths to which you should go in addressing them.

Moderate Conflict In this situation there are significant conflicts between required and observed preferences, but it seems, at least on first analysis, that they can be reconciled with something short of radical action. When you run into such conflicts it is useful to stand back and reassess the situation. Can you influence the manager's preferences to reduce the conflict to workable levels? Is it possible, for example, to modify the manager's preferences by exposure to the facts, reasoning, advocacy, or simple changes in job context? Are there nuances in the strategy itself that can be reworked to make it more acceptable, yet still consistent with your earlier environmental and resource considerations? Try working closely with the manager involved to craft a sensible compromise solution to the original conflicts. If this approach does not succeed, you will have to deal with the problem as a serious conflict that calls for more aggressive action.

Serious Conflict A serious conflict exists when it is impossible to find a moderate and workable accommodation of preferences and strategy. Persuasion, reason, better information, and modest changes in job context have not worked. One possible remedy in such a situation is to completely rethink and change the strategic proposal. However, the new proposal will have to be compatible with environment and resource considerations, and, not incidentally, the preferences of other influential managers. Other remedies lie in making major organizational changes, up to and including the reassignment of the manager involved.

These circumstances confront you with a potentially difficult situation. The manager in question may choose to fight the strategic proposal, particularly if he or she is in a position of power, on the grounds that the proposal is bad for the company. Strategic situations are often ambiguous enough that strong individuals may be able to colour the circumstances with their own biases. It is not too hard to imagine Harry Jantzen, for example, fighting the evidence of a changing market and arguing for an interpretation of the environmental conditions that support the strategic responses that he would like.

Another option for the manager experiencing such conflicts is to go along with the strategy and live with the discrepancy between it and his or her own convictions. Of course, that manager will probably not perform well over time with such suppressed inconsistencies. Your best options will probably boil down to organizational changes including the reassignment of the objecting manager. This move, while possibly painful in the short run, is probably best, both for the individual involved and for business performance.

The whole situation becomes much more problematic, however, if you report to or are otherwise dependent on the problem manager. Being forthright may be desirable, but it may also mean the end of your career! Remaining silent about the conflicts that you have identified or, worse, rationalizing your perception of the realities to fit the preferences might offer short-term relief, but will undoubtedly be counterproductive in the long run. In these situations, senior managers get the kind of advice they deserve. If their leadership style and management systems support candour, it will be relatively easy for you, as a subordinate, to discharge at least your minimum responsibility—which is to make it clear that the manager's strategic preferences are out of line with the strategic realities. If managers are repressive, it is unlikely that you will tell them the whole truth, unless you are a truly independent person, and even then it is unlikely that the message will be heard.

Gap-Closing Actions and Risks— Individual Managers

Many of the actions that you will want to take to resolve the conflicts of required and observed management preferences will involve organizational change. From the broad perspective of organization theory, the underlying problem is one of aligning business goals (strategy) and individual goals (preferences). Discrepancies between required and observed preferences affect the organizational abilities of the business—the collective ability of the people involved to carry out the required tasks. When you move on to the organization part of the Diamond-E analysis, you will need to ask whether the required abilities exist or can be developed in the time available. For now you need to set up that analysis by pinning down the capabilities that will be required to implement the actions. Using your experience with the Diamond-E framework and organization change from prior strategic analyses, you need to reject and/or recycle proposals that are simply too risky.

In the case of Harry Jantzen, the first step would be to provide him with a convincing picture of what is happening in his component system market and what the consequences will be for growth and profitability. You have some data and some serious concerns based on a very broadly based size-up of the situation, but it is unlikely that arguments at this level of abstraction will sway Harry Jantzen; you need tight and unequivocal evidence. This calls for an organizational capability to acquire and process the required information, which might look simple at first glance, but actually will be quite difficult to do. Why? Because the Jantzen organization has never really done this before—they have only looked at very narrow slices of information such as that gathered by their technical salesmen talking to their customers' engineering groups.

Suppose, further, that the new information strongly supports the case for change, but Harry Jantzen remains unconvinced. His preferences are frozen on the traditional formula for success and in various ways he indicates that he is not prepared to change his views. Now the conflict escalates to critical proportions. Should Jantzen step aside? If so, does the organizational capability exist to carry out such a difficult task? At a minimum, the board must believe that this is a necessary step and there must be a successor ready to move in and make the desired changes. (In reality such a step was not necessary.) Whether this capability is present or can be developed is, again, a question for subsequent organization analysis.

As you settle the list of the organizational capabilities required to address the fit of preferences and strategy, the analysis can move on to the subject of Chapter 8—do you have, or can you develop, the capabilities required to proceed with the strategy? Before we take this step, however, it is useful to review the common and complex challenges of bringing the preferences of a diverse group of managers into line with one strategy.

Framing the Gap-Closing Issues— Groups of Managers

You should not be surprised to find differences among the strategic preferences of the various managers of a firm. Each of these managers, after all, will be working from a somewhat different personal background and job context. As a matter of fact, you should expect that marketing and operations managers, for example, will read the facts of a situation differently, see different options for action, and weigh consequences unevenly. This is one of the prime arguments for articulating a strategy in the first place—to provide a unifying theme that will help to bring these different strategic preferences together, and establish a common basis for management action. But a good strategic process alone may not be enough to achieve and sustain a workable consistency of preference in a diverse management group.

It follows that you should identify the strategic preferences of the key management groups in a business and determine how consistent these preferences are with those required by the strategic proposal under consideration. This is anticipated in Table 7.3, which calls for analysis by management group. Again, the art of the analysis is to be carefully selective in choosing which particular groups and preference issues to study.

You will probably encounter some obstacles in the process of identifying the real preferences of diverse groups of managers. Some will be in subordinate and perhaps vulnerable positions and reluctant to openly express their views. In firms that have learned how to support an open expression of opinions and to avoid the difficulties of frozen preferences, this obstacle will not be a serious problem. Preferences may be carefully and even ambiguously posed, but they will be genuine. In relatively unhealthy firms, you may find that managers and groups operate more or less continuously with hidden agendas. Even senior and experienced people may be less than candid. In unhealthy businesses it is often difficult to tell what a manager's real position and preferences are, even when he or she openly supports a strategic initiative. The great fear is that the manager will nod yes, and then walk away and do nothing to help implement the strategy.

In our discussion we will assume that you are dealing with a management system that is healthy enough for the essential preferences of the managers to be identified, even if this takes careful diagnostic work. If a firm is so politicized that it is impossible to develop a reasonably valid impression of management preferences, the problem is so fundamental that it raises the question of the viability of the business, which is beyond our immediate scope.

The following paragraphs discuss the conflicts that might arise from differences within a management group in three increasingly difficult categories.

Minimal Conflict This is a situation that emerges when there are minimal differences among the strategic preferences of the key managers and groups in a business. Such a commonality of preference is an important feature of companies that have had strong leaders for some time, or that have otherwise built up clear traditions and culture. In these companies, the managers that succeed over time are those who conform to the dominant ethos.

Homogeneity across a management group can be a mixed blessing, however. It can be a powerful asset *if* the preferences line up with the strategic proposal under consideration. Minor conflicts can probably be ironed out easily, because the group is used to the give and take of working together. However, if these preferences are inconsistent with strategic needs, you now face the problems of what Irving Janis calls "groupthink," in which the concurrence of a cohesive group overrides a realistic appraisal of new realities.[28]

Moderate Conflict At this level it is often possible to bring diverse preferences into line with strategy by further documentation, persuasion, changes in the stakes for particular individuals, or changes in management assignments. A very important reason for having a strategic planning process in a business (and for having the process driven by line managers) is to work out preference conflicts as they happen. Even if a conflict still exists at the end of the process, the managers with problems will fully understand why the proposed course is deemed necessary, and may be more flexible in adapting to it.

It is difficult to resolve conflicts between strategic requirements and the preferences of a group of managers by modifying strategy; the most likely route to reconciliation is through organizational action. From a diagnostic standpoint this means, first, identifying the actions that are likely to bring preferences into alignment and second, identifying the organizational capabilities that will be required for implementation of the action.

Consider the task of bringing together differences of preference across business functions. It is commonplace for R&D, operations, and marketing managers to take a different view of strategic problems and of proposed solutions. Depending on the depth of the differences and the flexibility of the people involved, reaching a reasonable consensus may require, for example, providing better information about the market, changing incentives to emphasize joint performance, or, at the opposite extreme, restructuring to manage with smaller and more identifiably responsible leaders and teams. Each step of action across this spectrum puts increasing demands on the organization's ability to deliver and takes you further into the issue of whether those capabilities are in place or whether they can be developed.

There is also a catch in the process of using organizational action to address preference discrepancies. The current organization of a business is in many ways the creation of the managers you are dealing with and it reflects their preferences for how the business should be run. The execution of a new direction involves a capability on the part of the people in the organization to address and change those organizational preferences as well as the targeted strategic preferences. This is no small task. We shall return to it in our discussion of strategic change in later chapters.

Serious Conflict If managers are at such great odds with each other that there is no reasonable strategy that they can commonly endorse, you may be watching the total disintegration of an organization. The causes for the difficulties probably go far beyond the individual preferences of one manager or another. The management team may have tried in the past to paper over their differences, but the conflicts have kept re-emerging. The situation calls for a comprehensive review of the whole business and for action, as necessary, across an equally broad front.

MANAGEMENT PREFERENCES AND COMPETITIVE ANALYSIS

A corollary of the principle that strategy must relate to management preferences is that a competitor's strategy will also reflect its management's preferences. Analyzing the character, habits, ways of thinking, and stakes of a competitor's management team can help to predict the strategy that a competitor will employ and the conviction with which it will be pursued.

It is clearly important to understand the predispositions of the key managers in competitive firms. To this end it is useful to record and study their strategic initiatives and responses in prior circumstances. Most managers have a limited strategic repertoire, particularly when they have been rewarded for what they have done before. In 1994 Wal-Mart entered the Canadian market. Its strategy was highly predictable—to repeat the formula employed so successfully in the United States. It was up to the incumbent Canadian retailers to decide how to respond. Most tried to "out Wal-Mart Wal-Mart." In short order the Woolco discount chain was out of business (sold to Wal-Mart) and so was the Kmart chain (bought by Zellers). The largest remaining competitor, Zellers, fought on under its slogan, "Because . . . the lowest price is the law." But Zellers' sales and profits continued to suffer and in 1998 it capitulated, dropping the slogan and announcing that henceforth it would "out-flank" Wal-Mart and compete with an emphasis on fashion and style.[29] What the incumbent retailers seemed to have missed in all of this was the focus, conviction, and force with which Wal-Mart would proceed—which was just as evident as its visible strategy if you studied its U.S. management.

It is often possible to anticipate how a competitive manager is inclined to act on the basis of past personal history. This analysis should be coupled with what can be deduced about his or her personal stakes in the current situation. Is the manager on a fast track, looking for quick results? Is she or he near retirement? Are any unusual pressures being exerted by board members, shareholders, or bankers? Long-standing competitors use this understanding to predict strategy down to the finest nuances. By tracking new management appointments, such as when a competitor hires a new marketing vice president with a reputation for building market share by cutting prices, you can develop a pretty good idea about what is going to happen next.

A competitor's activities in a specific product market will depend on the number and nature of the issues with which its management is contending, and on the priority it gives to the specific market in question. It is often useful to analyze the relationships among functional and/or product groups in a competitive firm and to predict the response of this system to emerging threats. To the degree that competitors are harnessed by frozen preferences, their actions are predictable, and advantages can be gained by avoiding their areas of priority. The big hope of many of the new internet-based businesses, for example, from automobiles to books to banks, is that they can get a head start and build a defensible position before the conventional competitors in their industries notice and react with force.

SUMMARY

The object of management preference analysis is to identify conflicts between the motivations of key managers and the strategies that are important to their businesses, and to point to the actions that are required to resolve them. Conflicts arise when managers oppose a strategic proposal that is otherwise very desirable for the business, or when they freeze on strategies that are inconsistent with business opportunities and constraints.

The resolution of these conflicts calls for a careful analysis of the roots and changeability of the preferences involved and for action that is tailored to this understanding. It is sometimes possible to find strategic modifications that will accommodate existing preferences, but more often it is necessary to take organizational action to achieve consistency. Such action might range from persuasion to changes in job context to reassignment.

The final stage of analysis is to assess the feasibility of achieving consistency between preferences and strategy. In some cases the costs will be too high or the chances of success too low and you will have to recycle to generate new strategic proposals. On closer calls you will have to make judgments about the capacity of the business to develop new organizational capabilities, the subject of the next chapter.

Notes

1. Andrews, Kenneth R. "Ethics in Practice." *Harvard Business Review* 67 (September–October 1989): 99–105. Print.

2. Pfeffer, Jeffrey. "Shareholders First? Not so Fast." *Harvard Business Review* 87.7/8 (2009): 90–91. Business Source Complete, *EBSCO*. Web. 15 Aug. 2011.

3. Mitchell, R. K., Agle, Bradley R., and Donna J. Wood. "Toward a Theory of Stakeholder Identification and Salience: Defining the Principle of Who and What Really Counts." *Academy of Management Review* 22 (1997): 853–886. Print.

4. *Business Corporation Act of Ontario* Service Ontario, 2011. Web. 29 Sept. 2011. <www.e-laws.gov.on.ca/html/statutes/english/elaws_statutes_90b16_e.htm>.

5. Charreaux, G., and P. Desbrières. "Corporate Governance: Stakeholder Value Versus Shareholder Value." *Journal of Management and Governance* 5 (2001): 108. Print.

6. "A Trying Year." *The Economist Global Agenda*, (January 9, 2004): 1. Print.

7. McLean, Bethany. "Is Enron Over-priced?" *Fortune* 143 (March 5, 2001): 122–126. Print.

8. McLean, Bethany. "Why Enron Went Bust." *Fortune* 144 (December 24, 2001): 58–65. Print.

9. Zimmerman, John W. "Is Your Company at Risk? Lessons from Enron." *USA Today* 131 (November 2002): 27–30. Print.

10. Pound, John. "The Promise of the Governed Corporation." *Harvard Business Review* 73 (March–April 1995): 89–98. Print.

11. Gandz, Jeffrey, Mary Crossan, Gerard Seijts, and Carol Stephenson. *Leadership on Trial: A Manifesto for Leadership Development*. London: Richard Ivey School of Business, 2010. Print.

12. *The Financial Times* December 2, 2002: 21. Print.

13. *The Financial Times* January 20, 2003: 8. Print.

14. *The Globe and Mail* [Toronto] January 13, 2004: B17. Print.

15. *The Globe and Mail* [Toronto] January 13, 2004: B1. Print.

16. Carroll, Archie B. "Corporate Social Responsibility: Evolution of a Definitional Construct." *Business & Society* 38 (September 1999): 268–295. Print.

17. Margolis, Joshua D., and James P. Walsh. "Misery Loves Companies: Rethinking Social Initiatives by Business." *Administrative Science Quarterly* 28 (2003): 268–305. Print.

18. Friedman, Milton. "The Social Responsibility of Business is to Increase its Profits." *The New York Times* [New York] September 13, 1970. Print.

19. Andrews, Kenneth R. *The Concept of Corporate Strategy*. Rev. ed. Homewood, Illinois: Richard D. Irwin, Inc., 1980. 74. Print.

20. *The Globe and Mail* [Toronto] January 23, 1998. Print.

21. *The Globe and Mail* [Toronto] April 8, 1998, B1. Print.

22. *The Globe and Mail* [Toronto] March 12, 1998: B1. Print.

23. *The National Post* [Toronto] March 12, 1999: D3. Print.

24. "Wanted: A Manager to Fit Each Strategy." *Business Week* (February 25, 1980): 166–173. Print.

25. Hayes, Robert H., and William J. Abernathy. "Managing Our Way to Economic Decline," *Harvard Business Review* 58 (July–August 1980): 67–77. Print.

26. *The Globe and Mail* [Toronto] January 27, 1998. Print.

27. Guth, William D., and Renato Tagiuri. "Personal Values and Corporate Strategy." *Harvard Business Review* (September–October 1965). Print.

28. Janis, Irving L. "Groupthink." *Psychology Today* (November 1971): 43–46, 74–76. Print.

29. *Globe and Mail* [Toronto] May 20, 1998. Print.

Chapter 8
Strategy and Organization

By this point you have developed one or more strategic proposals that look good. They make sense given what is happening in your firm's external environment, and while you would probably have some resource and preference gaps to fill in order to execute any of the proposals, none of the challenges seem overwhelming. Now you need to determine what organizational changes, if any, would be required to implement each proposal, and if such changes are feasible in the time you have available.

Although we have worked through a process that begins with defining strategy, and examining the environment and resources, this need not be the sequence. There are many people who advocate that having a nimble organization is the essence of strategy. It is the organization that we should place on a pinnacle, not the strategy. For example, Reeves and Deimler state that "Traditional approaches to strategy assume a relatively stable world. They aim to build an enduring competitive advantage by achieving dominant scale, occupying an attractive niche, or exploiting certain capabilities and resources. But globalization, new technologies, and greater transparency have combined to upend the business environment. Sustainable competitive advantage no longer arises from positioning or resources. Instead, it stems from the four organizational capabilities that foster rapid adaptation."[1] They point to the ability to read the environment, experiment rapidly, manage complex interconnected systems, and motivate employees and partners. Clearly flexibility and agility are important capabilities in dynamic environments, but this does not negate the need for a sound, albeit nimble, strategy and the identification of the associated capabilities beyond agility and flexibility.

As well, there are many people who view decisions concerning the organization as part of execution—strategy is formulated and then executed through the organization. While we view the literature on execution as informative for the organization-strategy connection in the Diamond-E Framework, we think it is a mistake to relegate organization considerations as something that occurs after the strategy is formulated. Our focus in this chapter is on what we call organizational capabilities. By this we mean what your people are collectively capable of doing when they work together. Being quick at something, like developing a new product and getting it to market, is an organizational capability and so is the ability to innovate. In the language of the Diamond-E model, the people in your organization are resources, but what they are capable of doing together is an organizational capability. A decision to hire five automotive design engineers, for example, is a resource decision. What they are actually capable of, once they are working for you, is the addition they make to your capabilities. One firm may get a lot more from five new engineers than another.

As shown in Figure 8.1, we will address four sets of questions in this chapter: (1) What organizational capabilities would you need in order to execute the strategic proposal that you are considering? (2) What are the gaps between these needed organizational capabilities and the capabilities that you currently have? (3) What changes would you need to make in organization structure, management processes, and leadership behaviour to develop the organizational capabilities that you would need to fill these gaps? and (4) Would these changes in fact lead to the development of the new capabilities in the time available?

Before turning to these questions, however, we will discuss further the notion of organizational capabilities, and the relationship between capabilities, the culture of your organization, and the behaviour of your employees. These relationships are by no means simple, and the judgments that you are ultimately going to make—about the ability of your firm to develop new capabilities based on new behaviour and a changed culture—are as difficult as any discussed in this book.

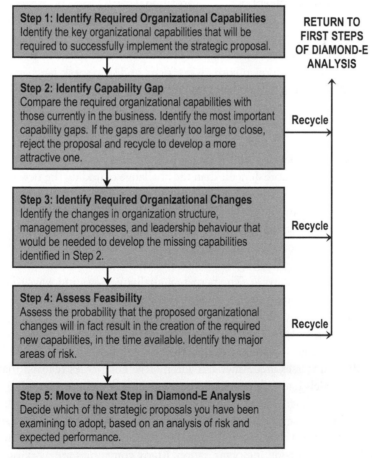

Figure 8.1 Strategy-Organization Analysis

ORGANIZATIONAL CAPABILITIES

New strategies usually require that new things be done well. You have already thought about the new resources that would be needed to support your strategic proposal, and the new preferences that would be required of senior management. But filling gaps in those two areas may not be enough. Your new resources, put into the hands of people who still act in the "same old way," may not be of much use. You might build a new factory, for example, but if the people in it do not understand that customer responsiveness is the key to your new value proposition, your strategy will never be properly executed.

Consider the case of Mattel Inc., the American toy company, when it sought to reduce its dependence on the U.S. market by doubling its international sales.[2] To do this, the company began to design and produce toys for individual foreign markets, rather than simply adapting U.S. products. The organization structure changed to give more prominence to international activities, and bonus incentives were tied to international growth targets.

Mattel's plan was ambitious, and definitely required new resources, new management preferences, and the development of new organizational capabilities. By way of example, let us focus on one aspect of the challenge facing Mattel: hiring non-American employees, and then learning to manage a more diverse, multicultural organization. In all likelihood, it would not be so difficult for Mattel to hire the needed new resources, in the form of people who understand foreign markets, foreign business practices, and who speak languages other than English. But Mattel's American employees would need to learn to work effectively with those of other nationalities, and vice versa. The company would also have to learn to create attractive international career paths and manage employees on foreign assignments. Developing the ability to work effectively across cultures usually takes some time. In this particular example we would judge that developing the new organizational capability (the ability to work across cultures) will prove more difficult than the challenge of finding the new resources.

There are, of course, many other types of organizational capabilities. In Chapter 1 we mentioned 3M's outstanding ability to innovate, a capability which has underpinned the company's strategy for the past 90 years. In other businesses the prized capability is to produce at the lowest cost. Aluminum companies, for example, routinely prepare and study histograms showing the relative cost positions of each of their smelters and those of competitors all over the world. The perpetual challenge is to find ways to move down the cost curve. Such an emphasis is common in industries in which the price of the end product is beyond the control of any individual player.

Another capability (see Table 8.1) that has gained prominence in recent years is speed. Firms have become aware of just how slow, in comparison to global industry leaders, some of their processes are. American automotive companies realized that the time to develop new models had to be cut by 50 percent. Jack Welch, former CEO of General Electric, proclaimed that "speed, simplicity, and self confidence"[3] were to become the hallmarks of GE businesses, and many other companies have tried to follow suit. Welch also highlighted "boundarylessness,"[4] meaning the ability to work effectively across boundaries inside and outside the organization. Many companies are working to develop this capability, but finding it difficult.

Table 8.1 Examples of Organizational Capabilities

Innovation

The capacity to stimulate and support strategies based on new ideas. Perhaps the creation of new markets, new products, new processes.

Prominent example: W.L. Gore.

Productivity

The capacity to stimulate and support strategies based on cost efficiency and price.

Prominent example: Wal-Mart.

Speed

The capacity to stimulate and support strategies based on speed. Perhaps to be first to market with new products, first to develop new technologies, first to gain government approvals, or to offer fast response to customer needs.

Prominent example: FedEx.

Cross-Cultural Effectiveness

The capacity to stimulate and support strategies based on unusually effective cooperation between employees of different cultures. The ability to gain a competitive edge by taking advantage of cultural diversity within the firm.

Prominent example: Nestlé.

Cross-Unit Synergies

The capacity to stimulate and support strategies that require seamless cooperation and support between different units within the company. Perhaps cooperation between business units, functional units, geographic regions.

Prominent example: Disney.

Capabilities such as those shown in Table 8.1 do not exist in isolation in an organization. They are based on the behaviour of your employees, which is in turn influenced and supported by the culture of the organization. We have illustrated these relationships in Figure 8.2. In this diagram, which is the basis for much of this chapter, we have also included three organizational leverage points that both support your existing culture, behaviour, and capabilities and act as your potential levers for change. As we shall discuss later, if you want to develop new capabilities you will need to change the behaviour and culture of your organization. These three leverage points are the means you have to make changes.

It is important to note that there are many organizational frameworks you could adopt. For example, Galbraith's "Star Model" depicts a five-point star with strategy at the top, connected to people, structure, rewards, and processes.[5] Many of these models take a very micro view of organizational processes, right down to the task level, and are particularly valuable in helping you understand the connectivity between these micro-processes. Our intent is to take a more macro view by focusing on structure, management processes

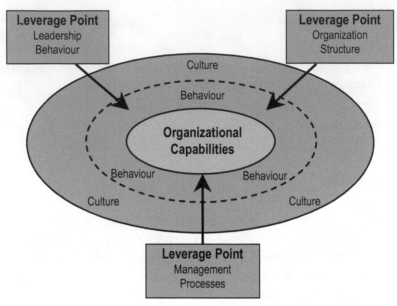

Figure 8.2 Organizational Capabilities Model

and leadership as three leverage points that affect culture, behaviour, and ultimately organizational capabilities.

Later in the chapter we will ask you to identify the changes in behaviour and culture that you would need to bring about in order to develop new organizational capabilities in your business. To help visualize such relationships, we have provided some examples in Table 8.2.

Table 8.2 Organizational Capability, Behaviour, and Culture

Organizational Capability	Related Behaviour	Supporting Cultural Belief
• The ability to be more often right than wrong with major capital investments	• Thorough data collection, thorough analysis	• We would rather be right than quick
• Quick and appropriate response to customer requests	• Decision making close to the customer	• We believe in delegation of responsibility and authority
• The ability to be a low cost producer	• Focusing on activities that add financial value	• Everything comes down to money
• Ability to innovate	• Financial and moral support for fledgling projects	• New product ideas are precious

Further examples are provided in the following sections in which we take a closer look at behaviour and culture.

BEHAVIOUR

When we speak of behaviour, we are talking of readily observable behaviour, not aspects of people's actions that one would need to be a trained psychologist to notice. When managers refer to the behaviour of others in their firm, they are generally thinking of how much energy they put into various aspects of their job, how they manage their subordinates, how much attention they give to external issues, how they relate to one another, and so on. One senior manager discussing the behaviour of executives who reported to him stated the following:

> All of my managers are pressed for time. Everyone has more things on their 'to do' list than they can possibly get around to doing. So for me the essence of behaviour is not about what time people get to work or how they dress, it is about what items come to the top of the priority list. Given all of the things that a manager could choose to spend his or her time on, which will they actually choose? If I am going to bring about change here, I have to begin by changing the things that come to the top of people's priority lists.

Clearly, the priorities of senior managers are an important element of behaviour, but you will have to cast a wider net to capture all of the key behaviour changes that would be necessary to develop a new organizational capability. A group of senior managers in a global chemical company, for example, wanted to develop new capabilities to support a move from commodity to specialty chemicals, and they went to some lengths to describe the behavioural changes that would be required. The four capabilities they were seeking were (1) the ability to recognize and assess changes in the external environment in a more timely fashion; (2) the ability to make better strategic choices—particularly a willingness to say no to more projects; (3) the ability to meet quality and delivery promises made to customers; and (4) an enhanced ability to understand where they were, and were not, performing well. The behaviours required to support these capabilities are listed in Table 8.3, alongside descriptions of current behaviour. Collectively they referred to the process of developing the new behaviours and capabilities as "getting more market focused."

The change in behaviour that these managers wanted to achieve in their company was going to be difficult, and they knew it. The problem, as one of them expressed, was that:

> We have a strong culture, which has resulted from our successful history, and it supports the current behaviour. We knew that if we were to change behaviour in anything more than a very temporary way, we were going to have to find a way to change our culture. I think many long established companies face the same problem.

Table 8.3 Inwardly-Focused and Market-Focused Behaviour

Internally Focused Behaviour	Market-Focused Behaviour
Assessing the External Environment	
We are absorbed by internal issues and indifferent to market-based information.	We need to be driven by external challenges, taking pains to acquire and share market information.
Making Strategic Choices	
We think of internal political realities when decision making.	We need to make choices in line with external realities and internal capabilities, based on judgments of future performance.
Achieving Operational Excellence	
We work in boxes and guard boundaries. Kick disputes upstairs.	We need to operate as a team. Solve disputes on the spot.
Assessing Performance	
We measure progress by internal standards.	We need to measure progress by external standards.

CULTURE

An organization's culture can have a major impact on the behaviour of everyone in the organization, and thus on its capabilities. When we speak of organizational culture we are referring to the values, beliefs, and core basic assumptions, more or less shared by people in an organization, that have worked well enough in the past to be considered valuable, correct, and true, so much so that they are taught to new employees as the proper way to think and to act.[6] In an organization with a strong culture, those values, beliefs, and core assumptions will be widely shared and strongly held.

As part of your organizational snapshot you should identify the key elements of your company's culture. Do not be concerned if you cannot be particularly precise. One writer described corporate cultures as having "the ephemeral qualities of flame or fog. You know they're there; you know they're real; but you can't grab hold of them or even describe them very well . . . "[7] We mentioned earlier 3M's continued capacity for innovation; here are some phrases used by 3M employees that capture important elements of the 3M culture:[8]

Listen to anyone with an original idea, no matter how absurd it may sound at first.

Encourage; don't nitpick. Let people run with an idea.

Hire good people and leave them alone.

Encourage experimental doodling.

Give it a try, and quick.

Try to make a similar list to describe your own company's culture, particularly those elements of it which are most strongly held. It will be critical, later in your analysis, that you be able to tell the difference between new organizational capabilities your culture could support and those it could not. If a strategic proposal would require capabilities that you judge would fit well with the existing culture, you will probably be confident of your ability to implement it. If this is not the case, you will need to be cautious.

When Sir David Simon at British Petroleum was trying to create a new culture in which all employees would understand that "everything comes down to money", he was up against a very strongly entrenched culture. He recounted a conversation between himself and a worker on an oil rig:

> I ask: 'How much money do you make?' An employee will reply: 'I can tell you how much oil we produce.' I say: 'Yes, but I am not interested in how much oil you produce, this is a factory for me. Where's the money?' Oil is only relevant in terms of money for shareholders, not in terms of barrels. That's very important. It's part of the change that can be implied by the direction the board takes. The board can say: 'We want this to be a performing culture, we want this culture to understand much more about the commercial than the technical merits of the business.' Those are very deep-seated cultural issues.[9]

Needless to say, a "deep-seated" culture, as Sir David put it, can be a real asset if it supports the behaviour and capabilities required by your current or proposed strategy. If a strong culture is inappropriate, it will be a major hindrance—and possibly disastrous.

Before leaving the topic of culture, we must emphasize that an organization's culture not only pushes "inward" (in Figure 8.2), impinging on behaviour and capabilities, but also has an "outward" force, influencing the choices that managers make about the organization structure, management processes, and the leadership behaviour of senior managers in the organization. Just as culture influences behaviour, so too is culture built, changed, and maintained by behaviour. We will examine this outward influence in more detail when we discuss the judgments you will make about your firm's ability to develop new capabilities, but to give one example now, consider the choices that managers make when making hiring and promotion decisions.

There is no doubt that hiring and promotion decisions are a vital aspect of corporate life, and have a major impact on the collective behaviour and capabilities of the corporation. So how are such decisions made? In many companies, new employees are hired because they look like they would "fit in," and they are promoted once it is clear they are competent, and are "our kind of manager." Herb Kelleher, the former CEO of Southwest Airlines, one of *the* success stories in the American airline business, expresses the views of many CEOs in the following statement:

> We'll take the person with less experience if he or she has the values we are looking for. . . . We look for attitudes. We'll train you on whatever you need to do, but the one thing that we can't do is change inherent attitudes in people . . . . Part of the purpose of the probationary period is to determine that. You may be an exceptional performer, but incompatible with our culture here. It doesn't mean there is anything wrong with you, there is just not a match.[10]

Clearly such decisions reinforce and support the existing culture. If that culture supports the capabilities that you need for the challenges that lie ahead, you are in great shape. If not, you may face a major challenge.

We are now ready to turn to the analytical steps outlined in Figure 8.1. As you work your way through these steps you may wish to return to Figure 8.2 from time to time, as your judgments about the relationships depicted there will play a crucial role in your assessment as to whether, and how, your organization could develop needed new capabilities.

STEP 1: IDENTIFY REQUIRED ORGANIZATIONAL CAPABILITIES

The first step in deciding if your organization is likely to prove capable of implementing a new strategy is to break the strategy into its four component parts, and identify the capabilities needed for each. We suggest that you do this by preparing a table like Table 8.4.

Table 8.4 Identifying Required Capabilities

Objective	Required Capability
Implement New Goals	What are the most critical organizational capabilities required by the goals of the new strategic proposal? (For example, an ability to stimulate and manage a faster rate of growth.)
Implement New Value Proposition	What are the most critical organizational capabilities required by the value proposition of the new strategic proposal? (For example, the ability to respond to customer requests within 24 hours.)
Implement New Product-Market Focus	What are the most critical organizational capabilities required by the product-market focus of the new strategic proposal? (For example, an ability to move aggressively into international markets.)
Implement New Core Activities	What are the most critical organizational capabilities required by the key activities of the new strategic proposal? (For example, the ability to manage outsourced activities, or to establish joint ventures.)
Close Resource Gaps	What are the most critical organizational capabilities that will be required to close the resource gaps that you identified in your resource analysis of the strategic proposal?
Close Preferences Gaps	What are the most critical organizational capabilities that will be required to close the management preferences gaps that you identified in your preferences analysis of the strategic proposal?

The difficulty you are likely to have in doing this is that your analysis will be hypothetical, meaning that you are guessing at what it would take to implement a strategy that you have never, in fact, implemented. There are several things to keep in mind as you do this.

Be as Specific as You Can About the Capabilities That You Will Need If your value proposition to customers, for example, is going to include "outstanding customer service," you will need the capability to deliver that. But what does "outstanding" actually mean? Remember that the quality of your service will be judged by customers, not by you, and their standard of comparison will be the service offered by others. "Outstanding" is too vague to be useful. So do some benchmarking. You may discover that "outstanding" means that you would need to offer 24-hour turnaround to a client needing repairs to a piece of equipment, anywhere in the world. That is a clear demand, and later you will have to assess whether or not you can develop the organizational capability to meet it. On the other hand, having a quick turnaround time for aircraft at the gate may be valuable in terms of a cost leadership strategy, but from the customers' point of view, all that matters is that the plane leaves on time. How long it takes to clean the cabin, refuel, on or off load luggage, etc., is irrelevant to the customer.

Cast a Wide Net When making your capability assessment ask people from different areas in your company to participate—not just one level in the hierarchy, and not just one functional area. Also ask outsiders: customers, suppliers, and others who know the market that you are proposing to enter.

As you can see from the bottom two rows of Table 8.4, you will also need organizational capabilities to close the resource gaps and preferences gaps that you identified earlier, and these should be included in your analysis. This may not be obvious at first glance, so consider the following examples.

Let us say that the strategic proposal you are considering would require more research and development effort in particular new product areas. You lack the resources to do this—in your earlier analysis you identified this as an important resource gap. When looking at how to close the gap, your first inclination was to hire more researchers, but for financial reasons that was not possible. The solution was to find a way to cut spending earlier on projects that are ultimately not going to be successful, and divert the funds to ongoing projects. This action will close the resource gap, but require a new organizational capability, as making an early identification of products that will ultimately fail is not easy. The capability has two parts: the ability to collect and assess new information; and the ability to make unpopular decisions that will be resisted by the researchers involved, with less solid information (because the decision is being made earlier) than was previously the case.

Identifying the organizational capabilities that would be required to close management preference gaps may require somewhat more subtle judgments. As we pointed out in Chapter 7, serious management preference gaps mean that there is conflict between managers. Adopting the strategic proposal you are considering would bring this conflict into the open, perhaps because some managers support it and others do not, or perhaps because it would mean that two organizational units would have to work closely together to make it succeed, and you know there would be conflict between the managers involved. The needed organizational capability is a willingness to acknowledge such conflict and to deal directly with it. In many organizations, strategy changes that would necessitate dealing with such conflicts are instinctively avoided—senior managers know that they do not have the capability to deal with the tension and stress that would result.

STEP 2: IDENTIFY CAPABILITY GAPS

Now that you have identified the organizational capabilities you would need to implement your strategic proposal, you need to compare those capabilities with the capabilities that you already have, and identify the most significant gaps. This is a relatively straightforward and focused exercise because you have already identified the capabilities that really matter. The question is whether or not you have these capabilities and, if not, the nature and size of the gaps that need to be filled.

As you do this, be careful to avoid flattering assessments of your organization's capabilities. Again we suggest involving a number of people in this exercise, from different functional areas and levels in the hierarchy. Be honest; this is no place for wishful thinking. Remember that capabilities are relative. There is no use comparing yourself to the worst performer in the industry if you are going to be competing head to head against the best. On the other hand, although the primary purpose of this exercise is to identify capability gaps, do be on the lookout for unique organizational capabilities that you possess that could form the basis of a new strategy others would find difficult to copy.

In Table 8.5 we included one task that we have not yet discussed, and that is the determination of the actions that would be required to close the organizational capability gaps that you have identified. It is to this major challenge that we now turn.

Table 8.5 Identifying Organizational Capability Gaps and Required Action

Required Organizational Capabilities	Existing Organizational Capabilities	Capability Gaps	Action to Close Gaps
Derived from strategic proposal, resource gap analysis, preferences gap analysis	Derived from observation	Derived from comparison of first two columns	Changes in organization structure, management processes, leadership behaviour required to develop new organizational capabilities

STEP 3: DEVELOP NEW ORGANIZATIONAL CAPABILITIES

Your capability gap analysis will give you a pretty clear picture of the new organizational capabilities that you need to develop. How to do it is much less straightforward, and as the annals of business failure suggest, fraught with danger. We are all familiar with companies that embarked on well-intentioned reorganizations that did more harm than good, managers who made changes in compensation systems to induce new behaviour that led to unanticipated dysfunctional consequences, and new strategies that never got off the ground because everyone ignored the "not very inspirational" messages coming from head office about how we are "all going to do things differently from now on." You are going to need to make some fine judgment calls about the best way to encourage people in your organization to change their behaviour as required to develop the new capabilities that you need.

To begin, we refer back to Figure 8.2 and the three leverage points which, as we said then, are your potential tools for developing new capabilities. For ease of exposition we discuss these sequentially and individually, while recognizing that the interaction and consistency between the three is important. The three leverage points are (1) *organization structure*, which captures the way you have grouped people around tasks and established reporting relationships, as reflected in your firm's organization chart; (2) *management processes*, which are the processes that you use to manage the company and the people in it; and (3) *leadership behaviour*, which is the way senior managers lead the company.

ORGANIZATION STRUCTURE

Your organization structure is reflected in your organization chart. It shows how you have chosen to group the people in your organization and to assign responsibilities. The way you have grouped people will make some tasks easier to carry out than others. This is a natural result of the fact that people working closely together will get to know one another's strengths and weaknesses, learn to trust each other's judgments, and will naturally focus on whatever tasks they have in common, be that developing a new video game or serving customers who are complaining about their recently purchased automobile.

No matter what choices you have made, your structure will not support every capability that you would like to have in the organization. There are always trade-offs to be made. Generally speaking, information and influence run most easily in a vertical direction, up and down whatever hierarchy you have created. The management challenge is usually to develop horizontal links across the organization. These will be outside the formal reporting relationships, and typically do not happen without active encouragement. Thus, if you have organized by product division (to be discussed) your challenge will be to get people in different product groups to communicate and cooperate. If you have organized in geographic units the challenge will be to get sharing of experience between geographic regions.

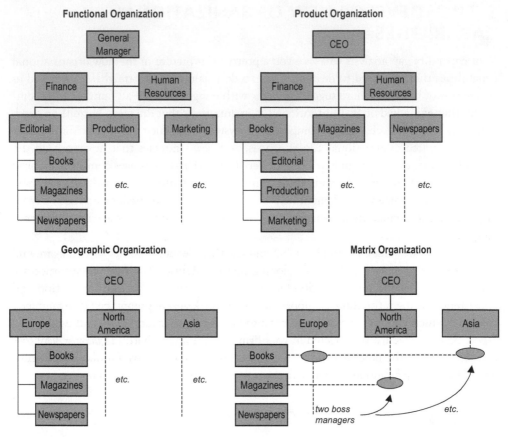

Figure 8.3 Basic Organization Structure (Partial)

In the following sections we have described some of the most commonly used organization structures, and the capabilities that they are likely to enhance. As a way of illustrating these basic structures, we have presented in Figure 8.3 the hypothetical case of a publishing company organized with a functional structure, a product organization, a geographic organization, and as a matrix. We refer to this example in each of the following sections.

Functional Structure

The traditional organizational building block is the functional unit, which consists of people working together within the same business function—research, engineering, manufacturing, marketing, sales, service, and so on—reporting to a general manager. Only the general manager is responsible for profitability. Small companies typically have such a structure, and the general manager is the president of the company.

Companies that grow while maintaining a narrow product line may stick with their functional structure, ending up with a worldwide functional organization. In the hypothetical publishing company of Figure 8.3, there would be a head of global manufacturing with responsibility for producing books, magazines, and newspapers; a global marketing department responsible for marketing these products around the world; and so on, each reporting to the chief executive.

A company with a functional structure is likely to be very good at coordinating activities and allocating resources within each function. Most of the major oil companies, for example, have a global exploration department, which reviews opportunities all over the world, before deciding where to drill. When the Swiss pharmaceutical company Novartis was formed from the merger of Sandoz and Ciba-Geigy, senior management took the opportunity to get rid of geographically run research centres, each of which had their own funding and research agenda.[11] Instead the company established seven therapeutic areas of research, each having a global mandate. As the head of research put it, "science is not local; it's global." Now Novartis makes global decisions with respect to the amount it wants to spend in each of the seven therapeutic areas; previously the decision was how much it wanted to spend in various areas of the world.

As these examples suggest, a global functional structure has many benefits to offer a company that is producing a standardized product for sale around the world. There one could expect to find such things as compact discs, a "world car," or computer software packages for global adoption, such as Windows Vista, being created, produced, and marketed in a global functional structure. This would offer the best opportunities for efficiency in worldwide design, production, marketing, and distribution. A global functional structure also offers the opportunity for low cost manufacturing, as world scale production facilities can be created, and then managed centrally, giving opportunities for optimal raw material sourcing, production scheduling, and other economies of scale.

The potential disadvantages of a worldwide functional structure may be a lack of sensitivity to local markets, slow decision making, and poor coordination between the functional areas. The problem may be that the engineers do not talk to the manufacturing people, the manufacturing people do not communicate with marketing, and marketing does not talk to the sales organization. The result is beautifully engineered products that manufacturing cannot produce, for which customers are not willing to pay, and creative marketing plans that bear no relationship to the product range that manufacturing can deliver. The challenge for companies with large functional organizations is to find formal and informal methods of horizontal communication between the functions, so that information passing between, say, an engineer working on a new product design and a marketer planning that new product's introduction does not have to go to the top of the hierarchy, across, and back down.

Most managers who are moving away from large functional structures say that they are doing so to enhance the speed and responsiveness of their organizations. They argue that by breaking the organization into smaller units they will get decision making closer to the customer, and faster. The usual resistance to such a change comes from the heads of the functional units, who see themselves as likely to lose status and power in such a transition.

Product Organization

If a company with a functional structure grows by adding new products, the structure will become awkward, as within each functional area there will be groups of people associated with each product, with different knowledge, different challenges, and different priorities. This would be true, for example, if our publishing company began life as a book publisher, then added magazines, and then newspapers. In the early days of a new product's life it is likely to suffer from a lack of attention, as most people in the functional structure will be preoccupied with the original product, which in all probability will be providing the bulk of the company's revenue. To avoid such problems, at a certain point a second product division will be formed around the new product. It will be a profit centre, headed by a general manager who will report to the CEO. If the product divisions do not need their own legal function, personnel department, or finance function, these groups may report in at a corporate level, as shown in Figure 8.3.

The advantage of a product organization is the focus that it gives to each product line in the company. The performance of each product area is visible, and resources can be allocated to each. This clarity and focus comes at a cost, in contrast to the large functional structure. The product organization represents duplication, as you now have a general manager, a marketing manager, manufacturing manager, and so on, for each product group. This is why the decision as to when to split an existing division into two is not an obvious one. Companies that focus on innovation, like 3M, want a lot of care and attention given to new products, and as a result tend to create new product divisions early.

The potential disadvantage of a product organization is that the divisions may not share knowledge and learn from one another. This may or may not be important, depending on the similarity of their technology, customer base, or the geographic markets they serve. Let us say, for example, that our publishing company had three worldwide product divisions (books, magazines, newspapers) each of which operated in Brazil. The result could be three senior managers located in Brazil, in different cities, not sharing any overheads, not coordinating their paper purchases or local employment practices, and not working together in representing their interests to various government agencies. The usual solution is to establish an informal horizontal liaison between the businesses, or to appoint a country president. The latter is a somewhat thankless job, however, as such presidents have very little power. Managers within the country report to managers in their product division elsewhere in the world, not to the president. As one disgruntled ex-country president recently put it, "I came in each morning to raise the flag and turn on the lights, and that was about it."

There is also a danger that customers will not be happy with a product-based organization, if they are buying from more than one product division. They may prefer a single point of contact, a single invoice, and a sales representative who understands all of their needs. One solution, described in some detail by Jay Galbraith,[12] is a front-back hybrid organization in which the "back" of the company (production, for example) may be organized into different product units, to achieve efficiency, but the sales activity is bundled such that only one sales person calls on a given customer. Such a structure has the potential to give manufacturing focus, while reducing sales force duplication and at the same time giving customers what they want.

Geographic Structure

In a geographically organized company, the level below the CEO comprises executives who are responsible for various areas of the world. Each is responsible for maximizing financial results within that area, for all of the firm's products. Nestlé's manager for Germany, for example, is responsible for the total company results in the country, and it is up to him or her to decide how much attention is to be given, for example, to frozen foods, chocolate, coffee, or pet food, within that market.

Managers and employees at all levels in geographically based organizations get to know their area well. They know the politics, the changing tastes of consumers, the local competitors, the labour market, and so on. Thus, a geographically based organization is likely to be skilled at tailoring products and marketing approaches to local conditions. So, if your strategy is to adapt your product and marketing approach to local tastes (as is common in the food industry, for example) a geographically based structure may be the way to go.

A geographic structure may also help if you are trying to learn how to do business in areas of the world that are new to you. For example, in a geographically based organization there would likely be a general manager for China, to whom the heads of all the company's businesses in the country would report. This would maximize the opportunity for learning among the businesses, and allow the company to have a "China strategy" that would not be possible if each business reported into a separate worldwide organization. Any contact between the businesses within the country would be at their own initiative, and not naturally fostered by the organization structure.

The disadvantage of geographic structures is that they do not naturally lend themselves to global efficiency. The management team in every country usually has a reason why its product, marketing approach, advertising copy, and so on, need to be different. Some of these claims may be entirely justified, but others may just be a bid for local autonomy, to keep decision making within the country unit and away from head office.

There has been a clear movement towards product structures, at the expense of the traditional geographic structure. Procter & Gamble (P&G) announced in mid-1998 that it would abandon its long standing regional structure of four geographic divisions, and create three new global product divisions: laundry detergents, diapers, and shampoos. Each global business unit would have full profit responsibility and "all the resources it needs to understand consumer needs in its product area and to develop innovative products to meet those needs."[13] The company judged that it needed to get new products to market in half the time that it currently took.

In its 2003 Annual Report P&G reported that

> We have the resources to interact with customers on multiple levels including finance, logistics, marketing, shopper understanding and a wide range of services. We bring deep category understanding with global consumer research. We create greater value through the total supply chain by pooling knowledge, expertise and reach. We designed the new P&G organization with an eye toward these core capabilities, and are focused more explicitly than ever on getting the greatest value from them. The restructuring is complete and the new organization structure is fully implemented. We have created an organization unlike any other in the consumer products industry and it is producing significant competitive advantage.[14]

Indeed, in 2003—the last year in which a re-structuring charge appeared on the balance sheet—P&G's sales grew eight percent (all organic growth) to $43.4 billion with earnings climbing 19 percent, and continued revenue growth to $76.4 billion in 2007. In our terms, the new capability that P&G developed is clear, and the reorganization is one of the tools specifically designed to bring that about.

Matrix

Matrix structures are used by companies that do not want to put one element of organization, say product line or geography, in a superior position to others. Rather than having one primary organizing logic, they have two, or possibly more, which results in a number of managers reporting to multiple bosses, as illustrated in Figure 8.3. Thus, a marketing manager located in France may report to the president of the French subsidiary, and to a vice president of a worldwide marketing function for the product line that he or she is selling. Managed properly, such a structure encourages managers to pay attention to both local needs and worldwide product strategies.

One historically successful user of a worldwide matrix organization was Asea Brown Boveri (ABB). This Zurich-based multinational operated in 50 business areas and 1,100 local geographic regions. For ten years the company employed a matrix structure in which the presidents of the 1,100 companies reported to two bosses—to a business area boss and to the president of the national company. Percy Barnevik, former CEO of this 240,000 employee company, commented on the rationale for the firm's matrix organization:

> ABB is an organization with three internal contradictions. We want to be global and local, big and small, radically decentralized with centralized reporting and control . . . . That's where the matrix comes in. It allows us to optimize our business globally and maximize performance in every country in which we operate.[15]

Offsetting these potential advantages, however, is the fact that matrix organizations are extremely complex, and tend to be slow moving. The major difficulty is the ambiguity that arises from managers reporting to multiple bosses. Responsibility and authority are diffused, and power balances are not as clear-cut as they are in straightforward hierarchical organizations. Matrix organizations require matrix-minded managers in a "matrix culture"—both of which are rare and difficult to develop. One study concluded: "If you do not really need it, leave it alone. There are easier ways of managing companies."[16] Goran Lindahl, who took over as CEO from Barnevik, seemed to agree, and the company soon moved to a straightforward product-based organization. Lindahl described the change as "an aggressive move aimed at greater speed and efficiency by further flattening and focusing the organization."[17] The age of the matrix organization may not be over, but it certainly seems to be in decline.

Cellular

On the increase is a relatively new organizational structure called the cellular form. Knowledge intensive industries such as biotechnology, information technology, medical instruments and devices, and software development companies for example, rely on R&D for discoveries and innovations that can be converted into new products. Given the rising costs (and decreasing returns) of "in-house" R&D investments, firms are finding new ways to organize to take advantage of knowledge and expertise outside the boundaries of a traditionally structured organization. The cellular structure is one way that firms use structure to tackle issues of costs, changing markets, flexibility, and the advances of technology and knowledge. In the cellular form the organization is essentially a cluster of loosely linked "cells" that may or may not be linked with other cells in the organization (Figure 8.4 represents a stylized cellular structure). Each cell is led by a project manager and might have one or only a few other employees of the company, but would likely have

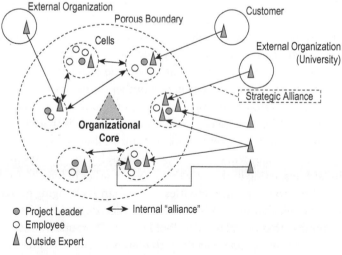

Figure 8.4 Cellular Structure

a larger number of contract employees, contract researchers, or "visiting" experts from external organizations.

An Australian information technology firm, TCG, has a cellular structure. When a new technology project starts up, it does so in the form of a self-directed cell under the leadership of a project manager who seeks the financing, human, knowledge, and other resources for the project. The cell might establish linkages with suppliers, and collaborative relationships with potential customers. The project leader may bring experts from industry or from universities into the cell on a contract, consulting, or other limited basis. They may form strategic alliances to fill knowledge or resource gaps. The advantage of cellular forms is their flexibility generated through a focus on entrepreneurship, self-organization and, usually, high degrees of ownership by the cell's members. For many senior managers a cellular structure is an uncertain proposition. The model requires decentralization including lack of central direction, a belief or philosophy that assumes that great ideas can be generated elsewhere than within the organization, and a well managed trust in others and other organizations which may involve sharing intellectual property while developing and leveraging new knowledge—a complicated, and for many managers, a risky, way to run an organization.

Strategic Alliances

One way many firms (and not just those that have cellular structures) attempt to extend and develop their capabilities is through strategic alliances. In summarizing the alliance literature, Barney discusses seven inter-firm synergies that can motivate strategic alliances: exploiting economies of scale, learning from competitors, managing risk and sharing costs, facilitating tacit collusion, low cost entry into new markets, low cost entry into new industries and new industry segments, and managing uncertainty.[18] He also points out three ways in which alliances can break down: "adverse selection" in which partners misrepresent the value or skills they contribute; "moral hazard" in which the value or skills are contributed but at a lower level than promised; and "hold-up" in which investments are made that are specific to the alliance with no economic value outside the relationship and are therefore vulnerable to unreasonable demands.

In deciding whether to form an alliance, or whether to incorporate an activity under the umbrella of the firm, transaction cost theory helps to frame the choice. As Collis and Montgomery point out, "the premise of transaction cost theory is that because people act in their own self-interest, if the market relationship allows them to do so, they will behave opportunistically—that is they will seek to benefit themselves at the expense of others...It is the possibility of firms acting in this way that causes market failure."[19] And it is market failure that causes firms to internalize activities rather than exchanging goods and services freely through market mechanisms. Where there is a high degree of asset specificity (i.e., specialized resources) so that one player can "hold up" another, uncertainties about supply and demand, and high transaction frequencies that are vulnerable to break down, there is greater potential for market failure.

Apple Computer's speed to market with its iPod portable music player and iTunes online music store has been attributed to its ability to line up partners successfully.

> To build the iPod, Apple persuaded a little-known Silicon Valley startup to provide customized key software and worked with Toshiba to come up with a tiny but capacious "hard disk". The product, which contractors assemble in Taiwan, came together in less than nine months. As for the online music store, the company parlayed its relative neutrality in the music industry to persuade all the major record labels to set aside their fears and rivalries, and to make their music available for download. Apple's payoff for being the first mover: the iPod claims the lion's share of all the revenues generated by sales of MP3 players worldwide, and the iTunes music store now accounts for nearly two-thirds of all legal music downloads.[20]

As firms extend their capabilities through strategic alliances, it is important to consider how the culture and management processes of one firm mesh with the partner. In many instances the culture and process are at odds, preventing the organizations from realizing the expected benefits from the alliance.

Choosing a Structure

For the most part organization structure evolves as an organization grows in size and perhaps the organization spreads geographically. Task forces, ad hoc groups, and project teams are often used to fill gaps in the structure as the organization evolves. However, there are points at which the stress and tension arising from a misfit between the strategy and the organization structure becomes so great that serious examination of the overall structure is required. As Goold and Campbell note: "Most executives can sense when their organizations are not working well, but few know how to correct the situation. A comprehensive redesign is just too intimidating. For one thing, it's immensely complicated, involving an endless stream of trade-offs and variables. For another, it's divisive, frequently disintegrating into personality conflicts and power plays. So when organization design problems arise, managers often focus on the most glaring flaws and, in the process, make the overall structure even more unwieldy and even less strategic."[21]

Goold and Campbell suggest nine tests or questions that managers should address in designing the right organization.

1. The Market Advantage Test: Does your design direct sufficient management attention to your sources of competitive advantage in each market?

2. The Parenting Advantage Test: Does your design help the corporate parent add value to the organization?

3. The People Test: Does your design reflect the strengths, weaknesses, and motivations of your people?

4. The Feasibility Test: Have you taken account of all the constraints that may impede the implementation of your design?

5. The Specialist Cultures Test: Does your design protect units that need distinct cultures?

6. The Difficult Links Test: Does your design provide coordination solutions for the unit-to-unit links that are likely to be problematic?

7. The Redundant Hierarchy Test: Does your design have too many parent levels and units?

8. The Accountability Test: Does your design support effective controls?

9. The Flexibility Test: Does your design facilitate the development of new strategies and provide the flexibility required to adapt to change?

Changes to organization structure are often fraught with serious complications and indeed many reorganizations end up having no effect while some actually destroy value. Blenko, Mankins, and Rogers reinforce that decisions should drive the organization. They suggest figuring out which decisions are most important and where in the organization they need to be made. Ensure that the structure supports the decisions and that the associated management processes enable decisions to be made quickly.[22] Neilson, Martin, and Powers also conclude that although many managers turn to restructuring as a leverage point to execute strategy, it is more often the information flows and decision rights that are the issue.[23] We turn to these management processes in the next section.

MANAGEMENT PROCESSES

During the past ten years managers have become much more conscious of the processes by which their companies make decisions and get things done. Spurred in part by advances in information technology, which allow fast and inexpensive communication inside and outside the company, many senior managers have tried to find ways to increase the speed of response in their organizations, while at the same time reducing costs and doing things more reliably. *Fortune* magazine suggested that the most significant innovation in the past 50 years is the modern corporation.

> When thinking of significant innovations of the past 50 years, an innovation that doesn't come readily to mind is the modern corporation. . . . It's all too easy to overlook the genuine creativity required to design and run an organization employing tens of thousands of people to consistently and efficiently develop, improve, manufacture, and deliver.[24]

There are many types of management processes to consider. For ease of exposition we focus here on three which generally have a major impact on a firm's capabilities: *decision-making processes*, *operating processes*, and *performance assessment and reward processes*. Decision-making processes are the routines and procedures that you go through for making the important decisions in your business: setting direction, determining objectives, allocating resources, deciding how to serve customers, and so on. Operating processes are the processes that create, produce, and deliver your products and services, including things such as your product development process, order fulfillment process, after-sales service process, and the like.[25] Performance measurement and reward processes are the ways

Table 8.6 Changing Management Processes to Develop New Capabilities

New Capability to Be Developed	Decision-Making Processes	Operational Processes	Performance Assessment and Reward Processes
e.g. **Faster Response to Customer Concerns**	Move customer-related decision making lower in the organization: closer to the customer.	Establish work routines that cut across functional boundaries.	Collect measures of customer satisfaction, as well as internal measures such as speed of response to customer requests.
e.g. **Increase Flow of New Products to Markets**	Make it hard to kill new product ideas early in their life.	Reduce the time to market by converting sequential processes to parallel processes.	Monitor the percentage of revenues or profits produced from new products in each business.
e.g. **Ability to Create Synergy Between Businesses**	Involve corporate-level executives in major decisions to ensure potential synergies are not ignored.	Create cross-unit information flows and joint execution of projects.	Monitor cross-business initiatives.

in which you measure the performance of businesses and people, and reward them. In Table 8.6 we provide examples of how you might change processes in each of these areas to develop a new organizational capability.

Decision-Making Processes

Whether we are talking of multi-billion dollar acquisition decisions or a hotel clerk deciding how to deal with an irate customer, decision-making processes are of vital importance to every organization. Companies trying to develop new capabilities to support a new strategy often find that they need to learn to make decisions faster, better, or both. "Better" in this context means decisions that support the company's strategy and when viewed with hindsight will prove to have been successful.

When considering ways to change their decision-making processes, companies often focus on who is involved in particular decisions, what information they have, and how they actually make decisions. Stewart argues that companies that manage in real time have a competitive advantage, and that advantage comes from the fact that they make decisions differently. "How can you possibly manage by command-and-control? A real-time company needs agility baked in. Yes, certain prudential matters—vision, values, strategic aims—need offline deliberation and must not be bounced about by stochastic hurly-burly infrastructure, especially the systems that feed supply and demand info, must be fast and 100% reliable. To manage real time means that every decision involves both time and money, so everyone must know that math. Everyone must get the data he needs."[26]

W.L. Gore, perhaps best known as the maker of Gore-Tex fabric, is also a major player in guitar strings, dental floss, medical devices, and fuel cells. Gore's approach to decision making has enabled it to leverage its success with fabric into a variety of other areas. Gore has a number of principles it follows: 1) ask your customers for help; 2) let employees figure out what they want to do; 3) leaders emerge as they acquire followers; 4) make time for dabbling; and 5) know when to let go. Notice how coherent these principles are. If you are going to let employees dabble in what they care about, you need to have processes in place that shut things down.

> But a capability Gore develops for a "no-go" business may end up solving someone else's problem. For example, Elixir guitar strings got their start in the early 1990s, when Dave Myers, a Gore associate in the medical division, invented ePTFE-coated bike cables. That business didn't get far. But Myers suspected that the cable's gunk-repelling coating might make it perfect for guitar stings . . . He was right: Gore strings maintain their tone three times longer. Today, Elixir is the leading brand of acoustic guitar strings in the U.S.[27]

In addition, having developed a superior dental floss, Gore realized it did not have the resources or capabilities to exploit the product fully and decided to sell the brand to Procter & Gamble.

Operating Processes

Operating processes govern the way that your employees work together to create, produce, and deliver products or services that your customers value. Generally, such processes work well if they are contained within a small organizational unit in a single location. Problems often arise, however, when coordination is required between larger units located in different places. The marketing group may make promises to customers that manufacturing cannot deliver; perhaps engineering designs products that manufacturing cannot produce at a reasonable cost; or the sales force in the West offers prices and conditions that are inconsistent with those in the East.

The new capabilities that many companies want to develop require closer coordination between organizational units than they have had traditionally. A global customer may be demanding seamless service around the world. Another customer may want to see only a single sales representative from the company who represents a number of business units. Perhaps the goal is cost reduction, and the links between product design and manufacturing, for example, have to become much tighter.

To increase cross-unit cooperation you may use informal mechanisms such as rotating personnel between the units where cooperation is desired, placing the units in the same physical location, holding frequent inter-departmental meetings, parties, and so on. If such measures are insufficient, the next step is to create more formal horizontal work groups, such as a new product development team, that cut across departments. Performance measurement and reward systems (to be discussed subsequently) can also be tailored to promote cross-unit cooperation.[28]

An organization that has done an excellent job of creating new capabilities in the past decade by fostering close cooperation between its component parts is the Walt Disney Company. Disney's intent is to create each year a core property that every unit in the company can use to generate profit, leveraging on the "character" produced and the Disney name. *The Lion King* is a prime example. This movie, costing a reported $50 million to produce, brought in more than $750 million in box office receipts in its first year, a clear success in itself, but was able to bring in more than *double* that amount from sales of home videos, books, music, television rights, and licensing fees for merchandising of everything from toys to pajamas.

To create this capability, Michael Eisner, then CEO of Disney, created a vice president of synergy whose job was to ensure that each of Disney's nine business units were aware of what the others were up to, and that all synergistic possibilities were fully explored. In addition to the synergy group at head office, there were also synergy representatives in each business unit. Two or three times a year, senior managers met from around the world to present and discuss plans—and each group was expected to present initiatives that involved other units of the company. Synergistic initiatives were also expected in everyone's business plans, and were explicitly rewarded at bonus time.[29]

Few companies have been able to create such strong bonds across units, but many are trying. The trick is to create processes that will encourage useful cross-unit cooperation, without blurring the responsibility that managers feel for the performance of their own unit. "Yes, my own group's results are down, but look what I did for a sister division" is not a statement that corporate managers want to hear.

Performance Assessment and Reward Processes

Many managers who want employees to behave differently change the performance assessment and reward processes in their organization. This seems a logical step, but it often leads to unintended consequences. Consider, for example, the commonly expressed desire to increase the level of teamwork in an organization, and its logical corollary, that employees should be paid on a team basis rather than on individual incentives. The case of Levi Strauss is a reminder to managers everywhere of just how careful one must be when trying to change behaviour by changing assessment and reward processes.[30]

In an industry where low wages and poor working conditions are common, Levi has prided itself on being an exception. It made a concentrated effort to pay its workers well, and at the same time keep plants operating in the United States when many companies were having jeans made in low cost offshore locations. In a bid to raise productivity, lower costs, and reduce repetitive strain injuries, Levi moved from its individual piece-rate pay system to a team-based approach in which workers would be paid on the output of their team of ten to 35 people. The teams would be self-managed, and decide for themselves how to organize their work.

The result was a disaster on a number of dimensions. Fights constantly broke out within teams as faster workers berated slower ones for dragging down the group performance. The average pay of the faster workers declined, yet Levi's costs increased, as less productive workers were better off under the new scheme. Morale plummeted, and so did productivity. In 1997 the company, still unable to regain its former cost levels, announced the closure of ten plants in the United States, and the layoff of 6,000 employees, one-third of its U.S. workforce.

Our suggestion is that you be very cautious in assuming that new capabilities can be developed solely by changing performance assessment and rewards. Most employees work for more than money; they also want praise, encouragement, opportunity to grow, and fairness in rewards, to name but a few. In fact, you may want to avoid hiring people who are only interested in money. As Jeffery Pfeffer points out by way of example in his article "Six Dangerous Myths About Pay,"[31] Tandem Computer, prior to its acquisition by Compaq, would not tell prospective employees what they would be paid if they joined the company, other than to say that salaries were competitive. The reasoning was that employees who come for money will leave for money, and they wanted new hires to join because they liked the work, the atmosphere, the people—the culture of the place.

If you decide that changing performance assessment and reward processes needs to be part of your program for changing behaviour and developing new capabilities, we suggest that you combine this change with other moves—in particular with changes in your own behaviour and that of other leaders in the firm. Otherwise, this risk of unintended consequences is very high.

LEADERSHIP BEHAVIOUR

Changes in organizational structure and management processes can be rather heavy, blunt tools for attempting to change behaviour. You may want to first try changing your own behaviour. If you are in a key position in the firm, this alone may have a dramatic impact. Ask yourself if your behaviour is representative of the behaviour that you believe is needed in the organization. Do you actively encourage your colleagues to adopt the required behaviour? In the vernacular, do you "walk the talk" and not just "talk the walk"? Have you made crystal clear, through your own behaviour and communication, the nature of the needed new behaviour?

An interesting example is provided by Quest, a former division of Unilever, in the flavours and fragrances business.[32] Viktor Rensing, the CEO, believed that he could create a high-performance culture in the organization, based on a strong set of shared values, which would yield a permanent competitive edge. This was especially important in Quest, as the company had made 11 acquisitions in various countries over a seven-year period, and there appeared to be few, if any, shared values throughout the whole of the organization. As a first step, Rensing created a task force to take on the job of determining what Quest's key core values should be. They began by asking the five-person senior management team "what behaviour would you be most proud of in the year 2010 if it were typical of a Quest employee at that time?"

As the task force proceeded with identifying the core values of Quest, an unexpected thing happened. Richard Sweeney, who was leading the project, decided that proceeding in the usual way to advertise the new core values through catchy slogans, a video from the CEO, articles in the company newspaper, lucite paperweights with the values inside, and so on, did not make sense. If behaviour was going to change, he reasoned, it had to start at the top. The real message was not what Viktor Rensing and his colleagues said, it was what they did—how they behaved. The campaign was stopped, the task force disbanded, and the ball put squarely back in Rensing's court. After some soul-searching, the process was restarted, with intense personal discussions among the members of the top team, and behaviour did change. Then the process was cascaded downward through a series of workshops. Results improved dramatically over the next several years.

In Table 8.7 we have recreated the list of organizational capabilities that we used early in this chapter and suggested some starting points for thinking about how

Table 8.7 Organizational Capability and Leadership Behaviour

Organizational Capability	Behaviour Needed to Develop Required New Capabilities	Actual Behaviour	Needed Changes
Innovation	e.g. Could you do more to encourage innovation and experimentation? Are you innovative in your own activities? How do you handle well-intentioned failure?		
Productivity	e.g. Could you do a better job of asking questions that will lead others to focus more intensely on productivity issues? Do you focus on the key cost drivers often enough?		
Speed	e.g. Could you do more to demonstrate speed in your own behaviour and activities? Do you talk about speed as a success factor? Could you delegate in such a way as to speed up decision making or operating processes?		
Cross-Cultural Effectiveness	e.g. Could you improve your personal cross-cultural effectiveness? Do you encourage international careers? Could you do more to ensure that race-based bias is eliminated in your organization?		
Cross-Unit Synergies	e.g. Do you personally work well across organizational boundaries and encourage the same in others? Do you encourage group behaviour, information sharing?		

you might change your behaviour to drive other behavioural change throughout the organization.

Do You Have the Right Leaders?

As you work through your version of Table 8.7, you should also be thinking about the other leaders in the organization, and whether or not you have the right people in place. Do you make the right promotion decisions? Do you remove the people that you should? In the first three years after taking over as CEO of Allied Signal, Larry Bossidy changed 75 percent of the managers in the top 140 jobs in the company. Craig Weatherup, whom we will discuss in the next chapter, changed all but two of his 12 direct reports in a four-year change process at Pepsi USA.[33] You may judge that to develop new capabilities you are going to have to remove some of your current leaders.

The related question is whether you should change your promotion criteria to get the leaders with the behaviour that you need. Bossidy commented:

> We used to reward the lone rangers in the corner offices because their achievements were brilliant, even though their behaviour was destructive. That day is gone. We need people who are better at persuading than barking orders, who know how to coach and build consensus. . . . This has a big impact on how you think about who the 'best' people are.[34]

Bossidy established promotion criteria that take into account how a manager achieves results, as well as the results achieved. A manager who achieves results and does it "our way," meaning that he or she exhibits appropriate behaviour, is a star. One who does neither is out. The more interesting questions arise when the manager behaves well but does not produce (usually given a second chance) and, most difficult of all, when the manager produces results, but not with acceptable behaviour. Bossidy argues that such managers have to leave the company in spite of their results, because otherwise the whole drive for new behaviour will be undermined.

USING ALL THREE LEVERAGE POINTS

If your organization has a strong culture and deeply ingrained behaviour that you judge inappropriate, change is not going to be easy. To have any success, you will probably have to make changes in all three of the leverage points—structure, management processes, and leadership behaviour—that we have been discussing. It is important that the changes you make in each area send the same messages to employees about the desired new behaviour. It is extremely counter-productive, for example, to have a compensation system that rewards one type of behaviour while managers are exhorting employees to do something different, or if managers behave in one way while suggesting that everyone else do something different.

Table 8.8 3M's Innovative Capability

Leverage Point	Support for Innovation
Organization Structure	• "Grow and divide"; as businesses grow they are split into smaller units, each a profit centre with an autonomous management team
Management Processes	• 30% of each year's sales must come from products less than 4 years old. Every business must meet this target.
	• "Pacing programs" identify development programs that could make a major difference to the corporation, and these receive priority funding
	• "While products belong to businesses, technology belongs to the company," meaning that technology must be shared. This is done via numerous scientific forums and technology-sharing awards
Leadership Behaviour	• "Thou shalt not kill a new product idea"
	• Acceptance of "well-intentioned failure," to encourage risk taking
	• Leaders must be capable of developing and managing teams
	• "People will make mistakes, but they will not be as serious as the mistakes management will make if it tries to tell people exactly how to do their jobs"
	• Technical people are encouraged to spend up to 15% of their time on projects of their own choosing

Sources: Adapted from Harvard case *3M: Profile of an Innovating Company*, #9-395-016, Bartlett and Mohammed, 1995.

Furthermore, consistency over time is critical. Frequent changes in structure, processes, or leadership behaviour will quickly breed employee cynicism, as they see "flavour of the month" initiatives come and go. To return to an example of a company that seems to have its act together, we look again to 3M, and have produced in Table 8.8 some of the main features of its structure, processes, and leadership behaviour that work together to support its innovative capability.

STEP 4: ASSESS FEASIBILITY

At this point you have made your best estimate of the changes that would be required in your firm's structure, management processes, and leadership behaviour to implement the strategic proposal that you are examining. Two questions remain: (1) Can these changes be made in the required time frame? and (2) Will they produce the desired result? The answers are seldom an absolutely confident *yes* or a definitive *no*. They are more likely to be an estimate based on the nature and magnitude of the required changes in organizational capability (and hence behaviour and culture) that you are trying to bring about, and the extent to which various parts of the organization will embrace or resist the proposed changes.

You are likely to find that some of your managers will support the changes you think are necessary, but others may resist. Recall that there is an arrow between management preferences and organization in the Diamond-E framework. This reflects the fact that managers may have strong individual preferences, and may not see the need for change the same way you do. This is a topic that we shall discuss in depth in the last two chapters of the book. For the moment, you should make a first estimate of likely support and resistance, and factor your thoughts into Table 8.9.

This is also the time to think hard about the problem of "unintended consequences" that we discussed earlier. If you change some element of your management processes—the way you pay people, for example—will it really generate the behaviour change that you want or might it produce a rather different reaction? Remember the cautionary tale of Levi Strauss. If you are sure that your change will produce the desired result, record that in the fourth column of Table 8.9. Often the answer is a less confident one, and that lack of certainty needs to be considered when you are judging the feasibility of creating the required new capabilities in the time available.

Congratulations! You have now made it all the way around the Diamond-E and, assuming that you have more than one viable strategic proposal in hand, it is time to make a choice. That is the topic of the next chapter.

Table 8.9 Assessing Feasibility

Leverage Point	Nature and Magnitude of Required Change	Ability to Make Change in Time Required	Probability That the Change Will Bring About the Required Change in Capability	Overall Feasibility and Risk
Organization Structure				
Management Processes				
Leadership Behaviour				

SUMMARY

In this chapter we discussed the penultimate step of the Diamond-E analysis, which is to decide if the strategic proposals that looked attractive during your environment, resource, and management preferences analyses could be implemented in the necessary time frame. This analysis involves identifying the organizational changes that would be necessary in the firm's structure, management processes, and leadership behaviour to develop the capabilities you will need to support the new strategy. You must then make a crucial judgment regarding how likely it is that the proposed changes would have the desired result, and could be implemented in the given time frame. This assessment gives you a basis on which to weigh the risks against the benefits of the proposal.

If you are working through the Diamond-E analysis in the order that we have suggested, you may now have several attractive strategic proposals that have made it all the way through your analysis. Choosing between them is the topic of the next chapter.

Notes

1. Reeves, Martin, and Mike Deimler. "Adaptability: The New Competitive Advantage." *Harvard Business Review* 89.7/8 (2011): 134–141. *Business Source Complete*, EBSCO. Web. 15 Aug. 2011.

2. Bannon, Lisa. "Mattel Plans to Increase Global Sales." *Wall Street Journal Europe* (February 11, 1998): U9A. Print.

3. Tichy, Noel, and Ram Charan. "Speed, Simplicity, and Self Confidence: An Interview With Jack Welch." *Harvard Business Review 67* (September–October 1989): 112. Print.

4. Ashkenas, R., et al. *The Boundaryless Organization: Breaking the Chains of Organizational Structure.* San Francisco: Jossey-Bass Publishers, 1995. Print.

5. Galbraith, Jay R. *Designing Organizations: An Executive Guide to Strategy, Structure, and Process.* San Francisco: Jossey-Bass Publishers, 2002. Print.

6. Our definition of culture draws heavily on that of Edgar Schein, *Organizational Culture and Leadership: A Dynamic View.* 3rd edition. San Francisco: Jossey-Bass Publishers, 2004. Print.

7. Leavitt, Harold J. *Corporate Pathfinders: Building Vision and Values into Organizations.* New York: Penguin Books, 1986. 16. Print.

8. Collins, J.C., and Jerry Porras. *Built to Last: Successful Habits of Visionary Companies.* London: Century Business, Random House, 1996. 152. Print.

9. Kets de Vries, Manfred F.R. "Transforming the Corporate Mind-set at British Petroleum: An Interview With Sir David Simon and John Browne." INSEAD case study 497-013-4 (1997): 10. Print.

10. Goldsmith, Walter, and David Clutterbuck. *The Winning Streak Mark II: How the World's Most Successful Companies Stay on Top Through Today's Turbulent Times.* London: Orion Business Books, 1997. 183. Print.

11. Fischer, L.M. "How Novartis Became Number One." *Strategy and Business* (Second Quarter 1998): 70. Print.

12. Galbraith, Jay R. *Designing Organizations: An Executive Briefing on Strategy, Structure, and Process.* San Francisco: Jossey-Bass Publishers, 1995. 89. Print.

13. Tomkins, Richard. "The What, Not the Where to Drive P&G," *Financial Times*, September 3, 1998: 16. Print.

14. *Procter & Gamble Annual Report.* Procter & Gamble, 2011. 4. Web. 29 Sept. 2011. <www.pg.com>.

15. Taylor, William. "The Logic of Global Business: An Interview With ABB's Percy Barnevik." *Harvard Business Review* 69 (March–April 1991): 90–106. Print.

16. Davis, S., and D. R. Lawrence. *Matrix.* Reading, Mass.: Addison-Wesley Publishing Company, 1977. vi. Print.

17. *Financial Times*, August 13, 1998: 1. Print.

18. Barney, Jay B. *Gaining and Sustaining Competitive Advantage.* Reading, Mass.: Addison-Wesley Publishing Company, 1997. Print.

19. Collis, J.C. and Cynthia Montgomery. *Gaining and Sustaining Competitive Advantage. By Jay B. Barney.* Reading, Mass.: Addison-Wesley Publishing Company, 1997: 105. Print.

20. Schlender, Brent. "The New Soul of a Wealth Machine." *Fortune* 149 (April 5, 2004): 102–107. Print.

21. Goold, Michael, and Andrew Campbell. "Do You Have a Well-Designed Organization?" *Harvard Business Review* 80 (March 2002): 117. Print.

22. Blenko, Marcia W., Michael C. Mankins, and Paul Rogers. "The Decision-Driven Organization." *Harvard Business Review* 88.6 (2010): 54–62. *Business Source Complete*, *EBSCO*. Web. 16 Aug. 2011.

23. Neilson, Gary L., Karla L. Martin, and Elizabeth Powers. "The Secrets to Successful Strategy Execution." *Harvard Business Review* 86.6 (2008): 60–70. *Business Source Complete*, *EBSCO*. Web. 16 Aug. 2011.

24. Schlender, Brent. "The New Soul of a Wealth Machine." *Fortune* 149 (April 5, 2004): 102–107. Print.

25. Garvin, David A. "The Processes of Organization and Management." *Sloan Management Review* 39 (Summer 1998): 33–50. Print.

26. Stewart, Thomas A. "Making Decisions in Real Time." *Fortune* 142 (June 26, 2000): 332–334. Print.

27. Harrington, Ann. "Who's Afraid of a New Product?" *Fortune* 148 (November 10, 2003): 189–190. Print.

28. Galbraith, Jay B. *Designing Organizations: An Executive Briefing on Strategy, Structure, and Process.* San Francisco: Jossey-Bass Publishers, 2001. chapters 4 and 5. Print.

29. For further details, see the Harvard Business School case series, Disney's "The Lion King" (A), (B) and (C), by Cate Reavis under the direction of Carin-Isabel Knoop and Professor Jeffery Rayport. 1998. Case numbers N9-899-041,-042 and -043.

30. King Jr., R.T. "Levi's Factory Workers Are Assigned to Teams, and Morale Takes a Hit." *Wall Street Journal* [New York], Wednesday, May 20, 1998: 1. Print.

31. Pfeffer, Jeffery. "Six Dangerous Myths About Pay." *Harvard Business Review* 76 (May–June 1998): 108–119. Print.

32. Dowd, Jim, and Mary Schweinsberg. "Quest Core Values" (A) and (B), IMD case GM 648-649, 1997.

33. Garvin, D.A. "Leveraging Processes for Strategic Advantage." *Harvard Business Review* 73 (September–October 1995): 83. Print.

34. Tichy, N.M., and R. Charan. "The CEO As Coach: An Interview With Allied Signal's Lawrence A.Bossidy." *Harvard Business Review* 73 (March–April 1995): 68–80. Print.

Chapter 9
Strategic Choice

Finally, you may be thinking, after all this analysis, it is time to make a strategic choice. Indeed, you may be in the happy position of having a very attractive strategic proposal to move forward with, or even several good possibilities from which to choose. This is typically the situation in classroom case analysis, for example, where the discussion focuses on making a particular strategic choice at a particular point in time. Fair enough, for strategy decisions in business sometimes come to such a definitive point as well.

On the other hand, you may have ended up with one or more uncertain propositions and you are faced with trying to decide whether you are ready to go ahead with a major commitment, or perhaps with a trial step, or even to recycle and refocus your analysis to see if you and your management team can come up with some better options. This is quite often the case in business practice and it leads to strategy being formulated and implemented in an ongoing process as compared to a one-time analytic master stroke. There are still strategic decisions being made, but they are being made in steps, over time, and they consider developing conditions such as the clarity and urgency of the situation, the readiness of the organization, and the capacity of the management team to implement change.

Thus, in this chapter, we begin the discussion of strategic choice by describing the dynamics of strategy formulation over time. We conclude that, whatever the process and dynamics, there are points of time at which considered strategic choice is essential. These junctures are the focus of our attention.

STRATEGY AS A DYNAMIC PROCESS

As Mintzberg, Ahlstrand, and Lampel point out, "strategy inevitably ends on a knife-edge. For every advantage associated with strategy, there is an associated drawback or disadvantage."[1] Mintzberg et al. provide examples linked to four functions of strategy: setting direction, focusing effort, defining the organization, and providing consistency.

Setting Direction

Advantage: Strategy charts the future course of an organization to help it negotiate its environment more smoothly and cohesively.

Disadvantage: Strategy—particularly a formalized one—can prevent an organization from seeing emerging dangers. A predetermined strategic direction in situations of environmental uncertainty may lead the organization astray. Setting a direction is important, but in uncertainty it is better to move slowly, constantly scanning the environment, so that an organization can respond flexibly to changing conditions.

Focusing Effort

Advantage: Strategy coordinates activities and behaviours. Without strategic direction, people may pull in a variety of different directions causing chaos.
Disadvantage: 'Groupthink' can form when effort is too tightly focused. Even an otherwise good strategy can become too focused and therefore too ingrained in an organization, inhibiting adaptability as circumstances change.

Defining the Organization

Advantage: Strategy provides a model for how people should understand their organization and what it does. Strategy provides meaning.
Disadvantage: Defining an organization too specifically may define it too simply so that the rich complexity of the system is lost.

Providing Consistency

Advantage: Strategy reduces ambiguity, and it structures and facilitates activities.
Disadvantage: Improvisation and creativity spring out of inconsistencies by finding and presenting new possibilities and new combinations. Any strategy is a simplification and therefore is a *model for* reality—but it is not a *model of* reality. Every strategy simplifies and in some sense reduces other possibilities.

There are great debates about how strategy *is* or *should* be formulated. Of the many aspects to the debates, one that tends to reflect the conflicts noted by Mintzberg et al. is the planning-learning debate.[2] The debate centres around whether strategy formulation is, and should be, a well-defined, analytical process, or whether strategy emerges, and should emerge, over time as a trial and error process of learning. Figure 9.1 illustrates the relationship between intended strategy, which reflects the former position, and emergent strategy, which reflects the latter position.

Mintzberg suggests that while many firms develop intended strategies, most of these strategies are unrealized for a variety of reasons. Sometimes they are not well-formulated and therefore do not anticipate significant customer, supplier, competitive, or resource issues that impede the strategy. Often the strategy is generally sound, but is poorly implemented. Alternatively, strategy can emerge based on the day-to-day decisions and actions of individuals in the organization. Ultimately, realized strategy is a blend of intended and emergent strategies.

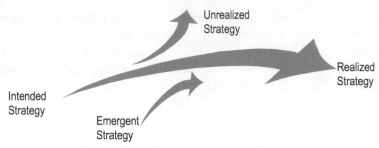

Figure 9.1 Intended and Emergent Strategy

Source: Mintzberg, H.; Ahlstrand, B.; Lampel, J.; *Strategy Safari*, New York: The Free Press, 1998.

Table 9.1 Intended and Emergent Strategy	
Intended Strategy	**Emergent Strategy**
Analysis	Action-oriented
Planned	Opportunistic
Controlled	Spontaneous
Thoughtful/reflective	Intuitive
Future-oriented	In the present
Top-down	Bottom-up
Episodic	Ongoing

To compare and contrast the intended and emergent approaches, we offer the descriptive points presented in Table 9.1. Please note that these are polar cases—the end points in a spectrum. Reality for the practitioner must be somewhere in between, because following a pure intended strategy process in a changing environment is futile and the pursuit of strategy by wholly relying on a purely emergent model is mindless. Every company and every industry will have a different mix of intended and emergent strategy. If you think of intended strategy as cold water and emergent strategy as hot water, you need to determine the appropriate temperature for your industry—how cold or hot does your industry run? The term "ambidextrous organization" is used for organizations that have capacity to do both, although the difficulty of doing so has been well documented.[3]

Strategy as Planning

From the intended strategy perspective, strategy would be formulated through a strategic planning process. Unfortunately, for many firms strategic planning deteriorates into an annual budgeting exercise, with very little real strategic thinking or analysis. Perhaps this is why countless studies have not been able to establish a relationship between formal strategic planning and performance. Simply put, it is not enough to have a formal strategic planning process. What matters is the quality of conversation that takes place in that process. As well, performance benefits will only be achieved if there is effective implementation. We contend that effective execution is also dependent on the quality of conversation in the planning process; it anticipates obstacles or challenges to implementation.

Grant studied the strategic planning processes of the major oil companies. He was interested in understanding the intended and emergent nature of those processes and the degree to which environmental turbulence and unpredictability affected the nature of strategic planning.[4] Grant found that for all of the companies engaged in a formal planning process (Exxon, Shell, Mobil, Texaco, ENI, Elf, BP) the principal stages of the planning process were common, as follows: (1) planning guidelines, i.e., an announcement by the corporate centre of the guidelines and assumptions to be used by the businesses in preparing their business-level strategies; (2) draft business plans; (3) discussions with the corporate centre; (4) revised business plans; (5) annual capital and operating budgets; (6) corporate plan; (7) board approval; (8) performance targets; and (9) performance appraisal. Note that this is really a "corporate" strategic planning process, which is built up from business-level strategies. Nonetheless, Grant has some interesting insights into the process as we discuss below.

Rocked by the precipitous decline in oil prices in the mid-1980s, strategic planning became less focused on single-point forecasts and more attentive to a range of possibilities using scenario planning. There also seems to been a shift from "strategy as resource deployment" to "strategy as aspirations and performance-goals." By the late-1990s planning became far more informal with less emphasis on written documents. Strategic plans became shorter as did the presentations that supported them. As well, there was a shift in decision-making responsibility from the corporate level to business-level managers, and a reduction in planning staff.

> The key priorities of the 1990s were speedier decision making to respond to fast-changing external circumstances and the increasing returns of shareholders. Strategic planning systems became less about planning the majors' long-run growth and stability, and more about squeezing increased profitability from mature, slow growth businesses.[5]

Consequently the tools of strategic planning shifted towards financial tools and away from analyzing the competitive environment, resources, and capabilities.

> By the late-1990s, strategy formulation was occurring, for the most part, outside of the companies' strategic planning systems. When interviewees were asked to identify the sources of critical strategic decisions that their companies had made in recent years—acquisitions, divestments, restructuring measures, and cost-cutting initiatives—it was apparent that few had their origins in the plans that emerged from the companies' strategic planning systems. The typical sequence was the other way around: strategic decisions were made in response to the opportunities and threats that appeared, and were subsequently incorporated into strategic plans.[6]

What role did strategic planning play then? Grant suggested three roles for strategic planning: (1) it influences the content and quality of strategic decision making; (2) it provides a mechanism for coordination; and (3) it provides a mechanism for control. In our view, we see this annual strategic planning cycle having evolved into a very narrow type of operational/budgeting process. The fact that strategic decisions are made outside of this process is not a surprise.

Unfortunately, Grant's study of the oil companies is reflective of many organizations who have found that the strategic planning process deteriorates into a budgeting exercise. The annual budgeting process is a fact of life in most organizations, and is often carried out at the unit level. The outcomes are specific with respect to measures of costs, revenues, and investments and the process is largely standardized so that managers have a clear grasp of what needs to be done and in what time frame. Typically, the budgets at the unit level are aggregated to achieve a financial forecast for the business. There is nothing strategic about the budgeting process; budgeting is a routine process, with reasonable clarity, that can usually be carried out at the unit level. In contrast, the strategic planning process is not routine. It is often quite ambiguous, and by definition it deals with the entire organization, not just the unit level. Furthermore, many managers feel it is beyond their grasp. As a result, there is significant danger of having the budgeting process overshadow or displace strategic planning. We recommend that you divorce these processes. At a minimum, this will ensure that you are not deluding yourself that budgeting is your strategy. Budgeting may provide input into a strategic planning process, by identifying the base case financial scenario, but more likely it will follow from a strategic planning exercise.

Many organizations have found it helpful to conduct an annual off-site strategic planning session. Getting away from the office to an off-site setting helps to free up more creative thinking and also reduces the distractions that can arise when you are close to the day-to-day business. Typically two days are taken to work through the analysis presented in the foregoing chapters with the proviso that many key pieces of the analysis have been prepared ahead of time. For example, competitive and customer analysis should be done in advance and it would be helpful to work up some financial analysis on various scenarios. The more "homework" that is done in advance, the more productive is the session. We have seen many management teams hit a roadblock in the session because they are missing vital information. In those instances, they shift into "what if" scenarios and carry out the analysis using different assumptions. One technique used by some firms is to have a case study prepared on their own company in advance of the session. The case is then used as the basis for discussion. Preparing the case helps the company identify critical pieces of missing information, and also helps to develop some shared understanding prior to the strategic planning session. The session can then be devoted to testing assumptions and fleshing out the various strategic options.

Who should attend a strategic planning session? Strategic planning sessions need the support and endorsement of the president, CEO, or most senior person in the business. That person needs to have a comfort level with the group who will attend the strategic planning session to ensure there is an open and honest dialogue. If having an open and honest dialogue means limiting the first round of discussions to a smaller group of more senior people, you should do so. You can always have a second round with an expanded group. There are two primary shortcomings associated with a smaller and likely more senior group. The first is that you miss vital input from people who are much closer to the action, be it customers, competitors, or your own operations. The second shortcoming is that it is not the senior group that faces the key execution issues, but rather those lower down in the organization, particularly middle managers. There are clear benefits to having a variety of perspectives represented in the strategic planning session, but you must ensure that the senior-most individual(s) buy(s) into the benefits. As well, those lower down in the organization need to be prepared to shed the hierarchy to become an equal partner in the dialogue. It is not uncommon for several levels of an organization to be present at a strategic planning session, and for more junior members to feel intimidated or lacking in confidence to express their views. We strongly recommend having an outside facilitator at the strategic planning session as the facilitator can help to keep the process on track and can also take an objective and constructive approach in helping you analyze some issues that may be critical, but sensitive.

When it comes time to write the strategic plans formally, they typically contain standard elements which we set out (below) with some references to the sections of the text that will help to provide the underlying analysis. Plans usually include:

- Executive Summary
- Overview of the Opportunity
  - This section should feature the proposed strategy as described in Chapter 2 including goals, product/market scope, value proposition, and core activities
  - Management team experience—particularly for small entrepreneurial organizations
- Market Opportunity and Industry Trends
  - Establish the potential value that can be created and how the organization will capture that value given the competitive landscape (this is the focus of Chapters 4 and 5)
- Specific Elements of the Plan—This is a comprehensive section that tends to cover the various functional elements of the plan. It arises from the analysis in Chapters 6, 7, and 8 and typically provides details on the following areas:
  - Marketing—e.g. product, price, promotion, distribution
  - Operations—e.g. facilities, logistics, technology, capacity
  - Organization and Human Resources—e.g. needs, structure, compensation
  - Financial Analysis—income statement, balance sheet, valuation, cash flow, sensitivity analysis
- Risk Assessment and Contingency Plans
- Implementation—timing and execution of key priorities (from the analysis in Chapters 9, 10, and 11).
- Conclusions.

It is understandable that there have been many critics of the strategic planning process, particularly if one focuses on some of the shortcomings we have highlighted above. However, we find there is no good substitute for managers getting together to have a deep dialogue about what is happening in their industry and their organization, and the implications for strategy. Whether we call this "formal planning" or simply "strategic thinking", it is imperative that there be a place on the corporate agenda for it to take place. For some organizations, this happens once a year and for others, it happens as often as it is needed. Much depends on the pace of change in the industry. However, critics of strategic planning suggest that the environment has become so unpredictable that organizations cannot plan, but rather need an inherent resiliency to be able to respond swiftly to the problems and opportunities that arise.

Strategy as Learning

Hamel and Valikangas argue that "in a turbulent age, the only dependable advantage is a superior capacity for reinventing your business model before circumstances force you to. Achieving such strategic resilience isn't easy."[7] They are not alone in what tends to be a chorus of writers advocating adaptability and resilience. Some even call adaptability the new competitive advantage.[8] Yet this is far from a new idea. De Geus, in his 1988 *Harvard Business Review* article, suggests that planning should be a learning process.[9] He argues that the only sustainable competitive advantage may be a firm's ability to learn faster than its competitors. When strategy is viewed from a learning perspective, the scope of individuals involved in strategy formulation increases. Whereas the intended strategy approach developed through a strategic planning process is largely top-down in orientation, the learning approach suggests there are individuals throughout the organization who have valuable input into strategy.

What makes this resiliency or learning orientation so difficult? Hamel and Valikangas suggest four tough challenges: (1) the cognitive challenge; (2) the strategic challenge; (3) the political challenge; and (4) the ideological challenge.[10] The strategic challenge is that resilience requires the development of competing strategic alternatives to the dying option, so it is no surprise that there is also a political challenge associated with diverting resources to new untested possibilities. The ideological challenge is that organizations need to embrace a process of renewal that is more continuous and opportunity-driven rather than episodic and crisis-driven. In many ways this last challenge is connected to the first challenge. Often individuals and organizations are not resilient because they do not perceive the threat or opportunity.

In the following section we delve into the black box of the learning process of strategy to reveal some of the underlying challenges in managing strategy as a dynamic process. We begin with a discussion of cognitive biases and provide some practical insight into how individuals and organizations can manage them. We then present a framework of organizational learning that reveals some of the key underlying processes and conclude with some approaches to reconciling the tensions that a dynamic perspective of strategy embodies, such as the coexistence of intended and emergent strategy.

Cognitive Biases[11]

There are many cognitive barriers that most of us are simply not aware of. According to Max Bazerman, biases can be viewed as "irrationalities" that blur our rational decision-making behaviour.[12] Having a bias can be defined as being partial to, or being prejudiced toward, some outcome. Cognitive biases lead to errors in judgment in decision making. It is important to note that everyone has their own biases. The critical issue is how well we recognize and manage them. Table 9.2 lists key individual biases that interfere with rational decision making of all people.

We can find evidence of all of the cognitive biases in strategic decision making. The information biases are problematic because they tend to limit strategic analysis to the information that is readily available. This is particularly true for customer and competitive analysis and in many cases is also a problem with respect to having appropriate financial data to make sound strategic decisions. The biases tend to have a negative compound effect when individuals inappropriately anchor estimates on available information and then aggravate the problem by assuming cause-effect relationships that may not exist. Furthermore, many of the assumptions are not checked because individuals falsely assume consensus on the approach.

Escalation of commitment is a very common temporal bias in organizations. It is difficult for people to let go of projects and ideas that have received substantial investment in terms of energy and commitment or perhaps financial investment, even though fresh analysis indicates it is time to shut things down. Even though the investments are "sunk costs," we have a tendency to want to take them into account when we analyze the merits of strategic options. Because of the hindsight bias, we tend to have difficulty learning from our mistakes. After the fact, when everything is clear, we tend to overlook the ambiguity or conflicts that may have been present when we were in the midst of strategic decision making. As a result, we often lose sight of where we went wrong.

Finally, we are all subject to judgment biases. Whether it be a tendency to seek or acknowledge information that confirms what we believe, inappropriately stereotyping others, or simply being over-confident about our own abilities, we need to be cognizant of the cognitive biases that affect strategic decision making.

There are a number of ways to mitigate against cognitive biases. At the group level, having a diverse management team serves to guard against the "groupthink" that can arise when management shares the same functional background, perspectives or cognitive orientation. However, you need to be able to tap into that diversity. Often, those with diverse points of view are censored by the custodians of the status quo.

As you consider whether you are falling prey to your own cognitive biases, consider the following questions: What biases are you most vulnerable to in decision-making? Are

Table 9.2 Cognitive Biases

Information Biases

Availability Heuristic	The tendency to make decisions based on pre-existing and hence most available information. People are reluctant to test new approaches to problem solving or to perform the research required to obtain new information.
Anchoring and Adjustment	Most people select round numbers or available numbers as an anchor and adjust it up or down in arbitrary increments. An initial offer in a negotiation can often be a figure that negotiators use as an anchor—whether or not the value is pertinent.
Gamblers' Fallacy	The belief that random patterns have a predictable sequence. People who do not understand statistics incorrectly believe that after a run of three heads in a coin toss, the likelihood of tossing tails is greater than 50 percent.
Framing	A tendency to evaluate an alternative as a potential gain or as a potential loss. Decision makers tend to be more risk-averse when evaluating gains and irrationally more risk-seeking when evaluating losses.
False Consensus	A person attributes his or her own beliefs to the group. Most people have the tendency to believe that others agree with them more than is actually warranted.
Illusory Correlation	The predisposition to relate two or more pieces of information simply because they are consumed within a similar timeframe (e.g. relating information from two completely different articles in a newspaper read during the same timeframe).
Unwarranted Causation	The belief that one event has caused the other without proof or consideration of other potential confounding factors. This is an extension of illusory correlation because the issues are not just related, but one is presumed to cause the other.

Temporal Bias

Hindsight Bias	Inferring the process once the outcome is known. Individuals overestimate the degree to which they would have predicted the correct outcome.
Escalation of Commitment	The tendency to continue on a strategic path to which you are already committed even though it may be irrational and can cause the company unnecessary losses.

Judgment Bias

Representative-ness	The more a person looks like the group stereotype the closer we associate them with that group, affecting how we might approach and evaluate them. Representativeness also brings forth the notion of cultural biases.
Confirmatory Evidence Bias	People tend to collect and value data that supports a currently held belief.
Just World	People believe good things happen to good people and bad to bad. As a result incorrect inferences are made about underlying causes.
Overconfidence	Underestimating the complexity of problems, creating an illusion that we have the management capabilities to deal with them.

Adapted from Ivey Business School teaching note by Vanden Hoven, F., Crossan, M., and Olivera, F., 2004.

you advocating an alternative just because it is the easy way out or because you are most familiar with its outcome? Are there facts to support your criteria and decision making rationale?

In helping your colleagues deal with their cognitive biases consider the following:

- Avoid information biases such as false consensus by asking why others may have a differing opinion and why that opinion might be valid.

- Attach a list of risks to each alternative and attempt to associate a likelihood of that risk happening. Include any further impacts from these risks including legal, medical, and ethical impacts.

- Be on the look out for "unwarranted causation" by asking questions regarding the root cause of issues as well as questions about information sources. Be sure to evaluate whether two factors are simply related or whether one actually causes the other.

- Be careful to dissect difficult strategic decisions. Avoid the "availability heuristic" trap by not using the information most readily available to make decisions. Ask difficult and penetrating questions about your available information and where it is incomplete.

- Seek out the most relevant information to make educated estimates based on real data instead of judgments based on arbitrary figures. Anchoring and adjustment errors are particularly problematic in negotiations. Initial offers in negotiations tend to be misleading and tend to limit your alternatives. Ensure that you generate as many alternatives as possible.

- As the expression goes—hindsight is always 20/20 and the decision maker assumes that the result was fated. The past is a powerful indicator of the future but it should not tether your opportunities. Be careful not to introduce past failures to crush the generation of alternatives in decision making.

- Remember that because a complex issue could be managed in the past that it may not be the case in the future. Be cautious of taking on too great a task and suffering from the "illusion of manageability". Be sure to have a complete list of potential risks associated with managing the alternative. Perform a resources check on each alternative (Is there sufficient money, assets, people, time?)

- "Over-confidence bias" strikes at the time one underestimates the likelihood of failure. Over-confidence can also limit the generation of alternatives. Taking a "devil's advocate" approach by arguing against your own alternative helps to reveal some of the flaws that would otherwise have been overlooked. For example, some firms employ a competitive gaming exercise by taking on the role of their competitors with a view to exposing the firm's vulnerabilities. In a group situation, publicly assigning the role of devil's advocate to someone can help to overcome "groupthink".

- The easiest way to underestimate a person's capability is to fall into the trap of "representativeness" by stereotyping that individual. Evaluate people based on skills, performance, and their broader experience.

- Avoid the problem of "frozen preference" by acknowledging that individuals will be partial to the alternatives they have generated. As in dealing with the overconfidence bias, it is helpful to have people play different roles that require them to expose the vulnerabilities of their own alternatives. In addition, as with several other types of biases, ensure you are utilizing as accurate and complete information as possible in support of your decision making.

Organizational Learning and Strategic Renewal

Viewing strategy as learning is more than applying a cognitive perspective to strategy. Learning is ultimately about how individuals and groups change both cognition and behaviour and how organizations themselves adapt. The 4I framework developed by Crossan, Lane and White, shown in Table 9.3, delineates the processes by which *intuitive* insights at the individual level in the form of images and experiences are *interpreted* as language develops to describe the experiences, and groups begin to *integrate* ideas to create a shared understanding. Ideas that gain some traction become *institutionalized* in the form of new structures, systems, strategies, and routines for the organization.[13] It is important to note that individual cognitive maps guide what is perceived and interpreted and those cognitive maps are also transformed in the process. The cognitive biases described above affect perception and judgment.

Table 9.3 4I Framework of Strategic Renewal

Level	Process	Input/Outcomes
Individual	Intuiting	Experiences
		Images
		Metaphors
	Interpreting	Language
		Cognitive map
Group		Conversation and dialogues
	Integrating	Shared understandings
		Mutual adjustment
		Interactive systems
	Institutionalizing	Routines
Organization		Diagnostic systems
		Rules and procedures

The levels and processes shown in the 4I framework are perhaps best understood by describing them in the context of the founding and growth of Apple Computer.

> By all accounts Steve Jobs, through an intuitive process, had the insights upon which Apple was founded. Jobs perceived patterns and evolved certain images about possibilities, which developed into a metaphor (e.g., the personal computer as an appliance; one in every home) that guided Apple during its early years. These were based, at least in part, upon his unique experiences and cognitive orientation. He provided much of the insight and energy that were the genesis of Apple. But these initial images were necessarily vague when it came to specific action. . . . On the basis of Jobs' own experiences and his perceptions of the events, along with Wozniak's technical expertise, they improvised actions as they went along.[14]

Admittedly, Jobs was insightful, yet he could not accomplish his vision alone. He needed others. The conversations and discourse, which helped to develop his understanding, also functioned to integrate the cognitive maps of the group. Shared understandings developed through those communication processes. Language plays, therefore, a critical role in the development of individual maps, and is key to integrating ideas and negotiating actions and meanings with others. Through conversation, areas of difference and agreement surface and groups come to share understandings and meanings.

> The organization naturally outgrows its ability to exclusively use spontaneous interactions to interpret, integrate and take concerted action. Relationships become formalized and routines develop. There is a need to ensure that the routines continue to be carried out, and the organization produces and performs. In the Apple situation John Sculley was brought in, at least in part, to provide the needed systems, structures, and other formal mechanisms. Individual and communal learning became institutionalized in the hope that it could be more systematically exploited. Institutionalization contributes to more efficient operations, enabling the organization to better deliver on the founder's original vision. It also may have hindered the organization's ability to renew itself by intuiting, interpreting, and integrating emerging patterns and new possibilities. Unable to realize his new vision within Apple, Steve Jobs left to start a new enterprise, appropriately called NeXT.[15]

Reconciling the Tensions in Strategic Renewal

The 4I framework and example of Apple Computer underscore the tension in strategic renewal between intended strategy and emergent strategy, planning and learning, and what many describe as a tension between exploration and exploitation.[16] The tension has been variously described as a tension between maturity and creation, and efficiency and flexibility.[17] March succinctly describes exploration, exploitation, and the balance between the two.

> Exploration includes things captured by terms such as search, variation, risk taking, experimentation, play, flexibility, discovery, innovation. Exploitation includes such things as refinement, choice, production, efficiency, selection, implementation, execution. Adaptive systems that engage in exploration to the exclusion of exploitation

are likely to find that they suffer the costs of experimentation without gaining many of its benefits. They exhibit too many undeveloped new ideas and too little distinctive competence. Conversely, systems that engage in exploitation to the exclusion of exploration are likely to find themselves trapped in suboptimal stable equilibria.[18]

We acknowledge that theses tensions exist, but believe that organizations can manage them. The first step is to understand that they exist. The second is to understand how they coexist. Crossan and her colleagues depict the tensions in the form of the Strategic Learning Assessment Map (SLAM) shown in Figure 9.2. As they expanded and developed the 4I framework they found that one of the major barriers to strategic renewal was the transference of learning across the three levels (individual, group, organization) and as a result SLAM focuses on the inter-relationship between the levels.[19] In addition, they found that managing the tensions described above was absolutely critical.

Across the diagonal of SLAM are the individual, group, and organization processes—the stocks of learning. The bottom right-hand corner represents the alignment of the non-human elements of the business such as the systems, structure, strategy, and procedures. It is through the feed-forward process that this institutionalized learning is renewed. Through the feedback process the organization is able to leverage and exploit what it has learned as the systems, procedures, routines, and strategy guide individual and group learning. In contrast to the stocks of learning that occur within a level, the feed-forward and feedback processes are the flows of learning across the levels. In a study of the Canadian mutual fund industry Bontis, Crossan, and Hulland found that the greater the gap between the stocks and flows of learning, the worse the performance of the organization.[20] As a result, strategic renewal depends critically on strong feed-forward and feedback flows.

The feed-forward and feedback flows represent the tension between learning and planning, exploration and exploitation, intended and emergent strategy. The reality is that organizations need all of these processes. They need to exploit what they have learned through feedback processes with a strong intentional orientation around how

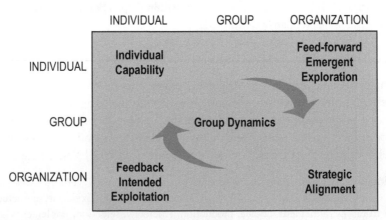

Figure 9.2 Strategic Learning Assessment Map

strategy, structure, systems, and routines guide what individuals do and pay attention to. For example, organization structure has a profound impact on who talks to whom in the organization. While you may pride yourself in your promotion of team development, if your structure and perhaps reward systems get in the way of having the right people work together, you will not fully realize the benefits of teamwork. The trick is that the various processes and routines that support your current strategy may impede the feed-forward, exploration, and emergent processes required for strategic renewal. In particular, budgeting and resource allocation processes tend to favour established projects since those projects have a documented track record and less ambiguity about market potential or competitive response, for example.

It is interesting to note that entrepreneurial organizations suffer from an excess of emergent strategy and need more intended strategy and stronger feedback processes while more mature organizations tend to become ossified in their feedback process. As a result, mature organizations find their emergent and feed-forward processes stifled by bureaucracy. Managing the tensions that exist in strategic renewal are therefore different for every organization. As previously mentioned, you need to assess whether your industry runs hot or cold to determine the appropriate balance. You also need to understand the stage of your organizational development as there are critical differences between start-up and mature organizations. However, we contend that, if receptive, it is easier to layer on the routines and procedures that support a more intended orientation to strategy than it is to rediscover the emergent feed-forward approaches that have tended to recede in mature organizations.

Many researchers have taken particular interest in how mature organizations better reconcile the tensions we have described. Brown and Eisenhardt suggest that firms need to compete on the edge of chaos[21] using a process of improvisation.[22] Improvisation, borrowed from jazz and theatre, has been successfully applied in business settings. Improvisation training has helped individuals and groups become more spontaneous and innovative, and has revealed important organizational characteristics that enable effective strategic renewal, such as having a tolerance for error, timely access to key information, a constant pruning of policies and procedures to reveal the minimal constraints that guide strategic decisions, and distributed leadership that supports innovation and learning.

The processes of organizational learning and improvisation are what deliver the kind of nimbleness that many people refer to when talking about what it takes to execute strategy well. For example, consider the points about information flow offered by Neilson, Martin, and Powers. They suggest that to achieve great execution "everyone has a good idea of the decisions and actions for which he or she is responsible," "important information about the competitive environment gets to headquarters quickly," "information flows freely across organizational boundaries," and "line managers have access to the metrics they need to measure the key drivers of their business."[23] There is a long laundry list of what needs to be done to ensure great feed-forward and feedback flow of learning in the organization in a timely fashion. Our experience is that the problems in executing strategy in a dynamic fashion have much to do with the individual cognitive and ideological challenges and the associated leadership required to enable organizational learning for strategic renewal.

LEADERSHIP FOR STRATEGIC RENEWAL

Reconciling the tensions we have described—to treat strategy as a dynamic process that encompasses planning and learning, exploitation and exploration, intended and emergent strategy, as well as the feedback and feed-forward processes—necessitates solid leadership. Crossan and Hulland found a strong correlation between the quality of leadership around organizational learning and the overall performance of the organization. It will come as no surprise that even in bottom-up distributed processes of organizational learning, leadership sets the context in which that learning occurs. Ultimately, it is the senior leadership that must endorse significant resource allocation decisions and who determine what learning gets institutionalized in the form of new strategies, structures, and systems.[24]

In the next chapter we delineate different types of leadership approaches associated with strategic change. In this section we provide a brief overview of some key leadership models as they relate to strategy. The tension between feed-forward and feedback, or exploration and exploitation focuses our attention on the need for different kinds of leadership. It is not surprising that *transformational* or *charismatic* leaders are best suited to situations that require transformation and change; the processes of feed-forward and exploration. *Transactional* leaders are ideal for managing the status quo or the processes of feedback and exploitation.[25] Transactional leaders set goals and expectations about how people will be rewarded for their efforts and commitment. They work to strengthen an organization's existing culture, strategy, and structure. Transformational leadership, in contrast, is charismatic, inspirational, and intellectually stimulating. Transformational leaders inspire others with their vision, create excitement through their enthusiasm, and puncture time-worn assumptions through their resolve to reframe the future, question the tried and true, and have everybody do the same.

Transformational leadership is closely associated with Rowe's notion of *visionary leadership* and transaction leadership is closely associated with his notion of *managerial leadership*. Rowe points out that *strategic leadership* is able to combine the visionary leadership associated with change and the managerial leadership associated with maintaining the business. Strategic leadership is the ability to influence others so that they voluntarily make day-to-day decisions that enhance the long-term viability of the organization, while at the same time maintaining its short-term financial stability. Visionary leadership is future-oriented and concerned with risk-taking. Visionary leaders are not dependent on their organizations for their sense of who they are. Under visionary leaders, organizational control is maintained through socialization and the sharing of, and compliance with, a commonly held set of norms, values, and shared beliefs. Managerial leadership involves stability and order, and the preservation of the existing order. Managerial leaders are more comfortable handling day-to-day activities and are short-term oriented."[26]

The theme differentiating leadership and management is longstanding. In 1977 Abraham Zaleznik provided a wake-up call to business and academia with his article "Managers and Leaders: Are They Different?" He admonished that our pre-occupation with managerial techniques was causing us to lose sight of key elements of leadership:

inspiration, vision, and passion. Kotter provided a succinct description of the differences between leadership and management.

> Leadership is different from management, but not for the reasons most people think. Leadership isn't mystical and mysterious. It has nothing to do with having "charisma" or other exotic personality traits. It is not the province of a chosen few. Nor is leadership necessarily better than management or a replacement for it. Rather, leadership and management are two distinctive and complementary systems of action. Each has its own function and characteristic activities. Both are necessary for success in an increasingly complex and volatile business environment . . . Management is about coping with complexity . . . . Good management brings a degree of order and consistency to key dimensions like the quality and profitability of products . . . . Leadership, by contrast, is about coping with change.[27]

In recent years, the management/leadership theme has expanded and there has been significant attention devoted to deepening our understanding of effective leadership. Jim Collins' study of the factors that enabled companies to transform themselves from "good to great" revealed that "the most powerfully transformative executives possess a paradoxical mixture of personal humility and professional will. They are timid and ferocious. Shy and fearless. They are rare—and unstoppable."[28] He referred to this type of leadership as "Level 5 Leadership". Other researchers have explored the softer side of leadership, advancing concepts such as *emotional intelligence* and *primal leadership*. It was found that an executive's emotional maturity (self-awareness and empathy) were positively linked to financial performance as was the leader's mood or emotional style.[29] In 2004, 18 leadership experts banded together to collaborate on an article entitled "Leading by Feel." They conclude that "empathy, intuition, and self-awareness are essential to good leadership, but they can be tricky to hone and dangerous to use."[30]

In summary, there is a role for strategy as more intended or planned, and strategy as more emergent or learned. There are natural tensions, paradoxes, and ambiguities that need to be managed and leadership is critical. As we begin to understand dynamic processes of strategy, new facets of leadership have emerged.

THE PRACTICAL MATTER OF STRATEGIC CHOICE AT A POINT OF TIME

Whatever the background process, from a ground-up strategy development process to a key decision in the ongoing flow of business, there comes a point for strategic choice and for considering implementation. At this time there is no avoiding the need to do a Diamond-E analysis, even if it is a quick review and check-off, as might be in the case in an emergent situation.

We suggest a summary format to help you pull together the most critical parts of your Diamond-E analysis in Table 9.4. Revisit each element of your work (strategy-environment,

Table 9.4 Strategic Proposal Performance Projections

Diamond-E Relationship	Major Uncertainties	Worst Case	Most Likely	Best Case
Strategic Proposal One				
Strategy-Environment				
Strategy-Resources				
Strategy-Management Preferences				
Strategy-Organization				
Cross-Category Impacts				
Proposal One: Performance Projections				
Strategic Proposal Two				
Etc.				

strategy-resources, strategy-management preferences, and strategy-organization) to iden-tify the major uncertainties associated with each. Then indicate the best case, worst case, and most likely outcome in each area of uncertainty. As you do this, you might find that events or outcomes in one area are linked to those in another. Pay close attention, as this is the first time that you have explicitly looked for links *between* the different areas of your Diamond-E analysis. We call this *cross-category impact*. The assessment of cross-category impact is the last logical step in your strategic assessment.

By way of example, let us say that your strategic proposal is to enter a new area of business. You know that one of the firms already in this business is working on a new tech-nology that could result in an improved product at lower cost. You are not sure, however, whether this technology will actually work or, if it does work, in what time frame the improved product could arrive on the market. You have considered various possibilities in your strategy-environment assessment. Your best case outcome is that your competitor's new technology is a total failure, and your worst case is that it is both more effective than expected, and arrives early.

The cross-category impact starts to emerge as you realize that if the new technol-ogy comes much earlier than expected you will have trouble raising the equity that you need to fund your entry into this business. Furthermore, your vice presidents of finance and engineering, who have been lukewarm about entering the new business from the start, might resist even more strongly, once they see the competitor's new product on the market, and not give the new strategy the support that it will require. Their lack of enthusiasm will be readily apparent to their subordinates, who will put tasks associated with the new entry low on their priority lists, and will not assign their best people to the new business area.

It is in this way that an external event, over which you have no control, might impinge on (1) your ability to raise new resources; (2) the likelihood that you will be able to change the management preferences of at least two key managers; and (3) your ability to marshal the organizational capabilities needed to support the new strategy. These are the types of linkages that you should be looking for as you prepare Table 9.4.

The final step in completing Table 9.4 is to create performance projections for each strategic proposal. These do not need to be extremely detailed, but they should include the key profit and loss and balance sheet items, under best case, worst case, and most likely conditions.

SUMMARY

At this point you should have a good feel for the potential risks and payoffs of each of your proposals. The choice is yours to make. Do not allow yourself to be paralyzed by risk. The challenge now is to balance the risks that you are taking against the enhanced performance that is likely to result. If you have followed the analysis that we have suggested thus far, you have done enough homework! It is time to make a decision. Remember that the biggest risk of all may be in making no decision, or deciding to wait for events to unfold.

To successfully implement your chosen strategy, you will need to initiate and manage change in your organization. You will need to determine the nature of the needed changes, the urgency for change, the support that will be available, and the resistance that you will face, and then determine best way forward. These are the topics to which we turn in the last two chapters.

Notes

1. Mintzberg, H., B. Ahlstrand, and J. Lampel. *Strategy Safari: A Guided Tour Through the Wilds of Strategic Management*. New York: The Free Press, 1998. 15–17. Print.

2. See *California Management Review* 38.4 (Summer 1996) for a series of articles on the planning/learning debate. Print.

3. Tushman, Michael L., Wendy K. Smith, and Andy Binns. "The Ambidextrous CEO." *Harvard Business Review* 89.6 (2011): 74–80. *Business Source Complete, EBSCO*. Web. 16 Aug. 2011. Print.

4. Grant, Robert M. "Strategic Planning in a Turbulent Environment: Evidence From the Oil Majors." *Strategic Management Journal* 24 (2003): 491–517. Print.

5. Grant, Robert M. "Strategic Planning in a Turbulent Environment: Evidence From the Oil Majors." *Strategic Management Journal* 24 (2003): 491–517. Print. 507.

6. Grant, Robert M. "Strategic Planning in a Turbulent Environment: Evidence From the Oil Majors." *Strategic Management Journal* 24 (2003): 491–517. Print. 510.

7. Hamel, Gary, and Liisa Valikangas. "The Quest for Resilience," *Harvard Business Review* 81 (September 2003): 52. Print.

8. Reeves, Martin, and Mike Deimler. "Adaptability: The New Competitive Advantage." *Harvard Business Review* 89.7/8 (2011): 134–141. *Business Source Complete, EBSCO*. Web. 15 Aug. 2011.

9. De Geus, A. "Planning as Learning." *Harvard Business Review* 66 (March–April 1988): 70–74. Print.

10. Hamel, Gary, and Liisa Valikangas. "The Quest for Resilience," *Harvard Business Review* 81 (September 2003): 52. Print.

11. The material in this section was based on the Ivey Business School teaching note developed by Vanden Hoven, F., M. Crossan, and F. Olivera, 2004.

12. Bazerman, Max. *Judgment in Managerial Decision Making*. 4th edition. New York: John Wiley & Sons, 1998. Print.; Neale, Margaret A., and Max H Bazerman. *Cognition and Rationality in Negotiation*. New York: The Free Press, 1991. Print.

13. Crossan, M., H. Lane, and R.E. White. "An Organization Learning Framework: From Intuition to Institution," *Academy of Management Review* 24.3 (1999). Print.

14. Crossan, M., H. Lane, and R.E. White. "An Organization Learning Framework: From Intuition to Institution," *Academy of Management Review* 24.3 (1999): 530–531. Print.

15. Crossan, M., H. Lane, and R.E. White. "An Organization Learning Framework: From Intuition to Institution," *Academy of Management Review* 24.3 (1999): 531. Print.

16. March, J.G. "Exploration and Exploitation in Organization Learning." *Organization Science* 2 (1991): 71–87. Print.

17. The tension has been variously described as a tension between creation and maturity, flexibility and efficiency (Lant, T., and S. Mezias. "An Organizational Learning Model of Convergence and Reorientation," *Organization Science* 3 (1992): 47–71. Print.); variation and selection (Ashby, W.R. *Design for a Brain: The Origin of Adaptive Behavior*. 2nd ed. New York: John Wiley & Sons, 1992. Print.)

18. March, J.G. (1991): 71. Print.

19. Crossan, M., and J. Hulland. "Leveraging Knowledge Through Leadership of Organizational Learning." *Strategic Management of Intellectual Capital and Organizational Knowledge: A Collection of Readings*. Eds. C. Choo, and N. Bontis. New York: Oxford University Press, 2002. 711–723. Print.

20. Bontis, N., M. Crossan, and J. Hulland. "Managing an Organizational Learning System by Aligning Stocks and Flows of Knowledge." *Journal of Management Studies* 39.4 (June 2002): 437–470. Print.

21. Brown, S.L., and K.M. Eisenhardt. "The Art of Continuous Change: Linking Complexity Theory and Time-paced Evolution in Relentlessly Shifting Organizations." *Administrative Science Quarterly* 42 (March 1997): 1–34. Print.; Brown, S.L., and K.M. Eisenhardt. *Competing on the edge: Strategy as structured chaos*. Boston: Harvard Business School Press, 1998. Print.

22. For further information on improvisation see the following articles: Crossan, M.M. "Improvisation in Action." *Organization Science* 9 (September–October 1998): 593–599. Print.; Crossan, M.M., et al. "The Improvising Organization: Where Planning Meets Opportunity." *Organizational Dynamics* 24 (Spring 1996): 20–35. Print.; Hatch, M.J. "Jazz as a Metaphor for Organizing in the 21st Century." *Organization Science* 9 (September–October 1998): 556–557. Print.; Moorman, C., and A. Miner. "The Convergence of Planning and Execution: Improvisation in New Product Development." *Journal of Marketing* 62 (July 1998): 1–20. Print.; Weick, K. E. "Improvisation as a Mindset for Organizational Analysis." *Organization Science* 9 (September–October 1998): 543–555. Print.

23. Neilson, Gary L., Karla L. Martin, and Elizabeth Powers. "The Secrets to Successful Strategy Execution." *Harvard Business Review* 86.6 (2008): 60–70. *Business Source Complete, EBSCO*. Web. 16 Aug. 2011.

24. Crossan, M., and J. Hulland. "Leveraging Knowledge Through Leadership of Organizational Learning." *Strategic Management of Intellectual Capital and Organizational Knowledge: A Collection of Readings*. Eds. C. Choo, and N. Bontis. New York: Oxford University Press, 2002. 711–723. Print.

25. Avolio, B.J., B.M. Bass, and D.I. Jung. "Re-examining the Components of Transformational and Transactional Leadership Using the Multifactor Leadership Questionnaire." *Journal of Occupational and Organizational Psychology* 72 (1999): 441–462. Print.

26. Rowe, Glenn W. "Creating Wealth in Organizations: The Role of Strategic Leadership." *The Academy of Management Executive* 15 (2001): 81–95. Print.

27. Kotter, John P. "What Leaders Really Do." *Harvard Business Review* 79 (December 2001): 85. Print.

28. Collins, Jim. "Level 5 Leadership." *Harvard Business Review* 79 (January 2001): 66. Print.

29. Goleman, D., R. Boyatzis, and A. McKee. "Primal Leadership: The Hidden Driver of Great Performance," *Harvard Business Review* 79 (December 2001): 42. Print.

30. Voices, "Leading by Feel," *Harvard Business Review* 82 (January 2004): 27. Print.

Additional Readings

1. Bass, B.M. *Transformational Leadership: Industry, Military, and Educational Impact*. Mahway, NY: Lawrence Erlbarum, 1998. Print.

2. Branzei, O., and C. Zietsma. "Temporary Cognitions of Entrepreneurial Love: Dancing with the Opportunity." *Frontiers of Entrepreneurship Research*. Babson Park, MA: Arthur M. Blank Center for Entrepreneurship, Babson College, 2003. 242–256. Print.

3. House, R.J., and B. Shamir. "Towards the Integration of Transformational, Charismatic and Visionary Theories." *Leadership Theory and Research: Perspectives and Directions*. Eds. M.M. Chemers and R. Ayman. San Diego, CA: Academic Press, 1993. 81–107. Print.

4. Tichy, N.M., and Devanna, M.A. *The Transformational Leader*. New York: John Wiley and Sons, 1986. Print.

5. Waldman, D.A., et al. "Does Leadership Matter? CEO Leadership Attributes and Profitability Under Conditions of Perceived Environmental Uncertainty." *Academy of Management Journal* 44 (2001): 134–143. Print.

Chapter 10
Implementing Strategy: Change Agenda and Starting Conditions

In previous chapters we have reviewed the analysis associated with all elements of the Diamond-E framework, and the associated tensions between what a firm "needs" to do, what it "wants" to do, and what it "can" do. This chapter is the first of two dealing with the implementation of strategic change. To this point we have focused on identifying and assessing strategic problems and opportunities, and deciding what changes in strategy would be most beneficial for your business. Now we turn to action. How do you go about making the changes that are necessary to implement your new strategy?

It is critical to recognize that the distinction between strategy formulation and implementation is artificial in many respects. In addition to the fact that they often occur simultaneously, it is dangerous to disconnect the "doing" of strategy from the "thinking" about strategy. As Martin points out, the view that there are those who formulate strategy and those who execute risks having "employees internalize the choiceless-doer model and stick to it faithfully."[1] The problem is that great execution comes from an intimate appreciation of the strategy and a freedom to operate within the bounds of that strategy. Furthermore, without the insight and engagement of front-line employees it is difficult both to formulate and execute strategy, as was discussed in Chapter 9. Many people equate implementation or execution with what we have incorporated under Organization in the Diamond-E Framework. We feel treating these elements of organization as part of implementation is a mistake and typically constrains strategy to doing an industry or environmental analysis. Much to our dismay, there are firms that say "we just had a consulting firm help us formulate a strategy, can you help us figure out the resources and capabilities we need for it?" By now, we hope you understand that strategy needs to encompass external and internal factors. Therefore, much of what has been written about execution, we have already incorporated into the chapter on Organization. What is important to consider around implementation is strategic change. Ultimately, great strategy formulation anticipates strategy implementation.

IMPLEMENTING STRATEGIC CHANGE

Managers wishing to implement strategic change face many challenges and choices. A common obstacle, for example, is that many people in the organization may not be ready for change. Thus, you might begin your change program by looking for some easy wins—small changes that will have a positive impact—to demonstrate that altering the usual way of doing things can be beneficial. On the other hand, you might judge that it makes more sense to tackle the big, more difficult issues immediately.

You will also face the challenge of deciding who should lead the change process, and how it should be led. It is unlikely that you will try to drive your change program alone. But should you spend your time and energy working with people who are most likely to agree with your proposed changes, or focus on those most likely to resist? Then there is the question of management style. Some managers lead change in a top-down, directive style, whereas others are more participative. Which is right for your situation?

This chapter and the next will help you develop a change plan to address such questions, but be forewarned that there is no generic set of "right answers" to the questions that emerge when managing change.[2] An appropriate change plan for you and your business will be unique to your situation, reflecting your particular change needs, and the conditions in which you are launching your change program.

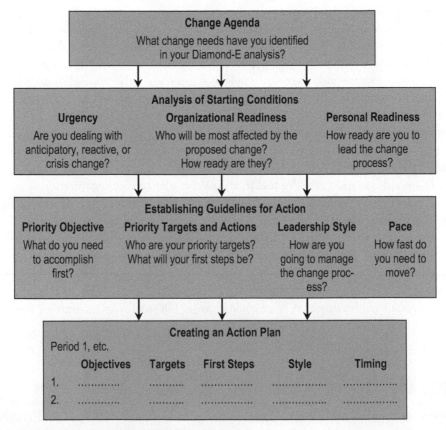

Figure 10.1 Creating a Change Plan

THE CHANGE PLAN

An overview of the steps for building a change plan is presented in Figure 10.1. In this chapter we discuss the first two: identifying the change agenda that has emerged from your Diamond-E analysis, and analyzing the starting conditions that will shape your program of change. These include assessing the urgency for change, the readiness of the organization to make the required changes, and your personal readiness to lead the change. In Chapter 11 we will discuss guidelines for action and your specific action plan for achieving change.

CHANGE AGENDA

At this point you have completed your Diamond-E analysis and chosen your preferred strategic option. In that analysis, you identified new resources, new organizational capabilities, and perhaps new management preferences that will need to be developed to implement your new strategy. You also determined how you might bring about the changes in behaviour needed to develop those new organizational capabilities through changes in senior management behaviour, management processes, organization structure, or management style.

As a first step in developing a change plan, we suggest that you collect the change needs identified in your Diamond-E analysis to prepare a change agenda, as shown in Table 10.1. To prepare such a chart, take the change needs that have emerged

Table 10.1 Change Agenda

	Change Needs Identified in Diamond-E Analysis		
	Non-Behavioural Changes Required	**Behavioural Changes Required**	**Potential Changes in Organization**
Develop New Resources			
Change Management Preferences			
Develop New Organizational Capabilities			
Change Strategy Components (e.g., new product market focus, value proposition, or core activities)			
Influence the Environment			

from each section of your Diamond-E analysis, separating those that will require behavioural change from those that will not, and list the organizational changes that you identified in the analysis of Chapter 8 that might bring about those behavioural changes.

We suggest this because behavioural changes are the most difficult to achieve, and this difficulty is often underestimated. The dangerous assumption is that if something makes sense (at least to the people proposing it) then everybody will fall in line and change their ways of doing things to conform with the new demands. Unfortunately, this seldom happens as easily as anticipated. People do not fall into line, sometimes because they just do not have the understanding and the skills required, and sometimes because they perceive, accurately or not, that the changes are not in their best interests.

ANALYSIS OF STARTING CONDITIONS

The first of the three categories of starting conditions shown in Figure 10.1 is the *urgency* for action—how clear and pressing are the forces driving the action that you have in mind? The second category deals with *organizational readiness*—who are the people who will be most involved in or affected by the change, and how ready are they to adopt and implement the prescribed changes? The third category has to do with your *personal readiness*—given the course of action being considered, how well-prepared and positioned are you to lead the process of change? We will discuss these starting conditions in order.

URGENCY FOR ACTION: THE CRISIS CURVE

Urgency refers to the pressure to implement the changes that you have in mind. Naturally, there will always be some urgency attached to these changes. The degree of urgency will vary, however, with the strategic performance of your business and the timing of the impact of the changing conditions. This relationship is demonstrated in the crisis curve of Figure 10.2, in which we have identified three categories of urgency ranging from the

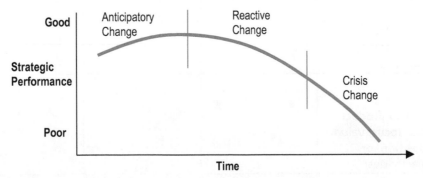

Figure 10.2 Urgency for Action: The Crisis Curve

relatively low pressure of anticipatory change to the absolutely immediate demands of crisis change.

A useful way to think about the crisis curve is by imagining a business that is doing very well, with performance improving over time as shown on the left-hand side of the curve. As some of the managers of this business look ahead, they suspect that significant changes will occur in the environment, but these changes are in the future and uncertain in their impact. To implement strategic change at this time would be an act of *anticipatory change*—management is acting in anticipation of future events.

Suppose that, for a variety of reasons, management does not act on the forecast changes and these changes start to have an effect. Performance plateaus and then begins to deteriorate. To implement strategic change in this span of time would be an act of *reactive change*—management is reacting to current environmental pressures.

Suppose even further that management fails to act or to act effectively in response to the continuing development of external events. Performance deteriorates at an accelerating pace, leading to a point of crisis from which recovery is improbable. To implement strategic change as a business falls down this slope would be an act of *crisis change*.

Understanding where you are on the crisis curve provides some helpful cues about management issues you will have to tackle and helps focus your analysis on the starting conditions with which you are dealing. In Table 10.2 we summarize the basic conditions

Table 10.2 Summary Characteristics of the Change Categories

	Anticipatory	Reactive	Crisis
Prevailing Conditions			
Strategic performance	Healthy	Sliding	Critical
Need for change	Uncertain	Becoming clearer	Clear
Time pressure	Little	Have to get started	Urgent
Internal commitment for change	Low	Mixed	High
Management capability	High	Mixed	Low
Management Issues			
Strategic	Is change necessary?	Where to start?	Achieving rapid pace of change
Organizational Personal	Lack of commitment Credibility	Dealing with resistors Power	Who to rely on? Links to past

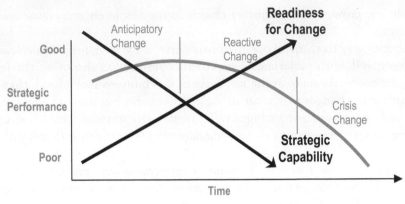

Figure 10.3 Readiness for Change and Strategic Capability

of each change category and the management issues that are typically associated with them. We will review these characteristics in the following paragraphs, but first we will elaborate on the "strategic performance" measure.

The objective of measuring strategic performance, as we pointed out in Chapter 1, is to capture an accurate picture of the progress and position of a business in its markets. The most accessible measures for this purpose are those of revenue and profitability and for the most part these are satisfactory indicators. But remember that financial measures such as these are *lagging* indicators of the true progress and position of the business. Revenue, for example, might continue to increase for some time after market share starts to fall because of underlying market growth, giving the illusion of progress. Similarly, market share can continue to increase for some time after the business has actually begun losing its position in the eyes of its customers, because of long-term commitments and inertia in purchasing habits and systems.

If you suspect that the financial indicators are indeed giving an optimistic reading of the true position of the business, it is very important to look beyond them to measures of market position and customer satisfaction. Otherwise the true urgency of the business situation will be misread.

The challenging dynamic of managing strategic transitions is that as the readiness for change increases, the strategic capability decreases, as noted in Figure 10.3.

Crisis Change

Crisis conditions are the most urgent and undeniable of the three change categories. The problems that you face are clear: an opportunity may be disappearing, sales may be in collapse, important customers may be cancelling orders, suppliers may be putting you on "cash on delivery," a cash crunch may be imminent, or banks may be on the brink of calling their loans. Fast, focused, and decisive action is required.

When Asda, one of England's largest supermarket chains, fell into crisis, its board of directors brought in 37-year-old Archie Norman to turn around the struggling business of 200 retail grocery stores.[3] As is usually the case in crisis, the symptoms were visible both inside and outside the company, and Norman knew he was walking into a tough situation. "Turning around Asda was *the* big challenge in British retailing," he commented. "Here was a business that was a recognized failure."

When Norman arrived, the Asda chain had suffered from 10 years of poor management as it tried to move the supermarket away from its once well-established position at the low end of the market. The supermarket's traditional value-oriented customers were deserting it, employee morale was low, profits were declining, the company's stock price had fallen by 50 percent in three months, and it was in danger of defaulting on its debts, which were more than £1 billion.

Norman wasted no time, addressing Asda's senior management team at 9 a.m. on his first day on the job. Like most managers dropped into a crisis situation, he did not mince words: "Incremental change is not enough," he stated. "There are no sacred cows. Our number one objective is to secure value for the shareholders and to secure our trading future. I am not coming in with any magical solutions. I intend to spend the next few weeks listening and forming ideas for our precise direction."

He also declared that liquidity was critical, and every possible source of cash would be exploited to the full. In addition, there would be a reorganization to shorten reporting lines to the stores, to build one management team, with the stores as the central focus. Interestingly, he also stated that there would be two experimental new store formats up and running within six months. These stores became "risk-free zones" where new ideas could be tried, and those that worked transferred to the rest of the chain. Norman described the experimental stores as "points of light" that everyone could look to, to see the future. Even before his short-term survival moves had shown positive results, Norman was working to build the future.

Crisis Change Conditions In crisis change, the business faces clear-cut external and internal challenges. In these conditions, people inside and outside your organization will usually be aware of the situation and will be expecting—even demanding—that changes be made to save the business. There may be some exceptions, but these people can usually be made to see the necessity for action quickly with the all too abundant and undeniable evidence of difficulty. The really tough issues are to come up with immediate actions that will stay the crisis and set the stage for subsequent recovery.

Management Issues In undertaking crisis change you will need to tackle a typical set of issues. Financial issues are usually a high priority, and the challenge will be to buy time. In a free-standing business, you have to convince bankers, suppliers, and perhaps customers to give you the benefit of the doubt and to postpone any precipitate action that would put you out of business. If the crisis is in a business unit in a large company, the challenge is to convince senior managers to give you the time and money you need for a turnaround. In either case, you need to demonstrate that you understand the gravity of the situation. Archie Norman did so by immediately terminating Asda's chief financial officer, and by instituting a pay freeze for all 71,000 employees, cutting off investment in new stores, and putting undeveloped store sites and a peripheral business up for sale—all within a period of one month. Asda's bankers recognized that Norman understood the financial difficulties facing the business, was taking appropriate action, and gave him their support.

An added difficulty in trying to manage your way out of crisis is that you are usually saddled with seriously depleted resources. As businesses slide through reactive conditions and into crisis, good people leave, assets are run into the ground, and external reputations are strained. There is a very real risk that this process may have gone beyond the point of no return.

You may also have to confront your own involvement in the business through the period of decline and fall. If you have been part of that period you will clearly have to break your links with the past—in your own thinking and actions and in the perception of others. The evidence suggests that outsiders may have the best chance of breaking the existing thinking, habits, and relationships that have led to the decline of businesses. Certainly the decision to appoint Terry Semel, who knew nothing about the internet, to take the helm of Yahoo!, must have seemed like a major gamble. But he dramatically reversed the company's fortunes—a task which an insider may not have been able to do.

If you are a new arrival, like Terry Semel or Archie Norman, you have probably inherited the management team that created the crisis. These may not be the best people to figure out how to save the business and work through the tough conditions of a turnaround. But one of the realities of crisis change is that you may be stuck with these managers, whether you like it or not; it is difficult to recruit new talent to a business that looks as if it is going down the drain. Archie Norman judged that he would be able to attract one or two senior outsiders to Asda, but for the first year or two he thought that he was going to have to depend heavily on people who, in his words, "could not really do the job."

Anticipatory Change

The circumstances of anticipatory change are at quite the opposite end of the spectrum from the clarity and desperation of crisis. This, unfortunately, is a mixed blessing. Anticipatory conditions allow you time to think and to act in a considered way; but the coincident lack of pressure or perceived urgency can pose a formidable obstacle to change. Consider the case of Pepsi's North American soft drink operations.[4]

The 1980s were a very successful period for the Pepsi business, as earnings growth regularly topped 15 percent per year. Pepsi North America, with its "Pepsi Challenge" advertising campaign claiming that consumers preferred the taste of Pepsi to Coke, was widely viewed as a more entrepreneurial organization than Coca-Cola. In 1990, growth and profitability were still strong, and the outlook for the new decade was for more of the same.

But Craig Weatherup, who had taken over as Pepsi's North American president, was worried by a number of factors, both inside and outside the company, even though they had not yet impinged on the business. His primary concerns were that the rate of growth of soft drinks, especially colas, was slowing, and private-label cola sales were starting to increase. In addition, Pepsi was not able to increase prices and still stay competitive with Coke, and Coke was widening its lead in terms of volume of cola sold, because of its extensive distribution through fountain sales in outlets like McDonald's.

By mid-1990 Weatherup definitely felt that "things weren't right," and he spent some months interviewing industry experts, customers, and employees to develop a better feel for the situation. In September he met with his ten direct reports to try and convince them of the urgency that he now felt for change. As he later stated, Weatherup was trying to get his managers to see overnight the unpalatable vision of the future that he had taken months to develop for himself. He painted a stark choice for his team. They could continue as they were and be a mediocre bottling company with a 5 to 10 percent annual growth rate, or they could strive for an annual target of 15 percent growth per year and be one of the premier companies in the United States.

Setting aside whatever misgivings they had (and Weatherup did admit there were areas of doubt in the external picture that he had painted for his team), Pepsi's senior managers began thinking about how to bring change to an organization that was performing well, and saw no particular need to change. An initial brainstorming session of the 10 managers produced a list of 35 potential "change levers," ranging from buying franchises to an increased focus on the customer, and they voted as to which would be the best place to start.

As might be expected, the change process was not as orderly and linear as first envisaged. Many employees did not see the need for change, and senior management did not want to push too far until everyone was on board. As a result, the journey took several years and led Pepsi North America into the creation of a vision statement; a major process re-engineering effort; the creation of a "total beverage" strategy, which took the company into iced tea, juice, and "new age" drinks; and finally to a reorganization which broke the business into 107 profit centres, where there had previously been one.

Weatherup's persistence paid off. Operating profit from Pepsi's domestic soft drink operations grew at more than 15 percent per year, and the operating margin grew by 25 percent. With hindsight one could argue that Weatherup's ability to manage "ahead of the curve" saved his business from an almost certain downturn in performance in the mid-1990s. Weatherup's persistence paid off in other ways as he received a series of promotions, becoming CEO of Pepsi-Cola in 1996 and then CEO of Pepsi Bottling Group (PBG) in 1999, taking it public with the fifth-largest initial public offering (IPO) in history. In 2001 he handed over the CEO position of PBG to Greg Carns, but remained as chairman.

Anticipatory Change Conditions In anticipatory change situations, strategic performance is healthy. A look out of the window at today's environment would reinforce today's strategy. The events of concern are events of the future; they have yet to have any impact on the business. Whatever the opportunities or problems that lay ahead, they are uncertain in their precise nature, their intensity, and their potential impact on the business.

Management Issues The strategic issues that you face in tackling an anticipatory change situation are the result of the uncertainties facing the business. The problem that you are dealing with is simply not that clear. Under these circumstances it is essential to figure out how you can balance the risks of omission and commission: to do nothing puts the business at risk of being late or unable to deal with the forecast developments. To go too far, however, might commit the business to strategic changes that turn out to be dead wrong. Did Pepsi need to change? How much? How fast? Was re-engineering an appropriate response to the issues the business faced? Was the total beverage strategy the right move—or should the company have put all its energy into its core cola products? All of these issues were hotly debated.

A second issue in managing anticipatory change is the lack of a sense of urgency for change among the people in the organization. The business has been doing well, after all, and most employees have been doing pretty well, too. It is one of the frustrations of anticipatory situations that you may be the only one who is convinced there is a need for change. Given the actual uncertainties of the situation, you have a limited ability to prove that change is necessary.

A third management issue in anticipatory change involves your personal credibility. The problems of managing in an ill-defined situation with minimal perceived urgency put a premium on credibility. To be effective in anticipatory change you need to have, or to build, and preserve credibility. It may be your prime resource as you try to marshal action in anticipation of the long-term challenges. In this respect, Craig Weatherup was well placed. He had led Pepsi during some very successful years, and was both well-liked and well-respected. A manager new to the business would probably have had a far more difficult task in persuading the organization that difficult times lay ahead. The reality for all managers is that the ambiguity of anticipatory situations means your credibility will always be tested. If you do not seem to have done your homework, or if you are wrong too often, you will lose the capacity to influence the direction of the business.

Reactive Change

The conditions of reactive change fall between those of anticipatory and crisis change. Strategic performance has gone over the top and is sliding. The need for change is becoming increasingly clear, but often not all executives see it, or they do see it, but respond too slowly. Consider the case of Scottish & Newcastle (S&N), the world's sixth-largest brewer, based in Edinburgh, Scotland.

In 2000, after selling a variety of non-brewing operations such as leisure parks and holiday camps, S&N embarked on an acquisition strategy to expand its brewing business beyond its mature UK home market. The first purchase was Kronenburg, at the time Europe's second largest brewer, and this was followed by smaller acquisitions in Portugal,

Greece, Finland, Russia, and the Baltic States. The rationale was to bring the acquired brands such as Kronenburg (France) and Baltica (Russia) into the UK market, and take S&N's big brands such as Newcastle Brown Ale and Fosters (for which S&N has the European rights) into the new acquisitions. To pay off some of the accumulated debt of more than £4 billion, the company subsequently sold its UK pubs division for £2.5 billion.

By 2002 it was clear that the strategy was not working. The acquired companies were running independently, much as they had before being acquired, and their financial results were not good enough, considering the amount S&N had paid for them. Furthermore, they were not providing much growth, as beer consumption was declining in most of Western Europe. (The one bright spot in growth terms was Russia.) Although still profitable, S&N was destroying shareholder value. By early 2003 the company's stock price was just more than half of what it had been 12 months earlier.

In response to the worsening situation, S&N's chairman decided an outside CEO was needed, and in the spring of 2003, Tony Froggatt, an Australian with extensive experience in the spirits industry, was hired as the new CEO. He spent his early months in S&N visiting all parts of the company's far-flung operations that by this time included joint ventures in China and India in addition to the European acquisitions. He commented that while the company was not yet in crisis, if it did not begin to move more quickly, it soon would be. Company personnel appeared to be receptive to change, he thought, but there was a "reluctance to move with any kind of speed, pace, or urgency".

Drawing together his observations of the company's situation and performance, Froggatt reached three major conclusions. The first was that there would be no more major acquisitions. The second was that S&N had to start operating as one company. When it had been operating pubs, brewing, and leisure parks businesses, it may have made sense to operate the company in a conglomerate fashion, but now that it was a focused brewing company Froggatt could see many opportunities for synergy and brand-building between the regional breweries. To begin the integration process he created three new corporate executive positions: group marketing director, group operations director, and group information technology director. These three positions, all to be filled by managers from outside S&N, would have responsibilities that cut across all geographic units.

Froggatt's third conclusion was that he had to increase dramatically the pace of change in the company. Change was taking place, but it was much too slow. The brewing industry was consolidating and there was every possibility that S&N was on the acquisition list of at least one of the world's major brewers. In fact, new rumours appeared monthly about who would be making a bid for S&N. The best defense against takeover, Froggatt believed, was to get the company performing well and raise the stock price. To increase the sense of urgency he put together a road show documenting S&N's poor performance vis-à-vis the competition and his own impatience for faster change. He then traveled Europe delivering the message to S&N's top 500 managers. Froggatt commented: "Initially, you have to use a lot of your own personal emotion and forcefulness to get things done. Once the sense of urgency becomes part of the culture, you don't have to do it anymore. But at the beginning, you need to be a driver."

Reactive Change Conditions In reactive change situations, strategic performance is sliding, the nature of the external changes is becoming evident, and the impact of these changes on the business is building. If you were to forecast performance at this time, assuming no adjustments by the business, you would project the business into crisis. The period of time before the situation becomes critical is your time to crisis. It establishes a tangible measure of urgency for action and quite obviously puts the ultimate time horizon on your work.

Management Issues In reactive change situations you need to concentrate attention on the core business. There may be a tremendous range of ideas in management about how to respond to the now recognizable challenges, but what the business needs is a focused and effective counter-attack in its key markets. S&N, for example, needed to invest more in its brands. In some areas Froggatt believed it needed to double its advertising and promotion budgets; but to get the money to do that, it needed to cut costs in other places. The most obvious opportunity was to make better use of its brewing capacity. S&N had quite a number of small and inefficient breweries, but these tended to be hundreds of years old and a source of pride and tradition to the towns—such as Newcastle, UK (where Newcastle Brown Ale was brewed)—that they supported. Managers needed to be persuaded that closing breweries was necessary and that strategic proposals that might make sense under other conditions, such as acquisitions or alliances, would only detract from the attention required by the core business.

The need for focus, the pressure of time, and the possibility of resistance mean that the power to press for change is important in reactive circumstances. You need power to make things happen. Froggatt, supported by the chairman and the board, had such power, but translating that into tangible action throughout the company is nevertheless a formidable challenge, particularly when one is new to the industry and the company.

ORGANIZATIONAL READINESS FOR CHANGE

Organizational readiness is the second critical variable defining the starting conditions for a change plan. Readiness refers to the commitment (or lack of it) that people feel to making the changes required by the situation the business faces, and their ability to perform the new tasks that will be required of them. To focus our assessment of readiness, we will work with *target groups* and *target group readiness*.

Target Group Identification

While most strategic changes will involve a wide range of people in a business, it is important to isolate the individuals and groups who will be particularly crucial at the start of the process. These might be senior managers whose support or resistance will most influence the success of the proposal. In Pepsi, for example, it was quite clear that Craig Weatherup would not get very far without the support of the most senior line people in the organization, and his first priority was to win them over to the 15 percent per year growth objective, and to convince them that this could not be achieved without significant change. In other situations the target groups might be plant managers, particular country organizations, or perhaps certain functional groups, who will have to be heavily involved in the change process.

As we will elaborate later, broad, unfocused change programs run into problems. By isolating a limited number of change targets—namely, the individuals and groups who are critical to the first steps of change—you can start to focus your assessment of readiness and increase the precision of your preliminary actions. This is a simple, practical necessity.

Target Group Readiness

It is useful to work with two stages of readiness in assessing how prepared your target group is for change. The first of these stages is the *sense of commitment* in the target groups: do they agree that the changes being discussed are necessary and appropriate, and will they play an active role in developing and supporting the changes, or will they resist the steps that are being put forward? The second is *capability*: given that they feel the changes are appropriate, do the target groups have the skills needed to undertake the changes being discussed? Commitment and capability are discussed further below.

Target Group Commitment A variety of factors will affect the commitment of your target groups to adopt and implement change. If they understand and accept the need for change, and feel that the proposed changes are appropriate and are not personally threatening, it is likely that they will collaborate and the changes will proceed with minimal difficulty. Unfortunately, change is seldom this tidy.

Lack of commitment to change can come from many sources. At the simplest level, your intended target groups may be unaware of the need for change. They may be deliberately or inadvertently isolated from the market and business performance data that indicate change is required. They may be focused on their local piece of the puzzle, without seeing the broader picture. It is not too hard to imagine regional executives in S&N, for example, focusing intensely on improving their local results, but paying scant attention to opportunities for improvement through cooperation with other countries and regions in the S&N empire.

Another concern is that individuals and groups may downplay or deny the urgency of a situation because they really do not want to face up to the realities. Some people in Asda, for example, may have seen signs that a crisis was developing before it arrived, but chose, consciously or not, to minimize its likelihood or impact because the alternative of responding to the signs may have seemed to be so disruptive and painful. Put several of these individuals together and you may end up with *groupthink*, in which members of the target group find common support for their perspective and add force to the denial of the need to change.

On the other hand, some people may see a need for change, but genuinely disagree with the direction that the change is taking. In the early months of Tony Froggatt's change initiative at S&N, for example, there was resistance to the idea that the solution for S&N was to create a more integrated company. Instead of focusing on integration, why not put more "heat" on the regional managers to improve their performance, and pay significant bonuses based on performance improvement? Beer is a local business, the argument went, and there were certainly opportunities for improvement within S&N's major operations in both the UK and France, for example. These issues needed to be debated and priorities set, as too many priorities or conflicting priorities, will kill any change process.

Others might resist because they think (perhaps rightly) they will end up losing position, power, compensation, prestige, or perks. People see themselves as potential losers as changes are made and they dig in to defend their positions. The best that you can hope for here is that the opposition emerges as open resistance, because then you can assess it and determine how to proceed. There may be ways to negotiate or to get the resistors onside, or you may have to move them out of the way. The task will be difficult. You may not win, but at least you know what you are dealing with.

The toughest situation is that of deliberate passive resistance, of which the most destructive form is compliance on the surface while foot dragging underneath. Jack Welch ran into an abundance of this in his work to transform General Electric. As reported by Tichy and Sherman: "Some business chiefs stolidly thwarted Welch's plans. . . . Rather than oppose the CEO directly, they would say yes, when they meant no, doing what they thought best for their businesses instead of pushing Welch's agenda of change."[5] Managers possess an enormous power in their capacity to do nothing, or at least to do nothing that really contributes to the direction of change. Such deliberate passive resistance is very hard to identify and to pin down, except over a period of time. You have to be aware that it can happen, watch for it throughout a program of change, and bring it to the surface. The potential for passive resistance also carries a warning for managers who would impose change by force. There are many ways, particularly in the short term, that people can avoid doing what you want them to do. In this respect, the effective balance of power is on their side.

All of these forms of resistance feed on ambiguity and are thus more likely to be encountered in anticipatory and reactive change conditions than in crisis. The uncertainty in both the Pepsi and S&N situations, for example, suggested that resistance would be a factor. The force of events in crisis, however, such as in Asda, helped to coalesce people around survival and to generate a willingness to get on with whatever needed to be done.

From an analytic standpoint, every potential key player in the change process needs to be assessed in terms of his or her commitment to change. Where there are problems, the diagnosis has to go deeper, to identify the source of the resistance and the power of that person or group to frustrate the change program. We will discuss this process further in the next chapter.

Target Group Capability In the Diamond-E analysis of your business you will have considered the broad capabilities of management and its support people and incorporated this assessment into your strategic decisions. The current analysis is different in two ways. First, it brings the focus down to the specific individuals and groups that are critical to your intentions for change. Are these potential target groups able to understand the situation and respond creatively and effectively to it? Do store managers at Asda have the skills required for a radical program of store renewal? Did anyone in S&N have the skills to be effective in one of the new group executive roles that would have to coordinate activities across the whole company? Clearly, Tony Froggatt decided the answer was no.

Second, your options for dealing with gaps between the available and required skills in your target groups narrow as you move from anticipatory to crisis change. In anticipatory change there is time for training and development and for the evolution of strategic responses to the external change. As the business moves towards crisis, however, there is less time for the development of new skills. In crisis you pretty well have to work with what you have—there is no time for training, and the possibilities of recruiting people with the required skills are limited by the crisis conditions. As we stated earlier, Archie Norman had to work with the management he had on hand at Asda and with the skills that they already possessed. This is one of the reasons why in crisis it is so common to shrink and focus the business—you are trying to simplify the business to the point where it can be run successfully by the existing talent.

At first glance the issue of capability is clear. You know what skills you need, and will devise ways to acquire or develop them in the time available. There is a second-order effect, however, that you should look out for: if managers do not possess the skills they think they will need to run the business in a different way, they have all the more reason to deny the problem, or to resist attempts to deal with it until it is in crisis. To this end, training does more than provide a new skill set. It provides people with the confidence that they will survive if they tackle the realities of the business, and an understanding that this is better done sooner than later.

PERSONAL READINESS FOR CHANGE

The third factor to be assessed in setting up the starting conditions for change is your own involvement in the situation. In an ideal world you would have the knowledge, power, and will to implement whatever changes come on the agenda. In reality, however, your strengths and weaknesses in relation to the change problem and targets are an inseparable part of the change conditions and should be an important influence on your choice of an action plan. These strengths and weaknesses define your personal readiness to lead the change process.

We will discuss personal readiness in terms of commitment and capability, just as we did in the organizational readiness section, with the major difference being that you have to work with these issues from two perspectives: your own and that of the prime target individuals and groups. Tony Froggatt, coming into S&N from Seagram, a drinks company, may be confident that he understands how to build brands and lead change in the brewing industry, for example, but the veterans in the company may think quite differently. You have to assess your readiness from both a personal and external perspective.

Personal Commitment This may seem like a curious item to raise since you are already positioned in the role of a change agent. But it is important that you assess your commitment to see the change through and to pay the price that this requires.

Changes do not come easily and it is well worth thinking about whether this is something you really want to do. This is more than a matter of personal preference. Others will sense your conviction, and test your commitment, and if they are not convinced then you and the change program will be in trouble. Tony Froggatt, who had lost out on a top job earlier in his career, made it clear why his drive to succeed at S&N was so strong. As he put it, "fear of failure for me is very strong. I have a point to prove to myself and others". It is best to think through your motivation carefully in advance and, if you are not sufficiently committed, to see what can be done to bring in others to deal with the situation.

As you assess your commitment for change, you should consider the related issue of the urgency with which the change is required. It is important to distinguish between the urgency that you feel—which will be a major factor underlying your commitment—and the urgency that actually attaches to the business situation. Aggressive managers may feel greater urgency than the business problem dictates, because of their personalities, perhaps, or their interpretation of their assignments. They want action now, but the business case is actually not that pressing. This is not necessarily a problem because, given a choice, it is better to press for earlier and faster change than later and slower change. But if urgency driven by personal motives is not carefully considered it can lead to premature and inappropriate actions.

As well, your personal desire to act quickly can give rise to resistance. If others think you are on a personal rather than a business agenda, the whole process of change might be stalled or become unnecessarily contentious. A reasonable example of this occurs in the foreign affiliates of many multinational companies. Local management becomes accustomed to new presidents and other senior officers being moved in and out by the parent. They also understand that these executives want to come in and change things quickly to make their mark before they move on to new assignments. The acid test that the locals will put to these rotating executives is simple: are they dealing with real business needs or their own career needs? The degree of local cooperation or, conversely, the degree of local resistance will vary accordingly.

The key point here is to be aware of the possibility of a difference between your personal urgency and commitment to change and that required by the external conditions. This may mean that you have to speed up if you are behind. It certainly does not mean you have to slow down if you are ahead, but in this case you have to consider the issues of being out in front and deal with them as part of your action plan.

Personal Capability In considering your own ability to lead the change program, ask yourself whether you have the skills to understand the circumstances and to act effectively to deal with them. If there are gaps in your knowledge, one of your first tasks will be to close them—by some personal education but also by recruiting people internally or externally who will bring the needed skills to the situation.

The target groups in your change situation will interpret your capability in terms of credibility and power and you must do the same. In your own view and in that of others, are you a credible agent of change? In your own view and that of others, do you have the ability to manage people effectively, the power to make things happen and, if necessary, to roll over opposition? The answers are obviously crucial to your approach and will affect the tactics that you can employ. In the Asda situation, for example, Archie Norman's previous experience at turning around Woolworth's, another struggling UK retailer, was well known to the management team he inherited at Asda, and was an important factor underlying his ability to move as quickly as he did.

THE VIEW FROM BELOW

Adopting a general management perspective, and furthermore managing or being part of strategic change at lower levels of the organization, poses some particular challenges. Uyterhoeven in his 1989 *Harvard Business Review* article[6], and Kotter in his 1999 *Harvard Business Review* article[7] address the role of general managers. Kotter adopts a top management perspective to delineate what effective general managers really do. In his study of 15 successful general managers, Kotter found that there are two fundamental challenges and dilemmas found in most jobs: figuring out what to do despite uncertainty and an enormous amount of potentially relevant information; and getting things done through a large and diverse group of people despite having little direct control over most of them. He suggested the key tasks of effective general managers are setting agendas and building networks. Finally, Kotter suggests that general managers need to utilize their networks to implement agendas.

Uyterhoeven moves down the ladder to examine general managers in the middle of the organization. Like Kotter, he focuses on managing relationships as a key task of the general manager. As you move down the organization there are three relationships that need to be managed: superior, subordinate, and equals. As Uyterhoeven suggests "managing the triple set of relationships is most demanding; it is analogous to a baseball player having to excel simultaneously in hitting, fielding, and pitching."[8] He points out that for the general manager in the middle of the organization, responsibility often exceeds authority. However, "the buck stops at the middle manager, who must assume the bilingual role of translating the strategic language of his or her superiors into the operational language of subordinates in order to get results."[9]

There is very little in the way of literature on the nature of strategic analysis and action from the point of view of employees at the lowest levels or fringes of the organization. Yet, the newer models of strategic management acknowledge the need for strategic thinking throughout the organization. We suggest that the most challenging position to exercise strategic thinking is from the front lines of the organization. Often individuals have little authority or credibility, and may lack knowledge of the overall strategic position of the organization. Yet they have important insights about the company and industry that need to be taken into consideration. In the absence of strategic thinking, it is likely that individuals may take decisions and actions that are very short-sighted in nature. In contrast, having a general management perspective does not ensure success. On the contrary, just as the most senior people in the organization need to consider their personal readiness in affecting strategic change, so too must individuals at lower levels of the organization. As noted, the challenge increases as you move down the organization.

SUMMARY

This chapter is the first of two dealing with the move from broad strategic prescriptions for change to the specific and detailed actions to put those changes into place. We presented a process for planning change that consists of four sequential steps: (1) identifying your change agenda; (2) identifying starting conditions; (3) developing guidelines for change; and (4) creating a specific action plan.

The chapter began with the recommendation that you create a change agenda, listing the broad changes that you identified in your Diamond-E analysis as necessary to support the strategy that you want to implement, paying particular attention to those that will require behavioural change.

Then we turned to starting conditions, which were discussed in terms of three considerations: the urgency for action, organizational readiness, and personal readiness. Urgency for action refers to the pressure to implement the strategic changes that you have in mind. Degrees of urgency are related to the strategic performance of the business and can vary from the immediacy of crisis situations to the low pressure and ambiguity of anticipatory change conditions. Organizational readiness depends on the commitment and capability of the individuals and groups who will be most instrumental to the change process. Personal readiness refers to the commitment and capability that you bring to the situation as the manager who is going to lead the change process.

The change agenda and starting conditions for every change project will be unique. There is no standard recipe that will lead to success in all change situations. You need to understand your particular change agenda and starting conditions well before you begin to establish guidelines for action and an action plan. These are the topics to which we turn in Chapter 11.

Notes

1. Martin, Roger L. "The Execution Trap." *Harvard Business Review* 88.7/8 (2010): 64–71. *Business Source Complete, EBSCO*. Web. 16 Aug. 2011.

2. A list of "eight steps to transforming your organization" is contained in John Kotter's article "Leading Change: Why Transformation Efforts Fail." *Harvard Business Review* 73 (March–April 1995): 59–68. Print. This is a good example of a generic approach to change. The steps are useful, but in any given situation some will be critical; others unimportant.

3. The Asda story is taken from Weber, James, and Michael Beer. "Asda." (A), (A-1), (B), (C), cases 498-005–498-008. Boston, Mass.: Harvard Business School, 1998. Print.

4. The Pepsi story is taken from Sull, Don, and David A. Garvin. "Pepsi's Regeneration, 1990–1993." case 395-048. Boston: Harvard Business School, 1994. Print.

5. Tichy, Noel M., and Stafford Sherman. *Control Your Destiny or Someone Else Will*. New York: Doubleday, 1993. 84. Print.

6. Uyterhoeven, Hugo. "General Managers in the Middle." *Harvard Business Review* 67.5 (September–October 1989): 136. Print.

7. Kotter, John. "What Effective General Managers Really Do." *Harvard Business Review* 77.2 (March–April 1999): 145–156. Print.

8. Uyterhoeven, Hugo. "General Managers in the Middle." *Harvard Business Review* 67.5 (September–October 1989): 138. Print.

9. Uyterhoeven, Hugo. "General Managers in the Middle." *Harvard Business Review* 67.5 (September–October 1989): 137. Print.

Additional Readings

1. Beer, Michael, Russel A. Eisenstat, and Bert Spector. "Why Change Programs Don't Produce Change." *Harvard Business Review* 68 (November–December 1990): 158–166. Print.

2. Ghoshal, Sumantra, and Christopher A. Bartlett. "Rebuilding Behavioural Context: A Blueprint for Corporate Renewal." *Sloan Management Review* 37 (Winter 1996): 23. Print.

3. Katzenbach, Jon R. *Real Change Leaders*. London: Nicholas Brealey, 1996. Print.

4. Pascale, Richard, Mark Millemann, and Linda Gioja. "Changing the Way We Change." *Harvard Business Review* 75 (November–December 1997): 127. Print.

5. Beer, Michael, and Nitin Nohria. "Cracking the Code of Change." *Harvard Business Review* (May–June, 2000): 1–8. Print.

Chapter 11

Implementing Strategy: Guidelines and Action

In this chapter we assume that you have worked through the material in Chapter 10, identifying your change agenda and starting conditions, and are ready to translate these into guidelines for action and a detailed implementation plan.

ESTABLISHING GUIDELINES FOR ACTION

In Figure 10.1 we proposed that you establish four guidelines for action: (1) priority objectives, which are those things that you want to accomplish first; (2) priority actions, which indicate your priority targets and the first action steps you will take with each; (3) leadership style, which establishes how you are going to manage the change process; and (4) pace, which determines how rapidly you should proceed. We will discuss these in order.

PRIORITY OBJECTIVES

At the outset of your change program you established a change agenda which resulted from your Diamond-E analysis. The items on your agenda included things like changing your organization structure or management processes to create behavioural change, hiring people with new skills, acquiring a new technology, stopping the negative cash flow in a crisis, and so on. We suggested that you pay particular attention to those items that were likely to require new behaviour, because these are all too often overlooked or underestimated.

Now, having assessed the urgency of your change situation and the readiness of key groups and individuals in your organization for change, you are ready to determine your most pressing objectives. Which of the items on your change agenda should you address first? How many items should you try to deal with at the same time? Should you focus intensely on a few objectives, or take a much broader approach?

Behavioural Versus Non-Behavioural Objectives

When preparing your change agenda you differentiated between items that were designed to produce behavioural change and those that were not. We continue that distinction here. Your priority objectives list will include items of each type, and you need to think carefully about how to blend the two. Some managers, for example, instinctively tend to shun the behaviour-related issues, preferring instead to focus on "easier to manage" issues such as making an acquisition or selling a business. If you find yourself focusing exclusively on items that do not lead to behaviour change, beware—you may be kidding yourself about what your true priorities should be.

For example, consider the situation facing Tom Stephens at MacMillan Bloedel ("MacBlo"). For many years, MacBlo had had the best inventory of trees on the West Coast of Canada, but its logging costs were the highest in the world, due in part to the adversarial relationship between the company and its unions. Rather than try to reduce costs by changing the behaviour of its managers or of the unions, previous senior MacBlo managers had chosen to diversify the company's efforts into other product lines, and other areas of the world. Stephens' approach was different. He decided that he would focus on the core West Coast business and work to change the traditional patterns of management and union behaviour.[1]

Stephens judged that without hitting the behavioural issues head-on, he would not make any real progress, and he decided to pursue simultaneously two sets of objectives: one involving portfolio changes, to be achieved by selling parts of the business, and the other to effect behavioural changes in the core business. He focused on empowering leadership at all levels of the organization, using his own behaviour to set the standard. He stated that "people tend to emulate their leaders, so if you want a broad organization to do things in a different way, you (the leader) must do things in a different way. You ask other people to emulate that and act in the same way. That way you get the cascading effect." He was very successful: the "People Project," which revolutionized MacBlo's labour relations and had managers and unions working together to co-design turnaround projects, was initiated by a low-level manager in the solid wood business. The SWIFT program, which taught business metrics and the factors that affected them to employees at all levels, was instigated and taught by a unionized operations employee and a lower-level manager.[2]

Stephens gets full marks for not making the common mistake of setting his objectives only in terms of substantive changes and underestimating the importance of changes required in behaviour. Stephens commented:

> In an organization, what you want are results. We want to decrease costs and increase productivity and achieve measurable results. Results are a function of human behaviour. Behaviour is a function of attitude. And, attitude is a function of the cultural environment in which we operate. If you want to achieve results, you must change the cultural environment. . . . You change the culture by laying out the principles and then walking the talk religiously.[3]

Our primary focus in this chapter is on the challenge of bringing about behavioural change in an organization. That is not to say that other changes are unimportant. In fact, you may want to make a significant substantive change—sell a business, raise new equity, or make an acquisition, for example—to demonstrate that you are serious about change.

But generally it is the behavioural changes that are the most problematic, and that is where we will concentrate.

ACTION PRIORITIES

As you set about determining how to achieve your key objectives, you must address two key questions: (1) whose behaviour do you want to change, and (2) how are you going to change it? The answers to these two questions make up your action priorities.

Priority Targets

In your analysis of starting conditions you identified the individuals and groups that will be most involved in or affected by the anticipated changes and assessed their commitment and capability for change. All of these people will sooner or later be involved in the change process, but the immediate question is with whom should you start; these people will be your priority targets.

An important first step in determining who will be a priority target is to assess each potential target in terms of his or her commitment to the proposed changes, and the capabilities that they could bring to the change program. Do not try to make this assessment for everyone in the company, however. If you judge, for example, that your plant management personnel are going to be critical to the success of your change program, focus on them, and decide who among them should become priority targets. To do this, take the plant managers and sort them into groups as indicated in Figure 11.1. The groups are described as follows:

Change Agents are people who believe that change is necessary, and that the proposed changes make sense. Furthermore, they have the skills and capabilities to help bring about the change. In short, they are competent and committed managers who are your potential allies in the change process. In most change situations, there are fewer individuals in this category than the others. In anticipatory situations it will be the commitment that is missing; in crisis, competence may be lacking.

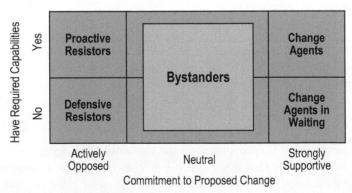

Figure 11.1 Assessing Potential Priority Targets

Change Agents in Waiting are those who would like the change program to be successful, but do not have the skills to be of much help. Given time and training, they might develop such skills, and whether you decide that these individuals should be priority targets will depend in part on how much time you believe you have to implement the change program.

Bystanders would prefer to wait and see how the change process fares before making a commitment to it. They may not have the energy needed to get involved, they may prefer to avoid the perceived risk of involvement, or they may be skeptical of "yet another initiative." Whatever the cause, turning a bystander into a change agent will take some convincing, and possibly some training.

Defensive Resistors are opposed to the change initiative, probably because they realize that they do not have the capabilities to play a meaningful role in it, and thus find the change program threatening. If the change program is successful, they could lose out. If these individuals are likely to be disruptive you may have to deal with them early in the process; more often, they do not receive attention until later.

Proactive Resistors are competent managers who think that your change initiative is inappropriate. They either believe that change is not required, or that the particular changes you are proposing are not the right ones. These people could be worth listening to, because they may be right. We know of one senior manager who spent time with such resistors early in his ("reactive") change process, rather than working with change agents (which would have been much more comfortable) because he thought he might have something to learn from them. In addition, he believed that if he could convert one or two of them into change agents (there were five active resistors) the others would feel isolated and, as an extra benefit, this visible change of commitment by active resistors might generate new commitment to the change process on the part of some bystanders. As it turned out, this approach was successful.

To decide which of these potential targets should get your early attention, you need to integrate the other starting conditions into your analysis—particularly the urgency for action and your power position relative to the potential targets. If you are dealing with anticipatory change, for example, there is little value in targeting resistors at the outset, since the case for change will be too ambiguous. Better to seek and to develop change agents and build momentum to influence the resistors. If you are in reactive change, however, you may have no option but to target and take on resistors and bystanders who are in a position to block progress. Here it is important to understand your powers relative to these targets and how they can be best employed in the limited time available.

In fact, you may not discover any attractive priority targets—people who can and will do what needs to be done in the time available. Schindler Elevator of Switzerland faced such a situation after it purchased the Westinghouse elevator and escalator businesses. The escalator business was performing poorly, and part of the problem was that it had been sourcing poor quality escalators from a Korean joint venture. One logical way forward would have been to move escalator manufacturing into an under-utilized former

Westinghouse elevator plant. But employees in this heavily unionized, high-cost facility in the U.S. Northeast were judged to be lacking both the capabilities and the attitudes needed to support the changes that would be required to produce escalators efficiently. The decision was made not to try and drive change in that plant, but to construct a new plant in the South, transferring former Westinghouse managers who seemed ready to try a new way of doing business, and hiring a new workforce. A huge amount of energy was focused on that plant, and both management and newly hired unskilled workers became the priority change targets.

Picking Starting Points for Action

Once you have chosen your priority targets, you need to decide what action you are going to take vis-à-vis each. There are two competing theories about this. The conventional approach is determined by *commitment and capability*: you start by preparing your priority targets for change by creating a sense of urgency, developing skills and commitment to the required changes, and then move logically through the structural or process changes designed to change behaviour. This is obviously a reasonable progression, but it can get bogged down in well-intended, but diffuse and ineffective action that has little ultimate impact on results. Schaffer and Thomson, for example, criticize the pursuit of this sequence as a "rain-dance" of activities that sound good, look good, and allow managers to feel good, but which have little impact on the bottom line. They cite as an example a three-year change program in a mineral extraction company that had accomplished 50 percent of its training goals, 50 percent of its employee participation goals, but only five percent of its results goals.[4]

In contrast to readiness-driven change is *results*-driven change, in which a set of precise and measurable results are specified, and people are made responsible for producing them. The results-driven approach does not ignore the obvious need for other organizational and readiness changes, but it develops them as necessary in a process that works primarily to support results. This approach keeps attention focused on the bottom line, but by forcing change and higher performance standards on people who are not ready for it, the whole endeavour may blow up in your face. Change is seldom risk-free!

In the end, you will tailor your starting points for action to the target in question, and to the starting conditions from which you are working. Thus, if you are in anticipatory change, like Craig Weatherup of Pepsi (Chapter 10), you have little option but to start with actions to improve readiness; if you are in crisis change, like Archie Norman at Asda (also Chapter 10), you are going to have to specify and achieve some immediate behaviour changes that will produce new capabilities and improved results.

As you work through your selection of priority targets and your intended starting points for each, collect your thoughts in a chart such as that shown in Table 11.1. As you do this, you should be asking yourself if you have focused too widely, or perhaps too narrowly. Do you have the balance right between focus and scope?

Table 11.1 Priority Targets and Starting Points

	Starting Points for Action				
Priority Targets	**Improve Readiness for Behaviour Change**		**Drive Behaviour Change**		
	Increase Capability	**Increase Commitment**	**Change Organization Structure**	**Change Your Management Processes**	**Change Ways of Managing People**
Target Group 1					
Target Group 2					
Target Group 3					

Focus Versus Scope

How much should you try to do at once? In a crisis, the answer is probably "a lot."[5] But in anything short of a crisis situation you will need to make some fine judgments about how widely to diffuse your time and energy. Singling out a small number of priority targets, for example, will permit you to focus your effort, but postpones work with people who will ultimately be important to the total program. Starting out with multiple targets, on the other hand, gives you the comfort of covering all the bases, but disperses your impact and may mean that your program will stall. Much will depend on the commitment for change across the potential targets, your own power, and the urgency of the situation. A high degree of readiness will allow you to work successfully with more people, whereas significant pockets of resistance will call for a more focused approach.

Avoid the temptation to take on too much at once. Evidence from studies of simultaneous multi-target, multi-objective change programs shows that they just do not work well—there is too much to manage and there are too many opportunities for slippage.[6] In the Schindler example just cited, the decision to focus energy on a single manufacturing facility proved to be a good one, as this plant became the low-cost producer in the industry and was selected by *Industry Week* magazine as one of the "ten best plants in the USA." Schindler then created rivalry between the new plant and others in the United States and Europe to drive change throughout the company.

Focusing change efforts often seems like a sacrifice at the beginning of a change program, because of the things that you are *not* doing, like improving the existing plants, but it is often a better way to begin. In many cases, the first order of the day is to get the company's portfolio of businesses right. Jack Welch did this in his early years at the helm of GE with his "number one, number two, fix, sell, or close" edict, which led to the sale and acquisition of many businesses. Similarly, Tom Stephens directed managers to "sell it, milk it or grow it – get off your lazy assets." In S&N (Chapter 10) Tony Froggatt came into a situation in which the portfolio reshaping had already been done. By 2003 S&N was an international brewer: the leisure parks had been sold, the UK pubs were up for sale, and the foreign brewing acquisitions had been made. The change challenge was not about strategy, it was about improving efficiency and execution. In simple terms, Froggatt's challenge was to get costs down and growth rates up. Like many managers, he started with costs, and that meant taking the emotionally difficult decision to close some very old breweries that had played a significant role in the history of the company. The good news was these early decisions signaled that he was serious about change and that there would be no sacred cows.

LEADERSHIP STYLE

Your leadership style determines how you intend to relate to target individuals or groups and what specific tactics you will employ. We have described two very different styles in Table 11.2. The particular approach that you choose will likely fall between these two

Table 11.2	Key Features of Directive and Participative Leadership Styles		
	Characteristics	**Benefits**	**Risks**
Directive	• Directive	• Fast	• Wrong diagnosis, wrong remedy
	• Assumes initiator understands problem, knows solution, has power	• Efficient	• Passive or active resistance
		• Economizes on initiator time, energy	• Pseudo-change
	• Tactics focus on communication of reasons, instructions, expectations		• High after-the-fact costs
Participative	• Participative	• Effective	• Too slow
	• Assumes that diagnosis and remedy will be developed in change process	• Flexible	• Potential to run off track
		• Develops and tests problem and people at same time	• Avoidance of tough decisions
	• Tactics focus on collaborative exploration of causes, development of remedies, building commitment		

extremes. The first style consists of a very *directive* approach to a target, with tactics that centre on instruction and pressure to create a change in behaviour. The second style is based on a *participative* approach to a target, with tactics that focus on guiding and facilitating changes in behaviour.

Some writers and consultants present one or the other of these styles as the single best way to achieve change. Our approach, however, is to focus on choosing the style that best suits the conditions with which you are dealing. Indeed, the question is seldom one of settling on a fixed style, but one of determining the right blend of styles.

Directive Leadership

There are a variety of simple terms to describe the directive style: autocratic, command, coercive, top-down, and so on. The crucial assumptions behind the style are that you understand the problems, know the solutions, and have the power to force compliance with your views. The tactical approach is straightforward, and involves (1) communicating the reasons for change to establish urgency; (2) defining the intended changes and telling people what to do (although targets might be given some participatory role in detailed execution); (3) training as necessary to perform the new tasks; (4) monitoring progress closely and adjusting instructions as necessary; and (5) implementing incentives and punishments to ensure that these tasks are executed and sustained.

If you operate as an impersonal, "cut and dried," mechanical leader, you will likely run into trouble. The directive style does not assume that you are, or that you should necessarily act, that way. There is room for variety in the approach you take to make it more acceptable to the people with whom you are dealing. Charismatic leadership, for example, is for the most part directive leadership, with emotion and enthusiasm serving as the foundations for the leader's power.

The benefits of a directive approach to change are substantial. If it works, you achieve change quickly and with an economy of effort. However, the change program can easily get off track or fail. There is not much room for correction as you go down this path. A perception that you are wrong, or on a power trip, or unable to sustain the pressure may encourage resistance. People may change their behaviour while you are around, and then revert to their old ways as soon as you move on. Finally, your relationship with the targets, and their willingness to work in the new situation and to contribute to the next change, may all suffer. These risk possibilities may sound severe, but there are situations in which directive leadership is both desirable and attainable.

The Choice of a Directive Style The most natural setting for a directive leadership style is in crisis change situations, when the circumstances of the business demand fast action. The people in the business, by and large, are waiting for decisive leadership; in fact, they are likely calling for it. These conditions confer power on the leader. The definite theme of action will be directive—quick decisions, clear orders, and a minimal tolerance for reluctant execution.

A second natural setting for a directive approach is during a reactive change, when a stand-off has developed between the proponents and opponents of change. In the meantime precious time is wasting. You have a mini-crisis situation on your hands. The sensible way to break the impasse is with a clear and focused application of power.

Finally, you would probably *not* want to use a directive approach in anticipatory change situations. On most of these occasions, if you are honest with yourself, you will admit that you simply do not know enough about the problems and the solutions to charge ahead into directed change. If you decide to do so anyway, the probability of minimal readiness and the possibilities for effective resistance will put you in a very difficult position. The possible exception is when you are trying to start a change process not because you see decay ahead, but simply because you feel that today's performance can be improved. In such a situation, you may be directive about the performance target, but participative when it comes to deciding how it might be achieved.

The Participative Style

The participative style can be characterized by a number of terms: bottom-up, collaborative, empowering, shared, and so on. The crucial assumptions behind the style are that an effective diagnosis and remedy can be developed in the course of the change process. The basic tactics of a participative approach are to (1) involve the target individuals and groups in studies of the situation to help clarify the reasons for change and to establish urgency; (2) collaborate, debate, and negotiate with these people to define the needed changes and the detailed steps of change; (3) train as necessary to perform the new tasks; (4) delegate significant responsibility for monitoring and adjusting implementation; and (5) install incentives and punishments to support the continuing execution of the new tasks.

The participative style is not a dereliction of duty. Rather, it requires you to think carefully through the steps of working with the targets and to exercise the patience and determination needed to see that process through. There will definitely be junctures at which you will have to take control and use directive tactics. A crucial skill is sensing when this needs to be done and how far you can go without poisoning the whole process. What you can expect is that it will be very hard work and make major demands on your time.

The merits of the participative approach are substantial. If it works as intended it produces effective solutions by employing the analytic and creative faculties of the people closest to the problems, and it harnesses the energy of those same people to implement and make the solutions work. However, there are substantial risks as well. Participative change is slow—at least compared with directive change. Furthermore, a participative approach is vulnerable to producing compromise solutions that the targets want (or perhaps just the compromises that they can agree upon) rather than the tough measures that the business needs. Finally, there is a chance that the sheer momentum built by the process will get out of hand and challenge the leaders to commit to directions that they are still quite uneasy about.

The Choice of a Participative Style The natural conditions for implementing the participative style are virtually the flip side of the conditions that favour the directive style. The most obviously appropriate conditions for using a participatory style are anticipatory change conditions, with their inherent need for better problem definition. There simply is not enough time in crisis change for participative measures. The conditions of reactive change may require a mix of styles: participative to mobilize those who want to get on with the job, and directive to deal with the targets that hesitate too long, resist, or otherwise create bottlenecks in the process.

PACE

Pace is a term to describe the amount of change that you want to accomplish in a given period of time. It encompasses both the scope and significance of the individual changes. A fast pace, for example, would be the pursuit of significant behavioural changes (perhaps new ways of handling specific issues) across a range of targets in a short period of time. A slow pace, in contrast, would be the pursuit of modest behavioural change (perhaps the recognition of some urgency for change) on the part of a few targets in the same time period.

Your decision about the pace of change has an important impact on your selection of action priorities and leadership style. A decision to try to work at a fast pace, for example, suggests aggressive objectives, a range of targets, and a directive style. The choice of a slower pace creates an opportunity to select less ambitious objectives, fewer targets, and a participative approach. Given its influence on the other change guidelines, pace should logically be the first of the guidelines that you settle on. We have dealt with it late in our order of presentation only because it is easier to understand its role after you appreciate the nature of the action priorities and leadership style guidelines.

Two key factors should be considered in setting the pace of change: (1) the urgency in the business situation, and (2) the urgency that you feel personally to press forward with the change. If the business urgency is high, as in crisis conditions, there is no room for personal choice—a fast pace is essential. But in anticipatory and reactive situations, business urgency only sets a minimum pace; there is room to move faster if you want to and if it makes sense. The time-to-crisis calculation in reactive change, for example, sets the time frame in which change must be accomplished, but it does not mandate that the process should take that long.

The decision to set a faster pace than business urgency dictates is a sensitive matter, as we discussed in Chapter 10. There are definite advantages in getting on with it, and moving to the next challenge. But if the haste of your personal agenda is likely to generate questionable decisions, or magnified resistance, the wise choice would be to slow down.

Implementing Pace Decisions

The best way to pin down the pace of your change plan is to think in terms of relatively short time periods, from perhaps a few days in a crisis situation to a maximum of 90 days in reactive and anticipatory change. By specifying how much you want to accomplish in, say, the first 90-day period, the second 90-day period, and so on, you build a plan that reaches from your starting point to your ultimate objectives.

A further advantage to specific, short time periods is that they allow you to break down a complex set of change requirements into workable projects based on what you intend to achieve and how you intend to achieve it. This helps you to move from general objectives to the specific practical actions required to achieve them.

By far the most critical time period is the first period. The decisions that you make about pace, action priorities, and tactics for this period will set the tone for your total program. Perhaps the most telling question that anyone can ask about a plan for change is: What are you going to do in, say, the first 90 days? The answers will reveal much more about where the change plan is going, whether it has been thought through, and its likelihood of success, than some lofty generalities about longer-term aims.

GENERIC GUIDELINES

In this section we will work through some guidelines for first steps in crisis, anticipatory, and reactive change to illustrate how to convert starting conditions into change guidelines and ultimately into detailed steps of change. These guidelines would be generally applicable in the early periods of change, and are summarized in Table 11.3. The normal caution is in order here: these guidelines are not intended to be fixed rules or even universally applicable. They simply represent thought starters for your consideration in planning specific actions in specific situations.

Table 11.3 Generic Change Guidelines

	Anticipatory Change	Reactive Change	Crisis Change	
Targets	• Supporters	• Pivotal Groups	• External	• Internal
First Steps	• Develop support and direction	• Organizational changes	• Buy time	• Make strategic changes
Style	• Participative	• Mixture	• Participative	• Directive
Timing	• Jog	• Run	• Sprint	• Sprint

Crisis Change

Crisis change demands urgent action; as Table 11.3 indicates, the pace of change will likely be a sprint. Further, while it is important to keep your actions simple and focused, multiple targets and multiple objectives will probably be necessary. Your tactical approach will also be mixed, encompassing a participative style with external targets and a directive style internally.

Preliminary Work The first item on a crisis agenda, curiously, is to look forward and visualize (at least roughly) the nature, strategy, and viability of the business to be salvaged. This objective serves three purposes. First, it helps answer the question of whether the business is worth the cost and risk of the rescue attempt. Second, by outlining the shape of the future business, it helps identify what needs to be saved and what is expendable. Third, it is helpful in obtaining the external support necessary to weather the crisis.

Two errors are commonly made at this point in crisis situations. The first is one of simply not planning, of reacting in an aimless way to the immediate pressures. Fate quickly intervenes to correct this error, often at the expense of the firm's existence. The second fault lies in trying to save too much. This latter error is understandable since most managers would like to preserve as much as possible of the business. Surgical cuts in personnel, product lines, and so forth are distasteful. But attempting to preserve too much will complicate an already hazardous venture and substantially raise the risk of failure.

External Targets Your negotiating position with external targets will usually boil down to balancing the costs for them of your going out of business, with the benefits for them of your staying in business. The up-side potential must exceed the risk and cost of continued support or they are better off to cut their losses and "run." If there is at least a reasonable case to be made for their support, then you can turn your attention to earning it. They may not exactly be willing partners, but like it or not, that is what they are, and you should set your tactics with them accordingly.

Securing support will require extensive face-to-face contact and a plan that passes muster under a critical eye. A probable condition for support by banks and other creditors will be plans and actions that reduce their exposure. Your recovery plan should anticipate this by liquidating redundant assets and pushing for operating efficiencies that will increase cash availability. Archie Norman put land that had been earmarked for Asda's future expansion up for sale. He also replaced his chief financial officer as part of his effort to regain credibility with the company's bankers.[7]

The support that you do obtain will likely be given on a very short-term basis, so an essential part of your plan must be to keep in contact with the key external parties over time, apprising them of progress and explaining your next steps. This task will be made more difficult by the usual pattern of performance in crisis, in which results almost inevitably get worse before they get better!

Internal Targets Within the firm, your plan for crisis must quickly focus on two action priorities: the strategic changes that are required to simplify and downsize your business and the identification of the people that you want to stay with the business to execute those changes. These strategic decisions are necessary to meet financial requirements and to minimize the demands on existing management and processes. They will usually involve cutbacks in product lines, market involvements, facilities, and so on, and will drive your handling of internal change targets.

First, decide who will stay and who will go, and act on your decision as soon as possible. Archie Norman dismissed his CFO on day one. As you will have minimal time and credibility to recruit new talent, the people whom you select to keep will be the team with whom you have to work. This reinforces the need to make strategic changes that simplify the demands made on management, and it sets up the tactics for dealing with the people selected to carry through with the turnaround.

The circumstances of crisis change call for a straightforward application of directive tactics inside the business. The strategic decisions and the personnel cuts have to be implemented quickly, and you will be directly involved in communicating needs, handling decisions, supporting managers, and generally tying loose ends together. None of this will be simple, and speed is essential. You cannot possibly get every decision right, and you are unlikely to get consensus for every action. One of the managers at Asda made the following comment looking back at the crisis the company had been through:

> In any change effort, one-third of the people are with you, one-third are unsure, but may come around, and one-third are not with you. Most of those not on board were rightly let go. Yet many of those who were unsure were also let go, never having been given the chance to change. Some of these people, I believe, were let go too quickly.[8]

After the Crisis Survival is your dominant goal at the time of crisis. Then, as the immediate threats are overcome, you need a period of time for stabilization. What is left of the business must be put on a solid footing. Changes should proceed at a slower pace and be directed at improving capabilities.

The reduced business base created by the survival actions will probably not be satisfactory for the long-term. Thus, as performance improves, you need to press for new areas of growth and development. You hope that the costs of survival—in human, financial, and competitive terms—will not encumber your prospects for new opportunities.

Anticipatory Change

The impetus for anticipatory change comes from a sense that strategic change is needed, rather than from concrete evidence. As you size up the future of your business, you come to an unsettling conclusion that it is not prepared for a changing environment and that performance will suffer. The requirements for change are not particularly clear, however, and in part because of this uncertainty, you know it will be difficult to develop a general sense of urgency about the situation.

The early approach to anticipatory change will usually involve measured steps with selected, reasonably friendly key players. The pace will generally be quite slow, reflecting the need to develop an understanding of the situation before major commitments are made and to maintain flexibility as the action proceeds. The action focus will probably be quite narrow to start, but it will become much more complex as progress is made because the ultimate strategic shifts will usually encompass a wide-ranging set of objectives and a growing number of key players in the process. Leadership will likely be participative and dominated by careful, purposeful, incremental steps. This approach is generally referred to as *incrementalism*.[9]

The primary problem with incremental change is that it takes a lot of time and effort. It may take years to develop and put a major change in place. This is naturally distressing if you are an impatient manager, but a desire for fast action must be weighed against the benefits of a slower incremental approach.

Quinn argues that incrementalism is the most appropriate model for most strategic changes, because it helps executives to (1) improve the quality of information available; (2) deal with the different change objectives, key players, lead times, and sequencing problems involved in strategic change; (3) build the organizational awareness, understanding, and psychological commitment necessary for effective execution; (4) overcome political and emotional barriers to change; and (5) improve the quality of their strategic analysis and choices by involving those people closest to the situation and by avoiding premature closure on the basis of potentially incorrect directions.[10]

One of the managers who participated heavily in the change process at Pepsi gave his view of the incremental process: "It was hell, because we couldn't map out everything in advance. We didn't know what we were going to do tomorrow until we had lived it today. Finally, we realized, 'We'll know as we go.'"[11]

Preliminary Work The earliest item in anticipatory change is building your personal conviction that change is needed. There are two routes to pursue in this respect. The first is the standard strategic analysis that we have developed in this text—assessing the current strategy and concluding, as you move through the Diamond-E analysis, that future performance will not be satisfactory. This process, of course, will stimulate ideas about what is needed to bring the business back on course. It is the uncertainty surrounding your forecasts and conclusions that puts you in an anticipatory position.

The second route is to do the foregoing analysis backwards: build a vision of the business at some future point and then ask yourself whether the firm is likely to get there on its present course. Thus, you might ask what you would like the main characteristics of the business (scale, financial performance levels, strategic commitments, etc.) to be in five years, and whether your current strategy can achieve this. For Craig Weatherup at Pepsi, the vision was simple: achieve a 15 percent year-on-year annual increase in earnings, forever. The challenge was to make his management team agree that achieving that goal was feasible, and would require major changes in the way they did business.

Long-term visions can motivate and channel anticipatory change. There is a danger, though, that these visions may escape reality and become the product of fantasy and little else. There is always a need, as we pointed out in Chapter 2, for applying the Diamond-E analysis to check for at least the vestiges of feasibility (remember, we are dealing with very uncertain conditions). Watch out, too, that your preliminary business definitions do not stimulate resistance from those who oppose that particular vision of the future. Both of these cautions support the idea of incrementalism, and of avoiding fixed destinations because they are risky to commit to in themselves and prone to spark resistance.

Target Groups The first item on your agenda as you tackle anticipatory change is to identify your priority targets. You are looking for people who might be disposed to work on the situation with an open mind, who carry some weight in the organization, and with whom you have a reasonable relationship. You might find there are few people who qualify in this regard, and the more difficult the situation, the more you should focus your choices. As stated earlier, Weatherup worked initially with his ten direct reports, and he decided that the change initiative would not be rolled down to the next 70 managers in the organization until those ten were fully on board. One of the managers recalled:

> We decided that we would not move forward until we were all aligned, until everyone supported it 100 percent. We would stop frequently for 'alignment checks' to make sure that we had all contributed, we had all had the opportunity to be heard, and that we were all committed to support the decision. It consumed our lives. . . . By the time we were done, it was tattooed on our chests.[12]

First Steps There are an almost unlimited number of specific approaches that you can employ in taking an incremental approach to change. However, beneath the detail there are some common action principles, including the following:

1. Go beyond the formal processes of planning and control in the business to sense strategic needs and develop early awareness and understanding.

2. Develop preliminary diagnoses, and implement partial, directional solutions to strategic problems, rather than attempting to determine and implement a final correct strategy.

3. Incorporate feedback at all stages of the process to further clarify what is needed, to respond to opposition and to capitalize on support.

4. Build commitment over time as information develops, problems clarify, partial solutions prove their worth, and initial obstacles recede.

The major challenge in nearly all anticipatory change situations is creating commitment to the idea that change is required, while it is still unclear exactly what that change should be. Weatherup used the "burning platform" speech, borrowed from a consultant advising the company to create a sense of urgency.

> It seems that a few years ago a North Sea oil rig caught fire. One worker, trained not to jump from the 150 foot high rig into the icy sea but to wait for help no matter how

bad things got, leaped anyway. He survived. Asked afterward why he stepped off the edge, the worker said he looked behind him and saw an approaching wall of fire and looked down and saw the sea. 'I chose probable death over certain death.'[13]

Reactive Change

The impetus for reactive change comes from a tangible deterioration in business performance. If the deterioration is not reversed it will lead to critical difficulties. The situation combines elements of anticipatory and crisis change: it may be difficult to establish both the need and the appropriate direction for change, but the deterioration creates a sense of urgency, and a need to act without delay.

The early approach to reactive change will likely be to deal with two quite different internal target groups—those who support the changes and those who are creating bottlenecks in the process. The priority objectives in the first periods of work will be organization changes that will help the supporters of change focus on the needed strategic developments and, at the same time, help you to deal with the resistors. The leadership style will probably be a hybrid of a participative approach with those on board and a directive style with resistors.

Preliminary Work Your first task as you prepare a plan for reactive change is to estimate the time that you have available. This is essentially a task of projecting the deterioration of the business and determining the point at which some form of crisis will thrust the business into chaos—a time-to-crisis calculation. This process will also be helpful in assessing the forces at work on the business and suggesting possible corrections. Remember that an established trend of deterioration tends to accelerate as competitors sense that you are vulnerable, and as good people leave because they see what is happening. The end may be closer than is first apparent.

Target Groups Reactive changes usually call for you to work on two target groups more or less simultaneously: supporters and resistors. Given the time pressure, it is critical that you identify and focus on the individuals or groups that are in a position to support or to resist the development and execution of the required changes—what we call the *pivotal change targets*.

The pivotal change targets in many reactive change situations will be a cross-section of relatively senior managers. If these managers are capable and flexible, they will be a positive force in implementing change. If, on the other hand, some or all of these managers are poorly equipped to deal with change, they will constitute an extremely difficult obstacle. They have power, by virtue of their positions and the constituencies they represent, to cause real problems. They can, at least in the short run, dilute, deflect, and distort change initiatives from above and below.

Since individual managers in the pivotal groups have the potential to exercise great leverage on change, it is important to do a thorough job in assessing their readiness for change and in particular their ability to implement or resist the program. In this way, you can tailor your tactics to individuals. Harvey Golub, who took over as CEO of American Express in the early 1990s, when the company was well down the crisis curve, commented on his early meetings with his management team: "I was listening to reports, and although I had zero data, I did not believe what I was hearing. The way people talked didn't match what I thought was reality, although I could not point to particulars."[14] He began to assess the readiness of individuals for change based on "how people were describing things to me. People use phrases that indicate their readiness levels. You get a sense for whether they know what to do but are simply unwilling to act, don't know what to do, or understand what needs to be done but don't know how to do it."[15] Golub judged that readiness was low, and strong leadership was required. He commented: "You can quickly back off if your assessment turns out to be wrong. But most people find it punitive if you start by under-leading and only later add structure.[16]

First Steps, Style, Pace If the priority targets in the business are all ready to go, then you can focus on directly developing the new behaviours, capabilities, resources, and preferences that you need to implement your new strategy. More likely you will face a mixed situation of supporters and resistors, making it difficult to move so quickly. In this case, you need to help the willing get on with the job and spend at least some time encouraging the resistors to see the light. If they cannot change, you will have to move them out.

The most difficult decision you will have to make as you move through reactive change is whether the pace of change is consistent with the growing urgency of the situation. As we saw earlier, one of the major challenges facing Tony Froggatt was to increase the pace of change in S&N. Many of his managers were willing to promise financial improvements in three years, but Froggatt insisted on improved results within 18 months. But at the same time, whatever was promised had to be delivered. There would be no more promises to analysts that were not met. The problem facing Froggatt and other managers in reactive change settings is that the downward momentum of the business cannot usually be reversed immediately, and the deterioration of performance will likely continue for some time, regardless of the action being taken. This factor has two major consequences.

First, you will have to make tough judgments early in the process regarding the performance of individual members of the pivotal group. Are they aware of and responding to the situation? Is their action consistent with the urgency of the situation? Financial results may not yet show improvement, so close personal monitoring is essential. One of the first steps taken by Golub at American Express, for example, was to change the way managerial performance was assessed. Traditionally, a manager's performance had been assessed by comparing actual financial results against a budget. Golub changed that, judging performance against:

> what you should have done, given the circumstances. That reduces the manipulative component of the budget process and . . . by taking into account how the results were achieved, I made the criteria both more subjective and more objective at the same time. For example, if you meet your net income goals by cutting advertising expenses, you won't get a very high score.[17]

Golub went further, recording his assessments in annual "report cards" that publicly graded managers on their performance in five categories: shareholders, customers, employees, re-engineering, and quality. Some managers liked the openness and clarity of this system; others did not. But it did change behaviour.

The second challenge that results from the fact that in reactive change situations "things are likely to get worse before they start to get better" is that opponents of the change program might seize upon the continuing performance deterioration and intensify their resistance. You do not have much time to accommodate such resistance and convert it to positive ends. You will have to deal with it aggressively. It is at this point that "heads are most likely to roll."

The conclusion is that in reactive change situations you will probably be called on to use a mixture of directive and participative styles. The precise mix will vary with the support you have and the resistance you face. One general manager who had, with mounting frustration, debated with his senior management team for months as to whether or not change was required in their organization finally "drew a line in the sand" when he stated at the next meeting they would discuss only what changes should be made, not if change should be made. Those who did not feel that was an appropriate agenda were not required to attend. The impasse was broken, and planning for change proceeded in a participative fashion.

CREATING AN ACTION PLAN

At this point you have established your guidelines for action, which means that you know your priority objectives, priority targets, first steps of action against each, your intended management style, and the necessary pace of change. The final step in the planning process is to detail the specific actions that follow logically from these general determinants. A format for this task is suggested in Figure 10.1. The first step is to decide on the time periods which are going to form the basis of your planning.

Time Periods To get to specific action you need to break down the total time span that you think will be required for change into relatively short periods, such as the 90-day intervals that we discussed earlier. The most important of the periods is the first one, the second most important is the second one, and so on. The span of the early periods should reflect the urgency of the situation. In crisis it may be necessary to work in periods of a few days or perhaps a week at a time. There is more leeway in anticipatory and reactive change, but the maximum length allowed should be 90-day periods. If the periods are any longer, there is a tendency to get less specific about particular actions and timing.

Focus hard on the first period or two. Get them right and you are on your way. Get them wrong and you will be in big trouble. It is difficult to plan the later periods in any detail, anyway, because they will rely so much on what happens at the outset. The planning approach that is most useful for these later periods is to develop some basic contingency notions and then, as things unfold, to fill in the appropriate detailed actions.

Priority Objectives and Targets This is where your identification of priority objectives and targets really counts. If the time period has been set correctly and you are realistic about what you can do, you will have a few focused objectives and targets on your first period list. In fact, if the list grows to more than a couple, you should reconsider your approach: your objectives may be insufficiently focused, or the time period that you have chosen to work with may be too long.

First Steps, Style, Timing For each objective and key target you will specify precise early action steps. Taken together, these steps should achieve the objective for the period. There is usually no risk-free way forward, but do not hinge the first steps of your change program on miraculous changes in attitude or behaviour if you can avoid it. Your planned sequence of actions is likely to be important, as you may want to achieve success vis-à-vis some objectives and targets before you move to others. On the other hand, many managers find that they need to work on several change streams in parallel.

Avoid the temptation of trying to do too much, too quickly. A big stretch is a necessary risk in crisis, but it is usually avoidable elsewhere. If you choose objectives carefully and act with a clear focus, your change process will build on itself and reach its destination in a sure and timely fashion. The stories of failed change are stories of overly ambitious objectives and expansive action. Perhaps the most important ingredient in achieving successful strategic change is the personal discipline necessary to focus your thinking and your action.

MONITORING PERFORMANCE

A key element of implementation is monitoring performance and cycling back to compare the actual performance against expectations. It is sobering to realize that most companies' strategy deliver only 63 percent of their expected financial value.[18] Closing the gap is two-fold. It requires having more realistic expectations of the strategy, but also having a better grip on the execution of the strategy. Mankins and Steele found that the 37 percent performance loss could be accounted for as follows: 7.5 percent to inadequate or unavailable resources; 5.2 percent to poorly communicated strategy; 4.5 percent because actions required to execute the strategy are not clearly defined; 4.1 percent because of unclear accountabilities for execution; 3.7 percent because organization silos and culture block execution; 3.0 percent as a result of inadequate performance monitoring; 3.0 percent due to inadequate consequences of rewards for failure or success; 2.6 percent and 1.9 percent to poor senior leadership and uncommitted leadership; 0.7 percent to unproved strategy; and 0.7 percent to other obstacles including inadequate skills and capabilities.[19]

The reasons for performance loss are inter-related. "In many companies, planning and execution breakdowns are reinforced—even magnified—by an insidious shift in culture. In our experience, this change occurs subtly but quickly, and once it has taken root it is very hard to reverse. First, unrealistic plans create the expectation throughout the organization that plans simply will not be fulfilled. Then, as the expectation becomes experience, it becomes the norm that performance commitments won't be kept. So commitments cease to be binding promises with real consequences. Rather than stretching to ensure that commitments are kept, managers, expecting failure, seek to protect themselves from the eventual fallout".[20]

Many of the shortcomings are associated with poor strategic analysis and unrealistic expectations. However, ensuring there are concrete milestones and rigorous monitoring to assess performance it critical.

SUMMARY

This chapter has outlined the required steps to move from the change objectives and starting conditions of a change program to a set of operational guidelines for action and thence to a detailed action plan.

The preparation of action guidelines in a specific situation is largely a matter of developing the implications of the change objectives and starting conditions (urgency, organizational readiness, and personal readiness) that were discussed in Chapter 10. It is useful to cast these implications in terms of three basic variable categories: (1) action priorities, which establish priority key players in the change process and objectives; (2) leadership style, which establishes the basic relationships and tactics to be used; and (3) pace, which establishes the required rate of change. Together these guidelines set up a definitive framework for specific actions.

The final step in the planning process is detailing the actions that follow logically from the guidelines. The major steps of this process are to (1) define a series of time periods; (2) indicate the key players that you wish to address within each time period; and (3) identify your priority objectives, tactics, and sequence of action within the time period. Ensuring there is a rigorous plan to monitor performance against expectations is critical.

Notes

1. Waal, Peter. "With a Vengeance." *Canadian Business* 71 (April 10, 1998): 35. Print.

2. Branzei, O., and C. Zietsma. "Temporary Cognitions of Entrepreneurial Love: Dancing with the Opportunity." *Frontiers of Entrepreneurship Research.* Babson Park, MA: Arthur M. Blank Center for Entrepreneurship, Babson College, 2003. 242–256. Print.

3. Searle, R. "Face-to-Face with Tom Stephens, CEO, MacMillan Bloedel." *Timber and Wood Products International* (October 31, 1998): 48–49. Print.

4. Schaffer, Robert H., and Harvey A. Thomson. "Successful Change Programs Begin With Results." *Harvard Business Review* 70 (January–February 1992): 80–90. Print.

5. See for example: Brenneman, Greg. "Right Away and All at Once: How We Saved Continental." *Harvard Business Review* 76 (September–October 1998): 162–179. Print.

6. Beer, Michael, Russel A. Eisenstat, and Bert Spector. "Why Change Programs Don't Produce Change." *Harvard Business Review* 68 (November–December 1990): 158–167. Print.

7. Weber, James, and Michael Beer. "Asda." (A1), case 498-006. Boston: Harvard Business School, 1998. 2. Print.

8. Weber, James, and Michael Beer. "Asda." (B), case 498-007. Boston: Harvard Business School, 1998. 16. Print.

9. Quinn, James Brian. *Strategies for Change: Logical Incrementalism*. Homewood, Illinois: Richard D. Irwin Inc., 1980. Print.

10. Quinn, James Brian. *Strategies for Change: Logical Incrementalism*. Homewood, Illinois: Richard D. Irwin Inc., 1980. Print.

11. Sull, Don, and David A. Garvin. "Pepsi's Regeneration, 1990–1993," case 395-048. Boston: Harvard Business School, 1996. 5. Print.

12. Sull, Don, and David A. Garvin. "Pepsi's Regeneration, 1990–1993," case 395-048. Boston: Harvard Business School, 1996. 3–4. Print.

13. Dumaine, Brain. "Times are Good? Create a Crisis." *Fortune* (June 28, 1993), as reported in Sull, Don, and David A. Garvin. "Pepsi's Regeneration, 1990–1993." case 395-048. Boston: Harvard Business School, 1996. 4. Print.

14. March, Artemis, David A. Garvin, and Harvey Golub. "Recharging American Express." case 396-212. Boston: Harvard Business School, 1996. 7. Print.

15. March, Artemis, David A. Garvin, and Harvey Golub. "Recharging American Express." case 396-212. Boston: Harvard Business School, 1996. 7. Print.

16. March, Artemis, David A. Garvin, and Harvey Golub. "Recharging American Express." case 396-212. Boston: Harvard Business School, 1996. 7. Print.

17. March, Artemis, David A. Garvin, and Harvey Golub. "Recharging American Express." case 396-212. Boston: Harvard Business School, 1996. 7. Print.

18. Mankins, Michael C., and Richard Steele. "Turning Great Strategy Into Great Performance." *Harvard Business Review* 83.7/8 (2005): 64–72. *Business Source Complete*, EBSCO. Web. 16 Aug. 2011.

19. Mankins, Michael C., and Richard Steele. "Turning Great Strategy Into Great Performance." *Harvard Business Review* 83.7/8 (2005): 64–72. *Business Source Complete*, EBSCO. Web. 16 Aug. 2011.

20. Mankins, Michael C., and Richard Steele. "Turning Great Strategy Into Great Performance." *Harvard Business Review* 83.7/8 (2005): 64–72. *Business Source Complete*, EBSCO. Web. 16 Aug. 2011.

Additional Readings

1. Augustine, Norman A. "Managing the Crisis You Tried to Prevent." *Harvard Business Review* 73 (November–December 1995): 147. Print.

2. Duck, Jeanie Daniel. "Managing Change: The Art of Balancing." *Harvard Business Review* 71 (November–December 1993): 109. Print.

3. Sadler, Philip. *Managing Change*. London: Kogan Page, 1995. Print.

4. Strebel, Paul. "Why Do Employees Resist Change?" *Harvard Business Review* 74 (May–June 1996): 86. Print.

Index

Costco, 29
costs: additional costs, 121; competitor cost structure, 69; cost disadvantages, 61; cost structures, 88–89; of failure, 122–123; sunk cost, 140, 191
Courtney, Hugh, 71
Coyne, Kevin P., 69
crisis change, 209, 210–212, 235–236
crisis curve, 208–216, 208*f*
cross-category impact, 200–201
cross-cultural effectiveness, 155*t*
cross-unit synergies, 155*t*, 175
Crossan, Mary, 113, 194, 196, 198
CTV, 32
culturally informed RBV (CRBV), 113, 113*f*
culture. *See* organizational culture
customers: bargaining power, 62–63, 96; as key stakeholders, 28; needs and preferences, 94–95; and value centers, 128; willingness to pay, 69; *see also* stakeholder interests

D

Daimler-Benz, 107–109
De Geus, Arie, 123, 190
decision, 57
decision making processes, 173–174
defensive resistors, 227
DeKalb Genetics Corp., 99
Delta and Pine Land, 99
demand, 94–96
deregulation, 101
design school, 36
Diamond-E analysis, 50–57, 93–103, 118–120; strategic analysis, process of, 54–57, 54*f*; strategy-environment linkage, 51, 93–103, 93*f*; strategy-management preferences linkage, 51–52; strategy-organization linkage, 52–53; strategy-resources linkage, 51, 118–120; *see also* environment analysis; management preference analysis; resource analysis; strategy-organization analysis
Diamond-E framework, 34, 36, 46–54, 47*f*, 53*f*, 111; *see also* Diamond-E analysis
differentiation strategy, 26
direction, 6–13
directive leadership style, 230*t*, 231–232
directors. *See* board of directors; corporate governance
Discipline of Market Leaders (Treacy and Wiersema), 27

Disney. *See* Walt Disney Company
disruptive technologies, 72
distinctive competence, 110
distribution channels, 61–62
Douglas, Paul, 113
Dow Chemical Company, 26, 110
downstream markets, 23–24
Dubai, 27
DuPont, 63, 99
dynamic resources, 123

E

eBay, 61
economies of scale, 61
Economist.com, 129
Edward Jones, 34
80/20 rule, 73
Eisenhardt, K.M., 197
Eisner, Michael, 175
Elf, 187
emotional intelligence, 199
employees, 128
Encana Corporation, 24, 50
ENI, 187
Enron, 129–130
environment analysis, 59, 71, 83, 84*f*, 104; Blue Ocean Strategy, 73–74, 74*f*; focused environment analysis, 83–93, 92*f*; forecast performance, 103–104; game theory, 67–69; global industry models, 75, 75*f*; math for strategists, 69–70; minimization of risks of focus, 91–93; new economy models, 71–73; PEST analysis, 70, 70*f*, 92; Porter's Five Forces Model, 60–64, 60*f*, 96, 97, 98; stakeholder analysis, 75–79, 78*f*; strategy-environment linkage, 93–103; value chain, 65–67, 65*f*
environmental risks, 49
escalation of commitment, 191, 192*t*
ethics, 131
Evans, Philip B., 72
execution, 57
Export Development Canada, 101
externalities, 76, 100, 102
Exxon Mobil, 78, 98, 187

F

failure, costs of, 122–123
false consensus, 192*t*, 193
feasibility assessment, 12, 179–180, 180*t*
FEMSA Cerveza, 121
financial resources, 119
Financial Times, 131
5Ps, 35

flexibility, 12–13
focus, 83–93, 185
focused environment analysis, 83–93, 92*f*
Ford, Henry, 10
forecasts. *See* performance forecasts
Fortune magazine, 7, 34, 119, 129, 172
4I framework of strategic renewal, 194, 194*t*
framing, 192*t*
Friedman, Milton, 132
Froggatt, Tony, 215, 216, 217, 219, 220, 230, 240
frozen preference, 140, 193–194
functional strategy, 38, 38*f*
functional structure, 164–166

G

Galbraith, Jay, 155, 167
Galvin, Christopher, 42
gamblers' fallacy, 192*t*
game theory, 67–69
gap-closing analysis, 121–123, 144–148
GE Healthcare, 49
General Electric (GE), 41, 154, 218, 230
general management, 1–13, 3*f*, 41–42, 164, 221
generic strategies, 26
geographic structure, 167–168
Gerber Products Company, 112
Ghemawat, Pankaj, 67–68
Gilden Activewear, 101
GLBT community, 113
global functional structure, 165
global industry models, 75, 75*f*
Globalive Wireless, 101–102
goals, 17, 19, 20–23, 21*t*, 86, 88, 104, 117*t*, 142*t*
Golub, Harvey, 240–241
Google, 10
Goold, Michael, 41, 171
government, 62, 100–103
Grant, Robert M., 187, 188
groupthink, 185, 191, 217
Gruber, Robert, 139
guiding philosophy, 8–10, 11
Guth, William D., 141

H

Hagel, John III, 73
Hamel, Gary, 110, 190
hard goals, 21*t*
Harlequin, 120
Hayes, Robert H., 137
HID Global, 10